T0326314

WRITING THE EARLY CRUSADES

WRITING THE EARLY CRUSADES
TEXT, TRANSMISSION AND MEMORY

Edited by

Marcus Bull and Damien Kempf

THE BOYDELL PRESS

First published 2014
The Boydell Press, Woodbridge
Paperback edition 2018

ISBN 978 1 84383 920 0 hardback
ISBN 978 1 78327 299 0 paperback

The Boydell Press is an imprint of Boydell & Brewer Ltd
PO Box 9, Woodbridge, Suffolk IP12 3DF, UK
and of Boydell & Brewer Inc.
668 Mt Hope Avenue, Rochester, NY 14620–2731, USA
website: www.boydellandbrewer.com

A CIP catalogue record for this book is available
from the British Library

The publisher has no responsibility for the continued existence or accuracy
of URLs for external or third-party internet websites referred to in this book,
and does not guarantee that any content on such websites is,
or will remain, accurate or appropriate

This publication is printed on acid-free paper

Typeset by Fakenham Prepress Solutions, Fakenham, Norfolk NR21 8NN

CONTENTS

Contents

ACKNOWLEDGEMENTS

This volume has its origin in a symposium, held at Liverpool in May 2011, that formed part of a research project on the historiography of the First Crusade, based at the University of Bristol and funded by the Arts and Humanities Research Council. The editors would therefore like to extend their warmest thanks to the Council for all its support, as well as to Brendan Smith, who generously assumed formal responsibility for the project in its latter stages. The editors also wish to thank all those who helped to make the symposium such a great success: Harald Braun, director of the Liverpool Centre for Medieval and Renaissance Studies; Brigitte Resl, then Head of the Department of History at Liverpool; and the staff of the University of Liverpool's Foresight Centre, which was an excellent venue. Although he did not give a paper, Dominique Iogna-Prat was an active and generous presence throughout the symposium, discussing papers and offering advice in ways that all the participants found very gratifying. Finally, it is, as always, a great pleasure to work with Caroline Palmer and the excellent team at Boydell and Brewer.

LIST OF CONTRIBUTORS

Laura Ashe	Worcester College, Oxford
Steven Biddlecombe	University of Leicester
Marcus Bull	University of North Carolina at Chapel Hill
Peter Frankopan	Worcester College, Oxford
Damien Kempf	University of Liverpool
James Naus	Oakland University
Léan Ní Chléirigh	Trinity College, Dublin
Jay Rubenstein	University of Tennessee, Knoxville
Nicholas Paul	Fordham University
William Purkis	University of Birmingham
Luigi Russo	Università Europea, Rome
Carol Sweetenham	University of Warwick

LIST OF ABBREVIATIONS

AA Albert of Aachen, *Historia Ierosolimitana*, ed. and trans. S. B. Edgington (Oxford, 2007).

BB Baldric of Bourgueil, 'Historia Jerosolimitana', *RHC Occ* iv, 1–111.

FC Fulcher of Chartres, *Historia Hierosolymitana (1095–1127)*, ed. H. Hagenmeyer (Heidelberg, 1913).

GF *Gesta Francorum et aliorum Hierosolimitanorum*, ed. and trans. R. M. T. Hill (London, 1962).

GN Guibert of Nogent, *Dei Gesta per Francos*, ed. R. B. C. Huygens (Corpus Christianorum, Continuatio Mediaeualis, 127A; Turnhout, 1996).

HBS 'Historia Belli Sacri', *RHC Occ.* iii, 165–229.

HVH *The Historia vie Hierosolimitane of Gilo of Paris and a Second, Anonymous Author*, ed. and trans. C. W. Grocock and J. E. Siberry (Oxford, 1997).

MGH Monumenta Germaniae Historica

MGH SS *Monumenta Germaniae Historica, Scriptores in Folio et Quarto*, ed. G. H. Pertz *et al.* (Hanover, Weimar, Stuttgart, and Cologne, 1826–).

OV Orderic Vitalis, *Ecclesiastical History*, ed. and trans. M. Chibnall, 6 vols (Oxford, 1968–80).

PL *Patrologiae cursus completus, series Latina*, ed. J.-P. Migne, 221 vols (Paris, 1844–64).

List of Abbreviations

PT   Peter Tudebode, *Historia de Hierosolymitano Itinere*, ed. J. H. Hill and L. L. Hill (Documents relatifs à l'histoire des croisades, 12; Paris, 1977).

RA   Raymond of Aguilers, *Le 'Liber'*, ed. J. H. Hill and L. L. Hill (Documents relatifs à l'histoire des croisades, 9; Paris, 1969).

RC   Ralph of Caen, 'Gesta Tancredi in expeditione Hierosolymitana', *RHC Occ* iii, 587–716.

RHC Occ   *Recueil des historiens des croisades: Historiens occidentaux*, ed. Académie des Inscriptions et Belles-Lettres, 5 vols (Paris, 1844–95).

RM   Robert the Monk, 'Historia Iherosolimitana', *RHC Occ* iii, 717–882.

WT   William of Tyre, *Chronicon*, ed. R. B. C. Huygens, 1 vol. in 2 (Corpus Christianorum, Continuatio Mediaeualis, 63; Turnhout, 1986).

INTRODUCTION

Marcus Bull and Damien Kempf

Whatever its substantive focus in any given instance and the particular problems that it is addressing, the study of the Middle Ages always comes down, sooner or later, to the study of the primary evidence that survives. As a scholarly discipline, medieval history requires sensitivity towards both the potentialities and the limitations of the source bases at its disposal, and a corresponding openness to new methodological and conceptual approaches that revivify the study of seemingly familiar, sometimes very familiar, materials.[1] Our understanding of the numerous narrative sources inspired by the First Crusade (1095–1102), as well as of those texts influenced by the language, imagery, clichés and cognitive assumptions of crusading discourses over the course of the twelfth century and beyond, is a case in point. The richness and range of the narrative corpus relating to the First Crusade and the early crusade movement has been recognized since at least the time of Jacques Bongars's *Gesta Dei per Francos* (1611), while the systematic study of that corpus in the modern scholarly era may be said to have begun with Ranke's star pupil Heinrich von Sybel's *Geschichte des ersten Kreuzzugs* (1841).[2] Studies of the narrative material have continued to appear, for example by Iorga in 1928, Hiestand in 1985, and Flori in 2010;[3] and

---

[1] For medieval sources, see, for example, R. C. van Caenegem and F. L. Ganshof, *Guide to the Sources of Medieval History* (Amsterdam, 1978); M. C. Howell and W. Prevenier, *From Reliable Sources: An Introduction to Historical Methods* (Ithaca, 2001), which is attentive to some of the challenges posed by medieval as well as post-medieval evidence; and the various useful papers in *Understanding Medieval Primary Sources: Using Historical Sources to Discover Medieval Europe*, ed. J. T. Rosenthal (Abingdon, 2012). See also J. H. Arnold, *What is Medieval History?* (Cambridge, 2008), pp. 23–56; M. G. Bull, *Thinking Medieval: An Introduction to the Study of the Middle Ages* (Basingstoke, 2005), pp. 62–98.

[2] J. Bongars, *Gesta Dei per Francos, sive Orientalium Expeditionum, et Regni Francorum Hierosolimitani Historia a Variis, sed illius Aevi Scriptoribus, Litteris Commendata*, 1 vol. in 2 (Hanover, 1611); H. C. L. von Sybel, *Geschichte des ersten Kreuzzugs* (Düsseldorf, 1841; new edn Leipzig, 1881); Eng. trans. Lucie, Lady Duff Gordon, *The History and Literature of the Crusades* (London, 1861).

[3] N. Iorga, *Les narrateurs de la première croisade* (Paris, 1928); R. Hiestand, 'Il cronista medievale e il suo pubblico: alcuni osservazioni in margine alla storiografia delle crociate', *Annali della Facoltà di Lettere e Filosofia dell'Università di Napoli*, n.s. 15 (1984–5), 207–27; J. Flori, *Chroniqueurs*

recently an interest has been emerging in the reception of some of these works as well as their social function as sites of memory.[4] Since the 1970s many of the major texts have been re-edited, sometimes for the first time since the *Recueil des historiens des croisades* in the nineteenth century, and more editions are in the pipeline, placing the study of the texts' origins, interrelationships and receptions on a much more secure footing. There remain, however, large gaps and areas of uncertainty in our understanding of this material, which means that a great deal more work is still to be done.

Such a scholarly project is all the more important because no other event in the Middle Ages stimulated such a large burst of historical writing. Because of their shared themes of military endeavour and long-distance travel, the histories that were produced to tell the story of Alexander the Great's campaigns seem to offer the most compelling points of comparison in the broad western, premodern narrative tradition. It is important to remember, however, that the Alexander material most closely equivalent to the eyewitness accounts of the First Crusade and the second generation derivatives of them written within living memory of the events recounted is no longer extant, and our knowledge of it is derived from much later, and sometimes fragmentary, literary recastings. In contrast, we can be reasonably confident that the surviving narratives of the First Crusade represent at the very least a substantial and representative sample of the forms in which the crusade found literary expression in the early decades of the twelfth century and thereafter.[5] Looking forward, one perhaps has to go as far as the narratives of the Spanish encounter with the New World in the sixteenth century to find a comparably rich body of material themed around travel-as-hardship, conquest and cultural collision, a comparison made all the more intriguing given the obvious influence of crusade language and motifs upon texts such as Bernal Díaz's *Historia verdadera de la conquista de la Nueva España*.[6] Within

---

et propagandistes: *Introduction critique aux sources de la Première croisade* (Hautes études médiévales et modernes, 98; Geneva, 2010). For helpful overviews, see also S. B. Edgington, 'The First Crusade: Reviewing the Evidence', in *The First Crusade: Origins and Impact*, ed. J. P. Phillips (Manchester, 1997), pp. 55–77; J. P. Phillips, *The Second Crusade: Extending the Frontiers of Christendom* (New Haven, 2007), pp. 19–28. See also M. G. Bull, 'The Western Narratives of the First Crusade', in *Christian–Muslim Relations: A Bibliographical History: Volume 3 (1050–1200)*, ed. D. Thomas, A. Mallett *et al.* (Leiden, 2011), pp. 15–25.

4   See J. C. Rubenstein, 'Putting History to Use: Three Crusade Chronicles in Context', *Viator*, 35 (2004), 131–68; N. L. Paul, 'Crusade, Memory, and Regional Politics in Twelfth-Century Amboise', *Journal of Medieval History*, 31 (2005), 127–41.

5   See L. I. C. Pearson, *The Lost Histories of Alexander the Great* (New York, 1960); N. G. L. Hammond, *Three Historians of Alexander the Great: The So-Called Vulgate Authors, Diodorus, Justin, and Curtius* (Cambridge, 1983); idem, *Sources for Alexander the Great: An Analysis of Plutarch's Life and Arrian's Anabasis Alexandrou* (Cambridge, 1993).

6   *Historia verdadera de la conquista de la Nueva España*, ed. J. Ramírez Cabañas, 7th edn (Mexico City, 1969). For the conquest literature in general, see now M. A. Arango Linares, *Proceso histórico-social en la literatura de los primeros cronistas de la conquista de América: Cristóbal Colón, Hernán Cortés, Álvar Núñez Cabeza de Vaca, Alonso de Ercilla y Zúñiga, Bernal Díaz del Castillo, Inca Garcilaso de la Vega, Juan Bartolomé de Las Casas, Juan de Castellanos, Juan Rodríguez Freyle, Pedro de Solís y Valenzuela y Sor Juana Inés de la Cruz* (Currents in Comparative Romance Languages and Literatures, 181; New York, 2011).

the narrower European experience of war, it is possible that the first occasion in which a closely comparable body of contemporary narrative material emerges is with the many accounts of some or all of the Thirty Years War, although one must bear in mind, of course, that by the time we reach the seventeenth century print and the (relative) spread of literacy have created a very different literary and cultural landscape from that of Europe around the time of the First Crusade.[7]

Closer to the First Crusade chronologically and culturally, perhaps the most compelling point of comparison in terms of the volume of material generated would be the many Lives of Thomas Becket written after his death in December 1170.[8] The 'flashbulb memory' quality of Europeans' shocked responses to the news of Becket's murder captures something of the more diffuse but probably no less profound impact that the launching of the crusade, reports of its achievements and its success in capturing Jerusalem made upon contemporaries. In both instances, the burst of writing was a response to a sense of the compelling irruption of the unusual and noteworthy (whether assigned a positive or negative value) into the normal run of affairs. On the other hand, it is important to remember that Becket's many 'biographers' were able to call up the ample resources of hagiographical tradition to guide their narrative strategies and to lend their work status and authority, whereas the earliest historians of the First Crusade had no one dominant cultural paradigm from which to work; in time their work became normative for those writing the histories of later crusade expeditions, but in the years immediately following the fall of Jerusalem no such convenient model was immediately to hand. As a result, one finds adaptive and imaginative blends of multiple influences and exemplars at play, including the Bible, of course, ranging from the Acts of the Apostles to the war books of the Old Testament, classical historiography, itineraries and pilgrimage texts, hagiography and works of Christomimetic devotion, deeds-of-rulers political narrative, and Latin and vernacular epic. The early eyewitness texts such as the *Gesta Francorum* can be seen eclectically exploiting these resources in creative ways, while the second generation histories that were largely derived from the eyewitnesses may be interpreted as, *inter alia*, attempts to streamline the range and cultural status of the intertextual reference appropriate to a telling of the First Crusade, what Jonathan Riley-Smith memorably summed up as the imposition of 'theological refinement'.[9]

Given the depth and range of the narrative corpus of the First Crusade, it represents a privileged 'laboratory' in which to pose questions about the nature of historical writing in the central Middle Ages, the formation and mutation of collective memory, the interfaces between oral and written cultures and the reception and mutual interplay of texts. In the light of such questions, it is all the

---

[7]   See B. von Krusenstjern, *Selbstzeugnisse der Zeit des Dreissigjährigen Krieges: Beschreibendes Verzeichnis* (Selbstzeugnisse ner Neuzeit, 6; Berlin, 1997); G. Mortimer, *Eyewitness Accounts of the Thirty Years War 1618–48* (Basingstoke, 2002).

[8]   See M. Staunton, *Thomas Becket and his Biographers* (Studies in the History of Medieval Religion, 28; Woodbridge, 2006). See also E. Walberg, *La tradition hagiographique de saint Thomas Becket avant la fin du XIIe siècle: Études critiques* (Paris, 1929).

[9]   J. S. C. Riley-Smith, *The First Crusade and the Idea of Crusading* (London, 1986), pp. 135–52.

more regrettable that scholars working on western European history-writing in the centuries either side of 1100 have tended to steer clear of crusade histories.[10] This is a major omission, one that probably cannot be reduced to a single cause. One reason is the incorrect but persistent assumption that the crusade movement was in some sense exotic and tangential to the main contours of European historical development. Another factor has perhaps been the equally false belief that because the crusade movement eventually petered out (though later than traditionally believed), the form and content of any written expressions specific to it would have made no enduring or significant impact upon mainstream European historical writing. Although writers such as Fulcher of Chartres and William of Tyre and his continuators stand in broadly the same sort of relation to the Latin Kingdom of Jerusalem as do the star names of the Anglo-Norman historiographical boom between the late eleventh and early thirteenth centuries or the earliest historiographers of the Capetian monarchy in Saint-Denis in relation to the political, ecclesiastical and social landscapes of north-western Europe, the fact that the Latin East emerged *de novo* and then did not endure in the long run seems to marginalize its historiographical legacy.[11] In contrast, the study of the politically focused, often regicentric, historical narratives produced in England, France and elsewhere – one thinks in particular of the important work of Gabrielle Spiegel – can slot into historiographical trajectories that begin in the early Middle Ages and extend into the early modern period.[12] A further problem lies in the fact that most crusade histories are of a narrow 'monograph' sort, tightly bounded substantively and thematically: most did not follow the pattern set by Fulcher of Chartres's history of the First Crusade, which mutated into a rolling political narrative of the Latin East. As such, they throw sometimes penetrating beams of light on relatively brief historical moments, often offering up a fineness of reconstructable human detail seldom attainable through other

[10] There is, for example, very little mention of crusade histories in Bernard Guenée's standard treatment, *Histoire et culture historique dans l'Occident médiéval* (Paris, 1980). Cf. among the most popular overviews in English B. Smalley, *Historians in the Middle Ages* (London, 1974); A. Gransden, *Historical Writing in England: I. c.550–c.1307* (London, 1974); D. Hay, *Annalists and Historians: Western Historiography from the Eighth to the Eighteenth Centuries* (London, 1977); C. Given-Wilson, *Chronicles: The Writing of History in Medieval England* (London, 2004). Rather more, but still not extensive, attention to crusade narratives, with a particular emphasis on Guibert of Nogent's *Dei Gesta per Francos*, is to be found in M. Kempshall, *Rhetoric and the Writing of History, 400–1500* (Manchester, 2011), esp. pp. 392–408.

[11] For Fulcher and William see V. Epp, *Fulcher von Chartres: Studien zur Geschichtsschreibung des ersten Kreuzzuges* (Studia humaniora, 15; Düsseldorf, 1990); P. W. Edbury and J. G. Rowe, *William of Tyre, Historian of the Latin East* (Cambridge, 1988) .

[12] See G. M. Spiegel, *The Chronicle Tradition of Saint-Denis: A Survey* (Medieval Classics: Texts and Studies, 10; Brookline, Mass., 1978) and the papers assembled in the second part of her *The Past as Text: The Theory and Practice of Medieval Historiography* (Baltimore, 1997). Cf. the remarks about the emergence of royal historiography in the twelfth century as a major turning-point within medieval historical writing in general in F. Lifshitz, 'Beyond Positivism and Genre: "Hagiographical" Texts as Historical Narrative', *Viator*, 25 (1994), 95–113. Although a great deal has been written about English historians and history-writing in the Anglo-Norman and Angevin periods, a monograph study of historiographical culture in England in the period *c.* 1075–*c.* 1225 would be very welcome.

medieval sources, but they do in seemingly isolated bursts. In this the First Crusade narratives can seem to resemble a closely contemporary text, Galbert of Bruges's marvellously illuminating and controlled account of the murder of Count Charles the Good of Flanders in 1127 and its consequences: packed with both rich substantive detail and evidence of historiographical craft and imagination, but resistant to easy categorization and difficult to situate within the conventional taxonomies that historians use to characterize their source repertoires.[13]

As a number of the contributions to this volume demonstrate, what the study of the First Crusade narrative corpus can bring to the study of medieval historio-graphical culture in general is much more than the addition of names and texts to appear on medievalists' source radar. It also enhances our understanding of the transmission and reception of historical texts, and by extension their status as cultural artefacts. As an emerging interest in the operations of historical memory in the Middle Ages is beginning to suggest, crusade narratives cannot simply be approached in a 'pointilliste' manner as moments of authorial creation standing on a given point on a timeline and in some fixed relation to the events and processes that they describe;[14] such texts had rich afterlives as they were re-read, copied, stylistically revised, structurally rearranged, anthologized with and reconfigured in relation to other texts in codices, and in some cases trans-lated. The First Crusade lived on in and through the transmission of its textual articulations. This fact has not received the scholarly attention it deserves. The debate some years ago about whether there were crusades in the twelfth century, for example, largely overlooked the fact that ticking away underneath the various utterances and events that supply the evidence, or not, for the existence of a crusade 'movement', the First Crusade remained an active site of memory through the sustained demand for copies of narratives of it – a demand that the distribution of datable manuscripts suggests the Second and Third Crusades certainly fed but did not in themselves create.[15] In other words, the First Crusade narrative corpus provides important evidence for the market and audience for near-contemporary historical writing in the twelfth century and beyond, as well as for the cultural, political and institutional stimuli (for example, royal ideology, subsequent crusades, ecclesiastical networks) that sustained, or sometimes revived, interest in the narratives. The presentation copy of Robert the Monk's *Historia Iherosolimitana* made for the emperor Frederick Barbarossa before his departure on the Third Crusade is fairly unusual in its combination of a striking (and much reproduced) illustrated frontispiece that stages the act of gifting the manuscript itself and showcases its status as an offering worthy of a great crusade

---

[13] Galbert of Bruges, *De multro, traditione, et occisione gloriosi Karoli comitis Flandriarum*, ed. J. Rider (Corpus Christianorum, Continuatio Mediaeualis, 131; Turnhout, 1994). See J. Rider, *God's Scribe: The Historiographical Art of Galbert of Bruges* (Washington, 2001); *Galbert of Bruges and the Historiography of Medieval Flanders*, ed. J. Rider and A. V. Murray (Washington, 2009).

[14] See N. L. Paul, *To Follow in Their Footsteps: The Crusades and Family Memory in the High Middle Ages* (Ithaca, 2012).

[15] Cf. C. J. Tyerman, 'Were There Any Crusades in the Twelfth Century?', *English Historical Review*, 110 (1995), 553–77.

leader in the making, the fact that we are informed who commissioned the copy (Henry, provost of Schäftlarn), and the frontispiece's overt acknowledgement of topical pertinence in its appeal to the emperor to drive Saladin's people from the Holy Land.[16] But it usefully stands for the many other manuscripts of Robert's text and other crusade narratives that are seldom so securely locatable in time and space, and which furnish only circumstantial evidence for why they were made, but which nonetheless cumulatively speak to the enduring traction of the memory of the First Crusade in the twelfth century and beyond. In brief, therefore, the First Crusade corpus is a major resource for research into the place of historical writing in medieval learned culture.

It is salutary to remember that the notion of the 'First Crusade' *eo nomine* is a post-medieval construct, and for this reason it is important to introduce a note of chronological, cultural and thematic elasticity when considering the crusade's historiographical and wider literary footprint.[17] Thus, for example, one of the papers in this volume considers the work of Anna Komnene, whose *Alexiad* is often pressed into service as an honorary telling of the First Crusade from the otherwise under-represented Greek perspective, but which, Peter Frankopan's paper reveals, is a far fuller and more complex text than historians' concentration on its crusade sequences tends to acknowledge. Similarly, Laura Ashe's paper considers vernacular literary texts from the twelfth and thirteenth centuries that are in important respects culturally cognate with many of the values and scripts familiar from crusade narratives, but also negotiated that affinity via multiple points of reference, such as chivalry, that cannot be reduced to crusading's particular cultural impress. William Purkis explores the extent to which the memories of the First Crusade, the sense of its novelty and the scale of its achievement, were registered in texts that are not ostensibly about the crusade but which nonetheless register it as a powerful cultural marker. Purkis demonstrates that the First Crusade was a rich source of evocation and allusion, inviting parallels, contrasts and reimaginings in a wide range of twelfth-century texts; but he introduces the important qualification that this was not an immutable or open-ended resource, for by around 1200 the Third Crusade (1187–92) was emerging as the dominant cultural reference point for those authors drawing upon the language and imagery of crusading.

Other papers in this collection engage in various ways with the central fact that a substantial number of more or less closely contemporary Latin narratives either take the events of 1095–99 (and sometimes the 1101–2 crusade expeditions and the embryonic years of the Frankish East) as their principal object or else embed substantial accounts of those events within larger historiographical projects. Given the richness and depth of this corpus, it is important to understand the transmission, reception and impact of the various histories of the First Crusade,

---

[16] *The* Historia Iherosolimitana *of Robert the Monk*, ed. D. Kempf and M. G. Bull (Woodbridge, 2013), pp. xlv–xlvii. See also Damien Kempf's paper in this volume. The manuscript is Vatican, Biblioteca Apostolica, Vat. Lat. 2001.

[17] Cf. G. Constable, 'The Numbering of the Crusades', in his *Crusaders and Crusading in the Twelfth Century* (Farnham, 2008), pp. 353–6.

and where necessary to differentiate between them so as to avoid misleading generalizations. Thus Damien Kempf's paper demonstrates how Robert the Monk's account of the First Crusade was the nearest thing to a 'best seller' among the many crusade narratives available to medieval readers, a text that transcended its francocentric ideological grounding to become hugely popular in German-speaking areas. Likewise, James Naus argues for the need to examine crusade narratives as discrete cultural artefacts, each reflective of the particular authorial circumstances and goals that shaped them – circumstances and goals that did not necessarily flow directly from the experience or memory of crusading, but which were nonetheless inflected by the opportunities that narrating the First Crusade afforded to revisit questions of power, status and authority back home in Europe. Thus Naus sees in Robert the Monk's *Historia Iherosolimitana* a political sensitivity to shifts in the relative prestige of churches and saints' cults clustering around the French monarchy, and a defence of the importance of Reims within the traditional configurations of secular and sacral power in northern France.

An understanding of the external influences acting upon First Crusade texts must be complemented by inward-looking examinations of their discursive dynamics, narrative strategies and meaning-making operations. Carol Sweetenham investigates the role of anecdotes within crusade authors' larger projects, arguing that vignettes were grafted onto the master narrative of the First Crusade at the intersections of oral memory, cultural script, literary convention and reader expectation in ways that equipped authors to draw upon the ethical frameworks of other textual genres such as *chansons de geste*, to individualize the crusaders' collective experience, and to optimize the crusade's exemplary potential. Steven Biddlecombe's discussion of Baldric of Bourgueil's history of the First Crusade, a work that was much more widely copied and read than scholars have traditionally supposed, explores the play of metaphor, specifically the notion of the *familia Christi*, within the text's adumbrations of an incipient crusade ideology. As Biddlecombe shows, Baldric's attachment to this metaphor speaks to a pronounced, and ideologically grounded, authorial warmth towards eastern Christians that most other Latin histories of the crusade did not share, at least to the same extent. In a similar metaphorical vein, Nicholas Paul isolates a powerful but hitherto overlooked motif within a number of crusade narratives, that of the closed gate, which serves as a point of entry into authors' under-standing of the crusade's place in larger temporal frameworks of past, present and future, the importance of liturgy and ritual in the attachment of meaning to places and events, and the migration of crusade memory into other genres such as princely dynastic texts. Léan Ní Chléirigh, similarly, explores the interstices between lived actuality, ritualized behaviour and discourse in asking whether the First Crusade may truly be characterized as a species of pilgrimage. In answering in the affirmative, contrary to some recent scholarly attempts to downplay this aspect of the crusade's ideological and pastoral self-construction, she shows how a close comparative study of the terminology of several texts, looking for lexical commonalities and shared assumptions about plot and agency, can complement a case-by-case analysis of what is distinctive in each individual narrative, in the process reminding us that discourses can transcend their individual articulations.

In the case of the First Crusade such discourses circulated, to a significant extent at least, beyond the texts that are now our sole evidence for them.

One of the ways in which ideas about the crusade circulated was, of course, by means of the appropriation and adaptation, even the recycling, of existing narratives, written and oral. The interrelationships between the various narratives of the First Crusade have long been a matter of scholarly debate, and are likely to remain so. Three of the papers in this volume consider aspects of this problem. Jay Rubenstein asks us to reconsider the complexity of Guibert of Nogent's historical project in his *Dei Gesta per Francos*. Guibert knew of, and positioned himself in opposition to, Fulcher of Chartres's account of the crusade and its aftermath, a positioning that a re-examination of Fulcher's text helps to elucidate; but, as Rubenstein goes on to argue, there are also a number of intriguing and compelling parallelisms between Guibert's plot details – some of them precisely the sort of anecdotes that Carol Sweetenham examines – and the *Historia Ierosolimitana* of Albert of Aachen, similarities that speak to the impact of orally transmitted capsule narratives, some of them perhaps the stuff of song, on the crusade-as-written. Luigi Russo's paper shows the importance of Monte Cassino as a centre of historiographical production, and the ways in which, as a result of the abbey's optimal location within communication networks between east and west, it participated actively in the adaptation, reworking, blending and dissemination of narratives of the First Crusade, the complexities of which scholars are only now beginning to disentangle. Finally, Marcus Bull revisits the relationship between Robert the Monk's history of the crusade and Gilo of Paris's verse *Historia Vie Hierosolimitane*, arguing that we should be guarded in our calling forth of lost 'common sources' in order to explain similarities between texts. Such putative shared sources can deflect us from fully appreciating the creativity and imagination on display in those texts that do survive.

It is probably fair to say that until recent years the study of the early crusade narrative corpus tended towards the methodologically conservative, and subordinated a wholesale engagement with modern theoretical perspectives to a mining of the texts for information or, if the texts themselves were foregrounded, analyses that privileged traditional and self-limiting intentionalist and instrumentalist readings (what did the author mean when he wrote such and such? what function does this text serve as 'propaganda'?). One of the ambitions for this volume is that it should participate in the process of helping the study of crusade historiography to catch up with, and by extension fully integrate itself within, the generally more adventurous and theoretically pluralistic approaches adopted by many scholars of ancient and medieval history-writing.[18] As the papers in this volume individually and cumulatively demonstrate, the historiographical response to the First Crusade and to the cultural diffusion of crusade motifs and ideas represents an unusually rich and under-exploited resource in this regard.

---

[18] See e.g. the showcasing of several leading scholars' methodological and conceptual approaches in *Writing Medieval History*, ed. N. Partner (London, 2005). For a good example of the benefits of reading crusade texts in new ways, see N. R. Hodgson, *Women, Crusading and the Holy Land in Historical Narrative* (Woodbridge, 2007).

BALDRIC OF BOURGUEIL AND THE
FAMILIA CHRISTI

Steven Biddlecombe

Baldric of Bourgueil reached the heights of influence and power in the north-western French Church in the last quarter of the eleventh and first quarter of the twelfth century. He was prior, then abbot of the rich Benedictine monastery of Bourgueil, in the Loire valley between Orléans and Angers, for over thirty years. He was appointed archbishop of Dol in 1107 and died in 1130 at the age of around eighty-four.[1] Alongside this career as a senior churchman he was variously a writer of poems, letters and elegies,[2] a preacher, teacher and sermonizer,[3] a hagiographer[4] and a historian of the First Crusade.

His Latin history of the First Crusade, the *Historia Ierosolimitana*, originally composed around 1105, was previously edited in 1879 in the fourth volume of the *Recueil des historiens des croisades: historiens occidentaux*. That edition was based on a collation of seven manuscripts. A new edition, produced by the present author, is derived from twenty-one extant manuscripts, and has identified a further three additional codices containing a version of this text, two in fragmentary form and one which was destroyed by fire. The *Recueil* edition relied exclusively on manuscripts produced in France in the twelfth and thirteenth centuries; in contrast, the new edition reveals a manuscript tradition extending into Anglo-Norman England and Spain, covering four centuries, and encompassing both a translation into Spanish and the transformation of the narrative into a French *chanson de geste*. In a very broad sense this significant

---

[1]   Baldric's life and works are discussed in H. Pasquier, *Un poète latin du XIIe siècle: Baudri, abbé de Bourgueil, archevêque de Dol, 1046–1130* (Paris, 1878); the modern edition of his poetry cited below (n. 2) expands on this history, and differs from Pasquier's reconstruction to some extent.

[2]   The most recent edition of his poetic works can be found in Baldric of Bourgueil, *Poèmes*, ed. and trans. J-Y. Tilliette, 2 vols (Paris, 1998–2002).

[3]   OV, v, 188–190.

[4]   For example, 'Vita s. Roberti de Arbrissellis', *PL* clxii, 1043–58. This Latin text has been translated into English in *Robert of Arbrissel: A Medieval Life*, trans. B. L. Venarde (Washington, 2003), pp. 1–21. Baldric's Life is also discussed in J. Dalarun, *Robert of Arbrissel: Sex, Sin, and Salvation in the Middle Ages*, trans. B. L. Venarde (Washington, 2006).

expansion of what we know of the text's manuscript tradition can be seen as a reflection of the popularity and influence of Baldric's *Historia Ierosolimitana*. As Neil Wright has pointed out, this text may not appeal to modern 'scientific' historians but it was very much to the taste of twelfth-century readers.[5] This paper will explore one of the key features of Baldric's narrative, one that may help us to understand the favoured status of his version of the events of the First Crusade; and will provide insights into one of the most significant questions facing western Christians in the immediate aftermath of the First Crusade. This key feature is his use of the extended metaphor of the *familia Christi* as a means of explaining the obligations that western Christians had towards those in the east who shared their faith. The significant question relates to how the relationship between the eastern and western limbs of the Christian faith could or should be maintained and whether their theological and administrative divergence could or should be ended following the success of the First Crusade.

Baldric writes in his prologue to the *Historia Ierosolimitana* that he had seen a book, written by some unknown compiler, that told the story of the First Crusade; this *libellus rusticanus*[6] conveyed the truth of what had happened, but its delivery represented such an *inculta et incompta lectio*[7] that even those with the simplest tastes would be put off reading it. Having been made aware through this book (which was without doubt the *Gesta Francorum*) of the narrative of the First Crusade, Baldric was outraged that its theological significance, its meaning to Christians and its potential as an *exemplum* to others had been made worthless (*viluerat*), because it had not been reported with the appropriate sophistication (*urbanitas*). He explains that he felt compelled to apply what talent he had to recapitulating this history, going over the main points of the *Gesta* again and adding the polish and elegance he felt it lacked.[8]

This added polish and elegance has been taken by some modern historians to simply mean improvements to the *Gesta's* 'literary style'.[9] This is an understandable response given Baldric's reputation as a poet, but Baldric thought the *Gesta* lacked something more significant, and that this lack undervalued the memory of the First Crusade, a view he shared with others.[10] For Baldric this was not just an issue of poetic language; for him the addition of flowery

---

[5] N. Wright, 'Epic and Romance in the Chronicles of Anjou', in *Anglo-Norman Studies XXVI: Proceedings of the Battle Conference 2003*, ed. J. Gillingham (Woodbridge, 2004), pp. 177–89.

[6] *Historia Ierosolimitana*, ed. Biddlecombe, p. 128 (BB *prologus*, p. 10): 'a rustic little book'. All references to Baldric of Bourgueil's *Historia Ierosolimitana* are to my PhD thesis, 'The *Historia Ierosolimitana* of Baldric of Bourgueil: A New Edition in Latin and an Analysis' (University of Bristol, 2010); references in parentheses are to the *RHC* edition.

[7] *Ibid.*: 'uncultivated and dishevelled text'.

[8] *Ibid.*

[9] S. Runciman, *A History of the Crusades*, 3 vols (London, 1951–4), i, 330; an even more dismissive, and more recent, point of view is Colin Morris's verdict that the *Historia Ierosolimitana* 'offered little that was not in the *Gesta*, beyond a more flowery style': 'Peter the Hermit and the Chroniclers', in *The First Crusade: Origins and Impact*, ed. J. P. Phillips (Manchester, 1997), p. 24.

[10] For example Guibert of Nogent noted that it was 'pieced together in words more simple than was appropriate': GN *praefatio*, p. 79. Robert the Monk called it 'uncertain and unsophisticated in its style and expression': RM *sermo apologeticus*, p. 721.

phrases, the use of alliteration and assonance and numerous classical and biblical quotations or allusions would not be sufficient to do justice to the great events that he was reporting. What Baldric added to the *Gesta* was not simply poetry. He dignified the memory of the First Crusade by introducing theological ideas, epic motifs and plausible characters that his audience could understand, relate to and be inspired by: all expressed in a language they would enjoy.

As with most contemporary writers on the First Crusade, Baldric's audience was primarily made up of well-educated ecclesiastics, scholars and others – the *litterati*: a very small minority who entirely dominated the written discourse of the medieval world.[11] Baldric was, at the time he began to compose the *Historia Ierosolimitana* in or before 1105, an experienced churchman: a poet who had written for and about many of the distinguished lords and ladies of the secular courts, the masters of the schools, and the bishops who ruled the episcopal palaces of the Loire valley and beyond. He himself was written about as a noteworthy figure, one who was making enemies and being considered for high office. As both a member of the *litterati* of north-western France and a significant contributor to its poetic output, it is likely that he would have been very familiar both to and with his audience. Baldric's audience may be considered to have comprised what Brian Stock terms a 'textual community', a group whose members may have been quite diverse in both social standing and role, but who demonstrated both a shared use of texts and a geographic closeness.[12] Gerald Bond points out, with regard to the audience for Baldric's poetry, that this community can be viewed through his epistolary poems.[13] His analysis has demonstrated that of the eighty-seven poems that Baldric addressed to fifty-three identifiable individuals, nine were to senior churchmen (bishops, abbots, priors or archdeacons), and four were to members of the secular hierarchy (kings, lords and other wealthy individuals), while forty were addressed to representatives of the lower ranks of the monastic or cathedral schools. Bond has also analysed where those in receipt of Baldric's epistolary poems were located geographically, finding that they were more or less radial to Bourgueil, and that most of the poems went to Orléans, Chartres, Caen, Bayeux, Le Mans or Angers. A poem, being shorter and therefore easier to carry, copy and disseminate, is clearly different from a substantial text such as Baldric's *Historia Ierosolimitana*; however, this type of audience, this mix of different people in different places, is probably a good sample of the initial audience who would have read, or were the intended readership of, the crusade history. Senior churchmen, literate secular lords and the cathedral and monastic schools would have formed such a 'textual community', with reading and writing at the centre of its interests, a forum for

---

[11] See M. Fumagelli Beonio Brocchieri, 'The Intellectual', in *The Medieval World*, ed. J. Le Goff, trans. L. G. Cochrane (London, 1990), pp. 181–211.

[12] B. Stock, *The Implications of Literacy: Written Language and Modes of Interpretation in the Eleventh and Twelfth Centuries* (Princeton, 1983), pp. 90–1.

[13] G. A. Bond, '*Iocus Amoris*: The Poetry of Baudri of Bourgueil and the Formation of the Ovidian Subculture', *Traditio*, 42 (1986), 143–93.

displaying skill and knowledge for students and masters, and wealth and culture for secular men and women.[14]

In his *Historia Ierosolimitana* Baldric strives to assess the meaning of the events of the First Crusade, and when writing about them he reveals attitudes to issues beyond those events. This is something that all authors writing about the First Crusade did to a greater or lesser extent. In their various histories they examined theological themes of salvation, the role of the Church in leading and controlling laymen, and the nature of the Church itself. One of the most significant issues facing the Church in the early part of the twelfth century was the relationship between its eastern and western halves, the schism that had developed between them, and the potential for reunification that existed in the idea of a crusade that would give aid to the eastern Christians. 'Eastern Christians' in this context means those from the Syrian, Armenian, Greek Orthodox, Nestorian and Maronite traditions who mostly lived in cities such as Edessa, Antioch and Jerusalem. It does not refer solely to the Byzantine empire or emperor, although it should be acknowledged that the reported actions of the emperor may well have influenced the attitudes towards other eastern Christians held by Latin historians of the First Crusade.

Each of the historians of the First Crusade explored the east–west relationship in light of the events of the crusade, reflecting attitudes and theological approaches to the eastern Church that varied significantly and revealing the diverse perspectives existing within the western Church at the start of the twelfth century. By comparing Baldric's attitudes towards the eastern Christians with those held by other First Crusade historians, these diverse perspectives can be assessed. In the process, it can also be shown how Baldric saw the *familia Christi* as a metaphor for the Christian Church, as a way of understanding the motivations of the crusaders, and as a means of encouraging support for and participation in a future crusade by his potential audience.

The attitudes that an ecclesiastic of this period might have adopted are revealed in the vision of Church and society that Baldric constructs in the *Historia Ierosolimitana*. He presents a view of the position and power of the Church in society and outlines the role of secular men as patrons of a 'Christian family', tasked with protecting its people and assets and enforcing its authority. By carrying out these tasks on crusade they become engaged in spiritual kinship both with each other and, for Baldric especially, with eastern Christians, in opposition to those outside the Christian Church. Baldric can thereby present a road to salvation for secular men on which they can turn away from fighting fellow Christians for personal glory and gain, and towards fighting the enemies of the Church on behalf of the faith they share with all Christians.

Peter the Venerable explained what he perceived as the increase in lay involvement in the Church through acts such as gift-giving or the presentation of sons as oblates as a way in which laymen could share in the spiritual merit of the prayers and good works of religious institutions, and thereby gain salvation

---

[14] Bond, 'Iocus Amoris', 189–90.

for their souls.[15] Similarly, most authors present the First Crusade as an opportunity for laymen to 'obtain God's grace',[16] whereby they could direct their skills and energies towards helping fellow Christians, a purpose that would bring them salvation without forcing them to abandon secular life. In the *Historia Ierosolimitana* Baldric approaches this from a perspective that distinguishes him from other First Crusade historians. He portrays the Christian Church as one family, and the armed pilgrims as the vigorous and vengeful defenders of that family; and he accepts eastern Christians and the eastern Church as an integral part of the family of the Church and the spiritual kin of the western Christians.

From the Council of Nicaea onwards a number of Christian theologians, rulers and churchmen had accepted, and some had even encouraged, splits in the Christian Church because of theological and political differences between different Christian communities, while many others had striven for unity despite these differences. The eleventh and twelfth centuries in particular saw 'both sharp disagreements and several high-minded endeavours to heal the breach'.[17] As far back as the fifth century Augustine of Hippo, taking his lead from the Gospel of St John, had written about the unity of the Church being more important than the secular divisions of imperial governments and language, saying:

> The Church, spread among the nations, speaks in all tongues; the Church is the body of Christ, in this body you are a member: therefore, since you are a member of that body which speaks with all tongues, believe that you too speak with all tongues. For the unity of the members is of one mind by charity; and that unity speaks as one man then spoke.[18]

Anselm of Canterbury, a contemporary of Baldric, was one of those who worked towards reconciliation between east and west; he believed that many differences were on unimportant matters, such as the priestly tonsure, bishops' rings or the use of unleavened, instead of leavened, bread in the Eucharist. On these matters he wrote: 'I think that these differences ought to be harmoniously and peaceably tolerated rather than being disharmoniously and scandalously condemned.'[19] Further, he urged that on the more important theological and liturgical matters, such as the use of the word *filioque* in the western Creed, agreement should be reached on the basis of reasoned argument and negotiation.[20] In the 1130s men such as Bishop Anselm of Havelberg, acting as a papal negotiator in

---

[15] Peter the Venerable, *The Letters*, ed. G. Constable, 2 vols (Harvard Historical Studies, 78; Cambridge, Mass., 1967), no. 28, p. 84.

[16] GN i.1, p. 87.

[17] H. Chadwick, *East and West: The Making of a Rift in the Church* (Oxford, 2003), p. 1.

[18] Augustine, 'In evangelium Joannis tractatus', *PL* xxxv, 1645, referring to John 14:2, Acts 2:4, and 1 Corinthians 12:27.

[19] Anselm of Canterbury, 'Ad Waleranni quaerelas responsio', *PL* clviii, 552. This is a letter to Bishop Walram of Naumburg, who was deeply concerned about the differing eucharistic practices to be found across the Church, including Palestine, Armenia, Gaul, Rome and Germany. Anselm's reassuring response is typical of his attitude to what he calls the 'administration' of the Church.

[20] Chadwick, *East and West*, pp. 222–7.

Constantinople, also echoed Augustine, arguing that diversity of usage did not compromise unity of faith.[21] This opinion was shared by an intermediary from the Byzantine side, Nicetas, archbishop of Nicomedia, who in the conclusion to his dialogue on the matter could state: 'Our disagreements are not in great but in very minor matters and, though not a help to charity, are no hindrance to the salvation of souls.'[22] So the tradition of tolerance and the acknowledgement and acceptance of diversity within the Church were not something that Baldric invented, nor did they end with him. There was not, however, universal agreement on this matter.

The various theological, political and cultural opinions among western Christians regarding the value of the eastern Church and its relationship to the western Church can be seen in the range of approaches to the eastern Christians taken by the various twelfth-century historians of the First Crusade. It is reasonable to suppose that they would have been aware to some extent of the history of the relationship between east and west and, when writing about events that had happened in the east, would be inclined to comment upon the nature of that relationship. In the following analysis the focus is not on the various anti-Byzantine and anti-emperor biases found in the narratives, but rather on their attitudes towards the Christian populations of Asia Minor, Syria and Palestine.

Guibert of Nogent, for example, is exceptionally harsh in his portrayal of the eastern Christians, presenting what he sees as the unchristian corruption of the eastern Church and the population as the reason why the Turks had been so successful in taking land in the east. He remarks: 'Since they fell away from faith in the Trinity, like those who fall in the mud and get muddier, little by little they have come to the final degradation of having taken paganism upon themselves, as the punishment for their sin.'[23] He even goes so far as to call the churches of Antioch, Jerusalem and Nicaea 'worthless',[24] observing that the faults exhibited by the churches had spread among the nominally Christian people of the east, who he says have become 'more wanton than the beasts of the fields'.[25] So not only are they corrupted and Christian only in name, but that corruption has brought upon them the punishment of subjection to non-Christians. The purpose of the crusade for Guibert is therefore twofold; to rid the land of the pagans and to restore a Christianity there that is free of unorthodox practices, follows the liturgy employed in the west, and acknowledges the pope's leadership of the whole of the Christian Church.

This hostility towards eastern Christians is echoed by a participant in the First Crusade, Raymond of Aguilers, whose very strong dislike of the Byzantines appears to have been extended to his brief acknowledgements of the existence of other eastern Christians. At one point he seems sympathetic, digressing to describe the suffering of the 60,000 Syrian Christians who 'were compelled to

---

[21] Anselm of Havelberg, 'Dialogi', *PL* clxxxviii, 1139–248.

[22] *Ibid.*, 1248.

[23] GN i.2, p. 92.

[24] *Ibid.*

[25] GN i.2, pp. 93–4.

forsake their country and Christian law' by the cruel Turks,[26] but then he cuts short his digression, saying: 'Why should I waste so much time on the Syrians? Surely this race plotted against the Holy of Holies and God's inheritance.'[27] Raymond is happy to see Christian lands and cities liberated, but the Christianity that will be brought back is not that which already exists in the Holy Land; it will be Latin Christianity.

The basis for many First Crusade narratives, and therefore the source for much of the information on the behaviour of the eastern Christians toward the crusaders that would shape or reshape the perceptions of later authors, was the *Gesta Francorum*, Baldric's *libellus rusticanus*. Here we find an author who participated in the First Crusade but rarely made a religious distinction between the peoples he met in the east; for example, he talks in the same sentence about Arabs, Saracens, Armenians, Syrians and Greeks, all being terrorized by the Turks.[28] Presumably the Arabs and Saracens he refers to are Muslim, the others Christian, but here he treats them as groups of people with different names but suffering the same terror. Elsewhere, the *Gesta* author has the Armenian and Syrian Christians walk a fine line between the Turks and crusaders; at Antioch for example they are spying for the Turks,[29] while at the same time bringing much-needed supplies to the crusader camp. However, these supplies are sold at extortionate prices, something they also try to do with the Turks.[30] They are reported as firing upon the Christian army from Antioch's battlements,[31] but also take the opportunity to ambush Turkish forces.[32] So their position in this narrative is ambiguous and the *Gesta* author, although he lists the crimes committed against them by the Turks, does not celebrate them as fellow Christians.

One author who also made the structure and events of the *Gesta Francorum* central to his narrative was Robert the Monk. His *Historia Iherosolimitana* survives in more than eighty medieval manuscripts, an indication that this was a very popular telling of the First Crusade, which is one reason why the attitude towards the eastern Christians taken by Robert is significant. He focuses on the land rather than the people in it, although he does outline, always in gruesome detail, the sufferings of 'those Christians'[33] whose lands have been invaded by 'her enemies';[34] for Robert, however, it is the land that 'begs and craves to be free, and prays endlessly for you (that is, western Christians) to come to her aid', not the Christians in that land.[35] He also emphasizes the quality of the land, saying it is 'more fruitful than any other, almost another earthly paradise';[36] but

26 RA, p. 129.
27 RA, pp. 129–30.
28 *GF*, p. 21.
29 *GF*, p. 29.
30 *GF*, p. 34.
31 *GF*, p. 41.
32 *GF*, p. 37.
33 RM i.1, p. 727.
34 RM i.2, p. 729.
35 *Ibid.*
36 *Ibid.*

he says virtually nothing about the quality of the Christian people who occupy it. He follows the *Gesta Francorum* in detailing the double-dealing of the eastern Christians, but excuses it as forced upon them by hostage-taking and scarcity. His approach seems sympathetic to the eastern Christians, but his focus is on liberating holy land and places, rather than people.

Robert the Monk was not a participant in the First Crusade, but one author who was an eyewitness to some of those events and who lived and worked first in Edessa and then in Jerusalem was Fulcher of Chartres.[37] He provides a testimony based on his experience of the east and seems to display a more positive attitude towards the eastern Christians; he has Pope Urban say: 'You must hasten to carry aid to your brethren dwelling in the east, who need your help for which they have often entreated.'[38] This reference to eastern Christians as brethren is positive and familial. Fulcher builds on this positive approach and has Pope Urban say: 'Oh what reproaches will be charged against you by the Lord Himself if you have not helped those who are counted like yourselves of the Christian faith!'[39] In his account the pope places an obligation on western Christians to aid those who share their faith. He also refers to the lands occupied by the Turks as 'our lands', indicating a shared inheritance. However, this sympathetic attitude appears to be contradicted by a letter included in the first recension of Fulcher's narrative.[40] It is addressed to Pope Urban from the crusade leaders and was purportedly written soon after the death of Bishop Adhemar of Le Puy in August 1098. It asks the pope to come to the Holy Land as 'father and head of the Christian religion' and to bring help to the crusaders to overcome the 'heretics, Greeks and Armenians, Syrians and Jacobites'.[41] The letter was included in the first version of Fulcher's *Historia Hierosolymitana* which was composed between 1101 and 1105, but is not included in Fulcher's later redaction completed between 1124 and 1127.[42] It has been argued that the insertion of this denunciation of the eastern Christians was done on behalf of Bohemond of Antioch, in order to lend support to his 1106 recruitment campaign in France.[43] The fact that it is not included in Fulcher's final version of his work is indicative of the much more positive attitude towards the eastern Christians reflected in the main body of his text, an attitude probably further influenced by the experience of living among them for an additional twenty years.

Another First Crusade historian who shares this positive approach is Albert of Aachen, but unlike Fulcher he has an independent perspective on the First Crusade in that he appears to have been unaware of other contemporary

[37] V. Epp, *Fulcher von Chartres: Studien zur Geschichtsschreibung des ersten Kreuzzuges* (Studia humaniora, 15; Düsseldorf, 1990) examines Fulcher's *Historia Hierosolymitana* in great detail.
[38] FC i.3, pp. 132–3.
[39] FC i.3, p. 136.
[40] FC i.24, pp. 258–64.
[41] FC i.24, p. 264.
[42] Fulcher of Chartres, *A History of the Expedition to Jerusalem 1095–1127*, trans. F. R. Ryan, ed. H. S. Fink (Knoxville, 1969), p. 107 n. 1.
[43] *Ibid.*

accounts, including the *Gesta Francorum*.[44] For him it is not a speech by the pope that marks the initial instigation of the First Crusade, but a complaint about the mistreatment of eastern Christians made by their nominal leader, the patriarch of Jerusalem. The complaint is made in a letter delivered by Peter the Hermit to Urban II, who is moved by this to preach an expedition to the Holy Sepulchre.[45] From Albert's perspective the First Crusade begins with the desire to end the suffering of the eastern Christians. Throughout his narrative eastern Christians take on positive roles, as co-operative local guides,[46] envoys[47] and scavengers for supplies.[48] They share the suffering of the crusaders, for example when the corpses of 'Gauls as well as Greeks, Syrians and Armenians mixed together' are found after Antioch is taken.[49] They welcome the crusaders into Bethlehem,[50] and mourn alongside them when Godfrey, the first Latin ruler of the city, dies in 1100.[51] This and other features indicate that Albert is ecumenical regarding the eastern Christians; as his most recent editor observes: 'He never mentions doctrinal differences and treats all as "fellow-Christians".'[52]

We see here a range of attitudes towards the eastern Church, from Guibert's condemnation of their practices and dismissal of their churches, and Raymond of Aguilers's rejection of them as not worthy of the efforts of the crusaders, through the ambivalent attitudes of the *Gesta* author and Robert the Monk, to the more positive assessment of Fulcher of Chartres and the ecumenical approach of Albert of Aachen. Some are more forthright in their views than others, but each expresses, either directly or indirectly, his opinions about the eastern Christians. This range of sentiments may reflect a similar variety of perceptions about the eastern Church in Latin ecclesiastical circles more widely, both before and after the First Crusade. It is therefore noteworthy that only Baldric takes the position of wholeheartedly embracing the eastern Christians as members of the same Christian family, celebrating the eastern Church as the source of the Christian inheritance, and describing it as the mother of the Christian faith.

Character utterance forms a significant part of Baldric's *Historia Ierosolimitana*; of its 35,500 words, 27% appear in passages of direct speech. This compares to a figure of around 18% for the proportion of direct discourse in the *Gesta Francorum* (many sequences of which are brief instructions or answers, rather than substantial orations). This is important because the set-piece speeches, of which there are many in the *Historia Ierosolimitana*, can be seen as the optimal vehicle for Baldric's authorial voice. They form the principal medium through

---

[44] AA, p. xxi; see also E. O. Blake and C. Morris, 'A Hermit Goes to War: Peter and the Origins of the First Crusade', in *Monks, Hermits and the Ascetic Tradition: Papers Read at the 1984 Summer Meeting and the 1985 Winter Meeting of the Ecclesiastical History Society*, ed. W. J. Sheils (Studies in Church History, 22; Oxford, 1985), pp. 79–107.

[45] AA i.5, pp. 6–8.

[46] AA x.28, p. 744.

[47] AA v.7, p. 346.

[48] AA vi.3, p. 408; vi.18, p. 426.

[49] AA iv.23, p. 282.

[50] AA v.44, p. 400.

[51] AA vii.21, pp. 514–16.

[52] AA, p. xxxiv.

which he expresses both his own view of what has happened and the views he believes those who participated would or should have held. They are not a direct or accurate report of what was actually said. In the longest and most powerful set-piece speech in the *Historia Ierosolimitana*, Baldric has Pope Urban II preach that French knights and noblemen should act as defenders of eastern Christians and the eastern Church: as their *couterini*, 'sharers of the same womb';[53] as *germani fratres nostri*, 'our true brothers';[54] and as fellow *membra Christi*, 'limbs of the body of Christ'.[55] This last phrase was probably inspired by Augustine's description of the unifying impulse that renders all Christians as the limbs of the body of the Church. Close to the end of the *Historia Ierosolimitana* there is a powerful sermon by an unnamed churchman, in which he refers to the participants in the First Crusade as *familia Christi*, and asks them to respond as members of that family.[56] The use of these words and phrases, and their positioning in set-piece orations, reveals Baldric's theological approach, and shows that he saw the Christian Church as a single entity encompassing both east and west, in much the same way as Augustine saw it, that is, as a unified body sharing the same faith, despite differences in how various Christians expressed that faith.

All of these formulations imply very close relationships: the crusaders and the eastern Christians are members of the same family or household, are born from the same womb, and form the limbs of the same body. Both the consistency with which Baldric uses these phrases and the context in which he places them indicate a strong theological emphasis on the Christian Church as the unified family of Christ and imply the duties of spiritual kinship that derive from membership of that family. The listener or reader is then struck by the strength of the metaphor, in which members of 'your' Christian family in the east are suffering, 'your' spiritual kin are being oppressed, and the heritage 'you' share with the eastern Christians is being used and abused by those outside the family. Penny Cole points out that Baldric's version of the speech by Urban was shaped, with its emphasis on familial relationships, in order 'to make his audience realize how profoundly these events touched their own lives'.[57] The implication in Baldric's version of the speech by Pope Urban is that it is the responsibility of the other members of the Christian family to right those wrongs, a message echoed and restated in even more direct terms by the unnamed sermonizer.

Baldric provides a preview of the language to be used by Urban when, before his version of the speech at Clermont, he refers to the eastern Church as *mater ecclesia*.[58] The first time Urban refers to the suffering of the eastern Christians, at the very beginning of his speech, they are distinctly acknowledged as 'our'

---

53 *Historia Ierosolimitana*, ed. Biddlecombe, p. 133 (BB i.4, p. 13).

54 *Ibid.*

55 *Ibid.*

56 *Historia Ierosolimitana*, ed. Biddlecombe, p. 307 (BB iv.13, p. 101).

57 P. J. Cole, *The Preaching of the Crusades to the Holy Land, 1095–1270* (Medieval Academy Books, 98; Cambridge, Mass., 1991), p. 16.

58 *Historia Ierosolimitana*, ed. Biddlecombe, p. 131 (BB i.1, p. 11).

Christians and 'our' brothers in both Jerusalem and Antioch. Baldric has Urban say:

> Audiuimus, fratres dilectissimi, et audistis, quod sine profundis singultibus retractare nequaquam possumus, quantis calamitatibus, quantis incommoditatibus, quam diris contritionibus, in Ierusalem et in Antiochia et in ceteris orientalis plagae ciuitatibus, Christiani nostri, fratres nostri, membra Christi, flagellantur, opprimuntur, iniuriantur. Germani fratres uestri, contubernales uestri, couterini uestri, nam eiusdem Christi et eiusdem ecclesiae filii estis, in ipsis suis domibus haereditariis uel alienis dominis mancipantur, uel ex ipsis exploduntur. [59]

The use of this metaphor of familial closeness by Baldric is repeated later in Urban's speech when he says of the eastern Church:

> Haec est enim de qua totius uestrae salutis emanauerunt gaudia, quae distillauit in os uestrum diuini lactis uerba, quae uobis propinauit euangeliorum sacrosancta dogmata. [60]

The portrayal of the eastern Church as the nourishing mother of Christianity works alongside the rhetorical argument that eastern Christians are spiritual brothers born of the same mother; they are metaphorical *couterini*, and the mother that bore them all is the eastern Church. [61] There are parallels here with the use of maternal imagery to depict God and Christ, of which numerous examples have been found in the works of twelfth-century authors such as Aelred of Rievaulx, Bernard of Clairvaux and Anselm of Canterbury, as described by Caroline Walker Bynum, who points out that:

> The maternal imagery of medieval monastic treatises tells us that cloistered males in the twelfth century idealized the mothering role, that they held consistent stereotypes of femaleness as compassionate and soft, and that they saw the bond

---

[59] *Historia Ierosolimitana*, ed. Biddlecombe, p. 133 (BB i.4, p. 13): 'We have heard, most beloved brethren, and you have heard what we cannot recount without deep sorrow, how, with great hurt and dire sufferings, our Christian brothers, the limbs of Christ, are scourged, oppressed, and injured in Jerusalem, in Antioch, and the other cities of the east. Your own blood brothers, your companions, your brothers of the same womb, for you are sons of the same Christ and the same Church, are either subjected in their inherited homes to other masters, or are being driven from them.' Translation based on that in A. C. Krey, *The First Crusade: The Accounts of Eye-Witnesses and Participants* (Princeton, 1921), p. 33.

[60] *Historia Ierosolimitana*, ed. Biddlecombe, p. 137 (BB i.4, pp. 14–15): 'She it is from whom the joys of your whole salvation have come forth, who poured into your mouths the milk of divine wisdom, who set before you the holy teachings of the Gospels.' Trans. Krey, *First Crusade*, p. 35.

[61] This is a complete reversal of the attitude expressed by Pope Leo IX in his letter to Emperor Constantine IX, in which the pope described himself as father and the Roman Church as mother to the emperor and the eastern Church respectively. See H. E. J. Cowdrey, 'The Reform Papacy and the Origin of the Crusades', in his *The Crusades and Latin Monasticism, 11th–12th Centuries* (Aldershot, 1999), no. I, p. 66. For the text of the letter, see C. J. C. Will, *Acta et scripta quae de controversiis ecclesiae Graecae et Latinae saeculo undecimo composita extant* (Leipzig, 1861), pp. 85–9.

of child and mother as a symbol of closeness, union, or even the incorporation of one self into another.[62]

Baldric uses similar imagery to make his audience more sympathetic to the eastern Church, and to imply that bonds exist between members of the Christian faith that should be as strong as those between family members.

He makes this even more implicit in the second speech, an inspirational, rabble-rousing oration addressed to the Christian army before the walls of Jerusalem by an unnamed churchman.[63] This speech acts as a confirmation, and a mirror, of the first long speech by Urban, reaffirming the validity of what Baldric reports the pope said. In this second speech the concept of crusaders as members of Christ's kin is combined with the preacher's assertion that eastern Christians are also members of that kin. Baldric has him say:

> Expergiscimini igitur, familia Christi; expergiscimini, milites et pedites expediti; et ciuitatem hanc, rem quidem publicam nostram, constanter capessite.[64]

After comparing what is happening to Christians inside the city to the suffering of Christ on the cross, the preacher then asks:

> Quid igitur agitis? Equumne est uos hec audire, uos ista uidere nec ingemiscere? Patribus et filiis et fratribus et nepotibus dico. Numquid si quis externus uestrum aliquem percusserit, sanguinem uestrum non ulciscemini? Multo magis Deum uestrum, patrem uestrum, fratrem uestrum ulcisci debetis, quem exprobrari, quem proscribi, quem crucifigi uidetis; quem clamantem et desolatum et auxilium poscentem auditis.[65]

Describing the crusaders as members of 'Christ's family', *familia Christi*, implies not just that they are fighting in the same army and share the same God, as in the

---

[62] C. Walker Bynum, *Jesus as Mother: Studies in the Spirituality of the High Middle Ages* (Berkeley, 1984), p. 167.

[63] Various names, including Arnulf of Chocques, have been put forward as the orator, but in all probability numerous sermons were made to the Christian army by various preachers. The likelihood is that this sermon was composed by Baldric himself to serve as an affirmation of the status of Urban's speech at the beginning of the narrative. As Orderic Vitalis pointed out, Baldric was a renowned preacher himself, and so he may well have considered what he would have said to the crusader army before the holy city: see OV, v, 190.

[64] *Historia Ierosolimitana*, ed. Biddlecombe, p. 307 (BB iv.13, p. 101): 'Rouse yourselves, members of Christ's family! Rouse yourselves, knights and foot-soldiers, and seize firmly that city, our common property!' Translation based on that in J. S. C. Riley-Smith, *The First Crusade and the Idea of Crusading* (London, 1986), p. 48.

[65] *Historia Ierosolimitana*, ed. Biddlecombe, p. 308 (BB iv.13, p. 101): 'What are you doing about these things? Is it right for you to hear these things, to see these things done and not to lament them? I address fathers and sons and brothers and nephews. If an outsider were to strike any of your kin down would you not avenge your blood relative? How much more ought you to avenge your God, your father, your brother, whom you see reproached, banished from his estates, crucified, whom you hear calling, desolate, and begging for aid.' Translation based on Riley-Smith, *First Crusade*, p. 48.

phrase *militia Christi*, used by all the other authors, but also that they are members of the family or household of Christ, the spiritual kin of the eastern Christians, and thus share the obligations, not just of *commilitones* (fellow soldiers), but of members of a spiritual family. By meeting those obligations secular warriors, as the limbs of the Christian Church, would be able to attain salvation.

The medieval Latin term *familia* usually refers to a whole household, including servants and attendants, not simply blood relatives.[66] As such it is an inclusive term, embracing a broad range of individuals of higher and lower status, and not exclusively limited by a shared ancestry. Its use in a crusading context is perhaps reflective of another aspect of Baldric's approach to explaining the events of the First Crusade, which typifies it as a communal enterprise. But given that Baldric usually refers to blood relationships, the *consanguinei* of mothers and daughters, fathers and sons, brothers and nephews,[67] it would be fair to assume that he is primarily using the metaphor of the *familia* to bring notions of blood-related kinship to the attention of the audience.

Baldric presents the First Crusade as an expedition to provide help to eastern Christians that is inspired by a desire for salvation, and an understanding of the obligations of kinship, which in eleventh- and twelfth-century France acted as a powerful uniting force.[68] With the Christian family facing external enemies who had injured members of that family, Christians in the west were told by Pope Urban to abandon their inter- and intra-familial quarrels and provide aid to their brethren in the east. This urge to provide mutual help was based on three obligations that the medieval aristocracy instinctively understood. Firstly, they were aware of the importance of communal defence and the guarding of each others' interests. When Baldric has Pope Urban speak of 'Your own blood brothers, your companions, your brothers of the same womb, for you are sons of the same Christ and the same Church... [being] subjected in their inherited homes to other masters, or driven from them', he is speaking about the need to relieve the suffering of spiritual kin, and of guarding or recovering the 'inherited homes' of the Christian family.[69] Secondly, aristocrats knew the value of maintaining their family estate. When the preacher exhorts the crusaders to take Jerusalem he says, 'Seize firmly that city, our common property.'[70] In the text this is described as *res publica nostra*, a phrase which would usually mean 'our state'; but having just referred to the crusaders as *familia Christi*, Baldric is clearly loading the speech with familial messages, not to do with citizenship, but with spiritual kinship; not to do with government but with a shared Christian family inheritance.

Thirdly, they knew that vengeance was required for any wrong done to a kinsman.[71] When the unnamed preacher at the walls of Jerusalem says to the

---

[66] C. B. Bouchard, *Strong of Body, Brave and Noble: Chivalry and Society in Medieval France* (Ithaca, 1998), p. 67.

[67] No mention is made of nieces or sisters in either of the speeches.

[68] M. Bloch, *Feudal Society*, trans. L. A. Manyon (Chicago, 1961), p. 135; see also G. Duby, *The Chivalrous Society*, trans. C. Postan (London, 1977).

[69] *Historia Ierosolimitana*, ed. Biddlecombe, p. 133 (BB i.4, p. 13).

[70] *Historia Ierosolimitana*, ed. Biddlecombe, p. 307 (BB iv.13, p. 101).

[71] Bloch, *Feudal Society*, pp. 125–30.

crusaders, 'If an outsider were to strike any of your kin down would you not avenge your blood relative?', he addresses this question to 'fathers and sons and brothers and nephews', because these are the members of the family who would be responsible for taking vengeance for violence against a kinsman. By listing the masculine family members he completes the metaphor of the eastern Church as the 'mother' of Christianity, reinforcing again the idea of familial obligation. Such an act of vengeance would be sinful if carried out against fellow Christians, but is given salvific meaning when carried out against non-believers.[72] This subject has been examined by Susanna Throop in her recent book *Crusading as an Act of Vengeance*, in which she observes that references in crusade narratives 'to the need to take vengeance for injuries to God and Christianity, couched in the terminology of family and lordship, confirm the relationship between social obligation and the idea of crusading as vengeance'.[73] She further points out a link between this obligation and the notion of just war in part elaborated by Augustine of Hippo and Isidore of Seville, for whom the justice of vengeful actions could be established by divine sanction; and for Urban's audience (of which Baldric was a part) his words were remembered as a confirmation of that divine sanction, and indeed acknowledged by shouts of 'God wills it', although Baldric himself does not report these. By extending the familiar obligation on laymen to avenge their kin to encompass vengeance for injuries done to eastern Christians, Baldric is both acknowledging the unity of the Christian faith and providing a theological justification for otherwise sinful acts.

Indeed, the kinship that Baldric has both Urban and the unknown sermonizer preach is based on shared faith and membership of the family of Christ. It appealed to motivations, emotions and instincts that were usually expressed in a secular form, through alliances and marriages, through warfare and feud between Christians, and through economic transactions such as inheritance. In the First Crusade these familiar and indeed familial motivations were given expression through an armed pilgrimage to bring aid to members of the Christian family in the east. Baldric accepts the diversity within that family, following the precepts of Augustine derived from his reading of the Gospel of John. He takes a clear ecumenical attitude towards the eastern Christians that is in accordance with the unifying message of his contemporary, Anselm of Canterbury. This sense of unification and co-operation was given concrete form by the actions of the most senior Latin churchman to participate in the First Crusade, the papal legate Bishop Adhemar of Le Puy, who in the crusader camp outside Antioch in October 1097 wrote a letter from himself and Patriarch Simeon of Jerusalem.[74] It was a joint appeal to Pope Urban II for more Christian soldiers to come to the Holy Land. The patriarch, probably with Adhemar's help and certainly with his approval, wrote a second letter of his own to the pope in January 1098.[75]

---

[72] M. G. Bull, *Knightly Piety and the Lay Response to the First Crusade: The Limousin and Gascony c.970–c.1130* (Oxford, 1993), p. 67.

[73] S. A. Throop, *Crusading as an Act of Vengeance, 1095–1216* (Farnham, 2011), p. 5.

[74] *Epistulae et chartae ad historiam primi belli sacri spectantes: Die Kreuzzugsbriefe aus den Jahren 1088–1100*, ed. H. Hagenmeyer (Innsbruck 1901), pp. 141–2.

[75] *Ibid.*, pp. 146–9.

As James Brundage has pointed out, this co-operation, the independent voice given to the patriarch, and the language of the two letters indicate 'a healthy working relationship' between the two men.[76] The second letter especially is written as though the patriarch saw no substantial difference between east and west, between the Greek and Latin clergy: all, to his eyes, were Christian and brethren.[77] Recent work by Christopher MacEvitt has shown that this sense of unity and co-operation was not a construct put together by men such as Baldric in the comfort of the scriptorium in Bourgueil, but a working and continuing reality in what became the Latin East during and after the First Crusade.[78] He characterizes the social interaction between the newly established Latin rulers and the local Christian population as 'rough tolerance', according to which the Latins exercised authority, sometimes violently, while allowing multiple religious communities to co-exist in a spiritually charged land.[79] Nor was this tolerance a geographically or historically isolated occurrence: in Spain what has become known as *convivencia* allowed for the interaction of Jewish, Muslim and Christian communities, while the status of *dhimmi* under Islamic law allowed for non-Muslim communities in areas under Muslim rule to practise their religion and to flourish to a limited degree. Norman Sicily provides yet another example of a form of multicultural interaction, and recent work by Graham Loud has indicated that the Norman kings of Sicily not only tolerated but financed the maintenance of Greek Orthodox churches on the island and in southern Italy.[80]

In fact the more one looks at the evidence the more one is struck by the idea that it is those who, like Guibert of Nogent and Raymond of Aguilers, emphasize difference and rail against the 'heresy' of non-western Christian traditions who are actually creating a theological or intellectual construct. While the First Crusade was a unique and violent set of events, Baldric attempted, by emphasizing the social obligations met by the crusaders, to ensure that it would be remembered as an act intended to right wrongs, avenge injuries and unite Christians regardless of the religious traditions of their individual communities. Thus, in writing his *Historia Ierosolimitana*, Baldric not only explained the theological meaning of the First Crusade, but also expressed a belief in a universal Church, diverse in language, practice and location, but unified in faith and kinship.

---

[76] J. A. Brundage, 'Adhemar of Puy: The Bishop and His Critics', *Speculum*, 34 (1959), 201–12.
[77] *Ibid.*, 210.
[78] C. H. MacEvitt, *The Crusades and the Christian World of the East: Rough Tolerance* (Philadelphia, 2008).
[79] *Ibid.*, pp. 22–5.
[80] See G. A. Loud, *The Latin Church in Norman Italy* (Cambridge, 2007), pp. 501–12.

GUIBERT OF NOGENT, ALBERT OF AACHEN AND FULCHER OF CHARTRES: THREE CRUSADE CHRONICLES INTERSECT

Jay Rubenstein

Guibert of Nogent wrote his crusade chronicle, *God's Deeds through the Franks*, in 1107–8, while living in his former monastery of Saint-Germer de Fly. Exiled from his abbacy in Nogent, he had a great deal of time on his hands, which he filled by writing a scholarly, elegant history of the crusade. His main source was the *Gesta Francorum*.[1] Like his contemporaries Robert the Monk and Baldric of Bourgueil, Guibert found the *Gesta Francorum* dissatisfying, particularly in terms of style.[2] On factual matters, by contrast, he stuck close to his source – sometimes to his frustration. The author of the *Gesta Francorum*, for example, fails to include the name of Bishop Adhemar of Le Puy, and somehow at Saint-Germer Guibert had difficulty tracking down anyone who knew it. Not until near the end of Book II could he write, according to a crusade veteran, 'that precious man was called "Aymar"'.[3] The passage is emblematic of Guibert's overall historical method: he rewrote the *Gesta Francorum* and supplemented it, where possible, with information from eyewitnesses. By the end of 1108, he had largely finished the book. Since his exile ended at the same time, he was able to return to Nogent to present the final product to Bishop Lisiard of Soissons.[4]

Very likely, though, the book offered to Lisiard contained an abridged version of *God's Deeds through the Franks*, as it exists today. It would have been uncharacteristically expeditious of Guibert to finish such a big project in only eighteen

---

[1]   J. Rubenstein, *Guibert of Nogent: Portrait of a Medieval Mind* (New York, 2002), pp. 94–6; see also Huygens's introduction to GN, p. 51, where he offers 1109 as a *terminus ante quem* for the chronicle.

[2]   See RM *sermo apologeticus*, p. 721; BB *prologus*, p. 10; and GN *praefatio*, p. 79. On these writers, J. S. C. Riley-Smith, *The First Crusade and the Idea of Crusading* (London, 1986), pp. 135–52; and J. Flori, *Chroniqueurs et propagandistes: Introduction critique aux sources de la Première croisade* (Hautes études médiévales et modernes, 98; Geneva, 2010), pp. 17, 105–6.

[3]   GN ii.13, p. 131.

[4]   GN, pp. 77–8.

months, even if he were living the tranquil life of an exile. For comparison, another of Guibert's works, the *Moral Commentary on Genesis*, took over thirty years to write. We further know from Guibert's autograph manuscripts that he was an assiduous editor, sometimes returning to finished texts, cutting up the quires and inserting whole new sections into them, or else composing lengthy additions in his books' margins.[5] Guibert may have rushed to finish a draft of *God's Deeds through the Franks* to coincide with his return to Nogent, but he did not necessarily stop working on it.

In fact, as late as 1118, Guibert was still adding to the text. Twice in Book I he references arguments made in later theological works, begun ten years after his crusade chronicle. The changes are minor. In one of them, Guibert notes that at least two churches claimed to possess John the Baptist's skull, and he mockingly suggests that the saint must have been two-headed. He makes the same joke in his 1120 book *On the Relics of Saints*. In another passage he wonders whether Judas received the sacrament in the handful of bread Christ offered him at the Last Supper, the subject of a letter he wrote in 1118 in the wake of a recent theological debate at Laon.[6] Probably no more than interlinear glosses, these phrases still indicate that Guibert continued to tinker with his greatest historical work long after he had presented a dedicatory copy to Lisiard at Soissons.

During this process of revision, Guibert also discovered two major new sources. His use of one of them, Fulcher of Chartres's *Historia Hierosolymitana*, is well known. His use of the other, by contrast, has gone unnoticed. Based on available evidence, he seems to have discovered one – or perhaps two or three – sources directly related to the *Historia Ierosolimitana* of Albert of Aachen. Drawing these several texts together will allow us not only to learn about Guibert's work habits but also to cast light upon Fulcher's and Albert's works as well.

Guibert originally intended to finish his crusade history about halfway through its seventh and final book. There, he describes the crusaders' victory at Ascalon, saying that even the poorest pilgrims left the field wealthy.[7] He follows the battle with a lengthy exegesis of Zechariah 12, demonstrating the prophetic significance of what had happened at Jerusalem. The Franks had waged their battle not for the sake of a city. Rather, they had cast seeds far and wide 'against the oncoming fury of Antichrist'.[8] In their conquests, the Franks had surpassed the achievement of the Old Testament Israelites. Admittedly, they continued to suffer in the Holy Land, because 'God tamed and tames them with frequent misfortunes'.[9] This observation leads him to the moral lesson of the crusade, very

---

[5] Rubenstein, *Guibert of Nogent*, pp. 28, 128–30.

[6] GN i.2, p. 91 (on the *bucella* given to Judas), and i.5, p. 103 (on John the Baptist's two heads); see also Guibert, *De pigneribus sanctorum*, ed. R. B. C. Huygens (Corpus Christianorum, Continuatio Mediaeualis, 127; Turnhout, 1993), p. 102. The analysis in Rubenstein, *Guibert of Nogent*, pp. 156–7 is flawed.

[7] GN vii.20, p. 300, with Huygens's note at ll. 899–900. Also the final scene in *GF*, p. 97.

[8] 'contra venturi rabiem Antichristi': GN vii.21, p. 304.

[9] 'creberrimis tamen infortuniis edomuit et edomat': GN vii.21, p. 307.

much in keeping with Guibert's exegetical writings. Using thorns of adversity, God recalls us to 'self-recognition' and teaches us to resist temptation.[10]

Thus the book reaches a dramatic and moral conclusion – except that Guibert continues, now regaling his audience with several anecdotes, many of them not found elsewhere. Among other things, we learn about armies of orphaned Christian children, formed during the siege at Antioch, where they occasionally fought mock battles against Muslim children.[11] We find in these chapters the earliest description of impoverished crusaders called 'Tafurs', whom Guibert slyly associates with acts of cannibalism.[12] We also meet a knight who had sold his soul to the devil – or rather, 'made homage to him' – in hopes of avenging a dead brother. The knight gained a temporary reprieve from this pact by vowing to go to Jerusalem. Sounding very much like a crusade recruiter, Guibert concludes, 'See! Recognize how much protection this noble pilgrimage offers to the pure of heart, since it grants safety and security to the wicked.'[13] These tales were probably afterthoughts in a technical sense: peripheral additions to what the author believed an already completed book.

Eventually Guibert draws this series of anecdotes to a close, too, sounding another valedictory note for the book: no king led the crusaders; God alone was their shepherd. 'He gathered the wolves whom he had turned into lambs under his own arm bringing them not by their arms into the safety of his lap and leading them, as children full of pious joy, to gaze upon the sights they had longed for.'[14] And thus the chronicle seems to end, again.

But it continues, to Guibert's evident frustration. 'I was about to put heels onto the body of the present history, with the blessing of the Author of this world, before I learned that a certain priest, Fulcher of Chartres, who served as chaplain to Duke Baldwin in Edessa, mentioned a few things I didn't know about. Other things he described differently from me, albeit falsely and with coarse language.'[15]

The copy of Fulcher's *Historia Hierosolymitana* that Guibert discovered would have been the first recension, completed and circulated in 1106 or 1107. No medieval exemplar of it survives. In addition to Guibert, only one other writer is known to have worked with it: a pilgrim usually identified as Bartolf of Nangis, who produced a slightly abridged but generally faithful version of the original.[16] Besides length, this 1106 version of Fulcher's text seems to have had a handful of substantive differences with later versions of the chronicle. Most notably, it contained a detailed description of the failure of the miracle of the

---

[10] 'ad sui recordationem': GN vii.21, p. 307.

[11] GN vii.22, p. 309.

[12] GN vii.23, pp. 310–12.

[13] 'hominium sibi facias' and 'Ecce pia ista peregrinatio pensemus quantum valuerit puris, quae tantum attulerit tutelae ac securitatis impuris': GN vii.30, pp. 325, 327.

[14] GN vii.31, p. 328.

[15] 'Presentis Historiae corpori, auctore mundi propitio, posituri calces, Fulcherium quondam Carnotensem presbiterum, qui Balduini apud Edessam ducis dudum capellanus extiterat, quaedam quae nos latuerant alia, diverse etiam a nobis aliqua sed pauca, haecque fallaciter et scabro, ut ceteri, sermone fudisse comperimus': GN vii.32, p. 329.

[16] The end of the 1106 recension corresponds with FC ii.35, p. 509; Bartolf's history is published as 'Gesta Francorum Iherusalem expugnantium', *RHC Occ* iii, 491–543.

holy fire to appear on Holy Saturday in 1101. The later, longer versions of the *Historia* describe this liturgical event with a single dependent clause: 'During the celebration of Easter, however, when everyone was worried because of the fire, which we did not have at the Holy Sepulchre on Saturday, the king set forth to Jaffa.'[17] Bartolf of Nangis and Guibert both indicate that Fulcher at one point described these events in greater detail – an impression confirmed in a much later copy of the *Historia*, usually identified as the 'L' manuscript.[18]

This 'L' manuscript contains an eccentric, heavily revised version of the *Historia*, with changes both stylistic and substantive. The most heavily edited passages appear in the first half of the text – that is to say, in those pages which correspond to the now lost first recension of Fulcher. The revisions are so significant that the editors of the *Recueil des historiens des croisades* elected not to incorporate them directly into their text but instead printed the 'L' text in the lower margin. Hagenmeyer chose not to use the manuscript at all. Its revisions, he concluded, were the work of someone other than Fulcher.[19] I will propose an alternative interpretation: based on comparison with both Bartolf and Guibert, the first half of the 'L' manuscript bears faithful witness to the substance of Fulcher's 1106 recension.

Specifically, in the passage on the holy fire, Fulcher in the 'L' manuscript speaks in the first person on two occasions. The first time, as crowds at the Holy Sepulchre begin to sing the *Kyrie Eleison*, he is so wonderstruck that he exclaims, 'And I, Fulcher, who had never heard a symphony of this kind, along with many others, new to this gorgeous uproar, turned my eyes toward heaven and rose from the ground, my heart overwhelmed with emotion, and hoped for that pure light to be kindled somewhere in the church.'[20] Later, when the flames failed to descend from heaven, Fulcher says that he and a chaplain hurried to Mount Calvary to look for heavenly fire. 'But neither here nor there did it appear.'[21] This mad dash to Calvary is one of the dramatic high points in the story. Bartolf of Nangis, however, fails to mention it.

Guibert does do so, albeit with an error. Working from a faulty memory, he says that Fulcher and the unnamed chaplain rushed to the Mount of Olives, where sometimes the holy fire had been known to descend.[22] It is an obvious geographic mistake. To reach the Mount of Olives, Fulcher would have had to walk across Jerusalem, exit the city and make the steep climb past the Garden of Gethsemane to the place of the Ascension. For Mount Calvary, he needed simply

---

[17] FC ii.8, pp. 395–6.
[18] Cambridge, University Library, MS 2079; Bartolf, 'Gesta Francorum', cc. 47–9, pp. 524–6.
[19] See Hagenmeyer's comments in FC, pp. 75–8. The writer is elsewhere called 'Pseudo-Fulcher': B. McGinn, '*Iter Sancti Sepulchri*: The Piety of the First Crusaders', in *The Walter Prescott Webb Memorial Lectures: Essays on Medieval Civilization*, ed. B. K. Lackner and K. R. Philp (Austin, TX, 1978), pp. 33–71.
[20] 'ego autem Folcherus, qui nunquam huiusmodi symphoniam audieram, multique alii, tumultui huic laudifluo moderni, oculis sursum erectis, cordibus compuncti de terra surrreximus et lumen almum alicubi in ecclesia iam accendit speravimus': FC, p. 831.
[21] 'sed nec huc nec illuc tunc venit': FC, p. 832.
[22] GN vii.42, pp. 342–3.

to walk a few steps away from the Holy Sepulchre and run up a staircase. This passage, despite the error, allows us to make fairly specific observations about the connections among these texts. First, because the 'L' manuscript describes Fulcher's ascent of Mount Calvary and Bartolf does not, we may say with confidence that Guibert was not working from Bartolf's version of the *Historia* but rather had direct access to the 1106 recension. Second, because of the overlap between Guibert's description and that of the 'L' manuscript, we can conclude that the latter manuscript provides a better witness to Fulcher's original draft than previous commentators have imagined.

We also are faced with a new question: if Fulcher originally wrote a lengthier account of what happened in 1101, why did he later excise it? Any answer is necessarily speculative, but it is worth considering whether Fulcher's historical mindset – about the holy fire and other subjects – might have changed between the first and second drafts of his chronicle. Hagenmeyer himself, albeit inadvertently when arguing against the reliability of the 'L' manuscript, suggests what some of these changes might have been. Unlike Fulcher, Hagenmeyer says, the L-writer was a royalist, apparently an imperial partisan in the Investiture Contest.[23] But would we expect something so different of Fulcher in 1106? As chaplain to Baldwin I, whose early reign was marked by an interminable struggle against Daimbert, patriarch of Jerusalem and papal legate, Fulcher was unlikely to be a simple reform advocate and papal apologist. The difference in tone between the two versions might thus indicate that Fulcher's attitudes not only about the holy fire but also about kingship evolved with the passage of time. And indeed the work of Meghan Holmes Worth seems to indicate that such a transformation in Fulcher's thought did occur.[24]

In recounting the holy fire in 1101, Guibert is content to paraphrase Fulcher. On other occasions, he wants mainly to ridicule him. His contempt, bordering on rage, grew mainly out of Fulcher's scepticism concerning the Holy Lance of Antioch, which he discusses in one short, misleading chapter in his *Historia*. Right after describing the capture of Antioch, Fulcher tells how a certain unnamed man claimed to have found the Lance of Longinus buried in a hole in the ground in an Antiochene church. The discovery caused much celebration, but after one hundred days the soldiers grew suspicious and forced Peter Bartholomew to undergo an ordeal by fire. Badly burned, Peter died twelve days later, causing everyone but Raymond of St Gilles to lose faith in the relic.[25] This passage, to Guibert's mind, is appalling evidence of Fulcher's ignorance, if not impiety. 'Will the arguments of that priest Fulcher, who at the time was being fêted and feasting at Edessa, even as our men were starving at Antioch, prevail against the people who were actually there?'[26] Guibert then cites a letter from

---

[23] See Hagenmeyer's comments in FC, pp. 76–7.
[24] M. H. Worth, '"To Write about Kings:" The Creation of Kingship in Outremer', Ph.D. dissertation in progress, University of Tennessee, Knoxville.
[25] FC i.18, pp. 235–41.
[26] 'Numquidne Fulcherii presbiteri, qui, nostris apud Antiochiam fame periclitantibus, feriatus epulabatur Edessae, tot prudentium, qui interfuere dum reppeiretur, ingeniis prevalebit argutia': GN vii.34, p. 332.

Baldwin of Edessa vouching for the Lance's authenticity and adds how, at the final battle of Antioch, no less a figure than Adhemar of Le Puy carried the Lance into battle, using it like a talisman against the enemy. Peter did later die during an ordeal, Guibert admits, but he adds, 'I'll explain how he died – and the cause is by no means certain – as soon as someone tells me why, according to Gregory the Great, a man who had received the gift of speaking in tongues lacerated his own limbs with his teeth.'[27] The reference is to Gregory's story of a boy named Armentarius who died as Guibert describes. Gregory himself says only that it happened according to the secret judgements of God.[28]

Setting aside the specifics of this debate, Guibert's criticism of Fulcher reveals something surprising and revealing. Guibert, as much as he would have hated to admit it, had not known about Peter Bartholomew's ordeal until he had read Fulcher. The story was not in his source material, the *Gesta Francorum*. Both of his fellow Frankish historians, Robert the Monk and Baldric of Bourgueil, do not describe the ordeal either. It is a reminder of how tenuous the lines of communication between Europe and the Levant were. The trial of Peter Bartholomew, a moment that ignited fierce controversy among the crusaders and continues to inspire historical debate today, passed unnoticed in Europe by men who had dedicated themselves to the task of recounting the crusade in its immediate aftermath.

Despite what Guibert says here, his narrative as now constituted does contain an earlier, brief description of Peter Bartholomew's ordeal, along with an explanation for why he died.[29] Similar to Raymond of Aguilers, Guibert argues that Peter emerged from the flames unharmed, but was badly injured during the confusion and celebrations that followed. As the crowds tore at Peter's clothes and body, 'they ripped away his soul'.[30] Opinions on this point were divided, Guibert admits, but Bishop Adhemar, he stresses, was so devoted to the Lance that he asked to be buried in the hole where Peter Bartholomew had first found it.

This passage would seem to be a later addition to the original text. If it were not, why in Book VII would Guibert refuse to explain how Peter Bartholomew died when he had already offered such an explanation in Book VI? The textual location of the story provides further indication that it was an insertion in Guibert's original text. Guibert situates Peter's death between the arrival of a fleet of ships laden with supplies and an account of the death of Anselm of Ribemont. These two events follow immediately upon one another in the *Gesta Francorum*.[31] In his original draft, Guibert probably copied them out one after the other, too. Later, when he learned the details of Peter Bartholomew's trial, he returned to his chronicle and added them at the appropriate point in the story.

---

[27] 'dicam quomodo iste obierit, de quo incertum est an Iesus fuerit, si dicat michi cur is, qui apud beatum Gregorium linguas omnes acceperat, propria dentibus membra disciderit': GN vii.34, p. 333.

[28] Gregory the Great, *Dialogues*, iv.26, trans. O. J. Zimmerman (Fathers of the Church, 39; Washington, DC, 1959), pp. 222–3.

[29] GN vi.22, pp. 262–4.

[30] 'animam extorserunt': GN vi.22, p. 263.

[31] *GF*, p. 85.

His experience of reading Fulcher thus inspired Guibert not only to add material onto the end of *God's Deeds through the Franks*, but eventually to go back and revise certain earlier sections of his book accordingly.

But Fulcher was not Guibert's only new source. His description of the ordeal by fire, as noted, immediately precedes Anselm of Ribemont's death – a scene that he describes in greater detail than does either the *Gesta Francorum* or Fulcher.[32] From the *Gesta* we learn simply that Anselm suffered martyrdom at Arqa. Fulcher says more specifically that Anselm died when struck by a stone.[33] Guibert works harder to set the scene: the Franks sought to undermine one of Arqa's towers by digging a tunnel beneath it. The Frankish women courageously helped, carrying away rubble from the tunnel's entry. Anselm of Ribemont, realizing that these efforts would fail, ordered catapults set up. The Saracens responded in kind, hurling stones from the city walls, and 'to the great loss of the Franks' army, Anselm, if not the best knight then at least one of the best, was struck down'.[34]

None of Guibert's likely sources provided him with these details. The only contemporary or near-contemporary version of the story which comes close to his is in Albert of Aachen's *Historia Ierosolimitana*. Albert does not precisely follow what Guibert says, but he does associate Anselm's death with Frankish siege machinery. Using mangonels the Franks bombarded the city walls, but the Saracens put up an unbelievable resistance with the same machinery, leading to Anselm's death. Albert also describes how the Franks tried to undermine one of the city's towers by digging a tunnel. Unlike Guibert, he attributes no role to the Frankish women.[35] The two stories do not precisely match, but there are enough similarities to suggest a connection or common influence.

The same can be said of the two historians' description of the trial of Peter Bartholomew. Albert gives fewer details about the pyre than does Guibert. Albert also reports that Raymond Pilet, along with Count Raymond of St Gilles, took custody of Peter after he survived the fire, a fact that Guibert does not mention. (Raymond of Aguilers, by comparison, does note Raymond Pilet's role in the ordeal.)[36] Albert also is more equivocal in his judgements than Guibert. Some say, Albert reports, that Peter 'emerged without injury', but the crowds treated him roughly – exactly the same explanation for Peter's death that Guibert gives. Albert, however, further notes that, according to some, Peter 'died shortly thereafter, worn down because of the conflagration'.[37] The two writers thus work from the same information, though Albert is more cautious in his conclusions than is Guibert.

Unlike Guibert's use of Fulcher of Chartres – confined to one long passage near the end of *God's Deeds through the Franks* – instances of shared information

[32] GN vi.23, pp. 264–5.
[33] *GF*, p. 85; FC i.25, p. 270.
[34] 'ad maximum totius Francorum exercitus dampnum Ansellus isdem aut primus aut inter primos ipse percutitur': GN vi.23, p. 264.
[35] AA v.31, pp. 376–8.
[36] Compare GN vi.22, pp. 262–4 to AA v.32, p. 378. Also, RA, pp. 122–3.
[37] 'illesus abiuit … exustione adeo fuisse aggrauatum ut in breui mortuus': AA v.32, p. 378.

with Albert are scattered throughout the chronicle. In the earliest example, both Guibert and Albert note the enthusiasm generated in northern Europe in 1096 by a wondrous goose. According to Guibert, it began in Cambrai, where a wretched woman announced before the congregation that her goose was leading her to Jerusalem. From there she travelled to Lotharingia, soliciting funds all the way.[38] Albert of Aachen writes more generally about how stupid people believed that a goose was 'filled with a holy spirit'.[39] Other writers outside the chronicle tradition mention this bird.[40] But among first-generation Latin historians, Guibert and Albert are alone in their testimony.

The two historians also offer similar descriptions of how Baldwin of Boulogne became count of Edessa. Following the *Gesta Francorum*, Guibert says that Baldwin and Tancred separated from the main army and went into Cilicia, where for a time they feuded over control of the city of Tarsus.[41] After telling this story, Guibert says that he has reached the best place to insert – literally, *insinuare* – some other material about Baldwin.[42] He likely used the word 'insert' literally, adding a bifolio to the end of Book III, where he places Baldwin's Edessan adventures. The prince of Edessa, he says, adopted Baldwin as his son in a strangely public ceremony in which the two men were nearly nude. Neither Fulcher nor the *Gesta Francorum* gives these details, but Albert does.[43] Later, Guibert reports, the citizens of Edessa rebelled against their old lord and proclaimed their wish for Baldwin to become their prince. Baldwin tried to defend the old man, but his recently adopted father 'begged him with countless prayers to desist from all resistance'.[44] Worn down by the burdens of office, he preferred for Baldwin to succeed, even though it meant a violent death at the hands of the mob. Albert's account does not exactly match Guibert's. He says, for example, that Baldwin did initially try to put a stop to the rebellion by offering the Edessans a substantial bribe, but they refused to accept any money. Albert also imagines the prince dramatically lowering himself from an upper window into the midst of an enraged mob. Whatever the discrepancies, the points of overlap between Guibert and Albert are striking enough to suggest, again, some sort of connection or shared influence between them.[45]

After Baldwin's takeover of Edessa, Guibert describes how, during the celebration of Christmas, certain citizens entered into a new conspiracy, apparently planning to kill Baldwin at mass. When Baldwin learned of their intentions, he ordered his Frankish bodyguard to accompany him to church in full armour.

---

[38]   GN vii.32, p. 331.

[39]   AA i.30, p. 58.

[40]   Ekkehard of Aura, 'Hierosolymita: De oppresione, liberatione ac restauratione Jerosolymitanae ecclesiae', *RHC Occ* v, 19; R. Chazan, *European Jewry and the First Crusade* (Berkeley, 1987), p. 56.

[41]   Compare GN iii.13, pp. 161–2 with *GF*, pp. 24–5.

[42]   GN iii.14, p. 163 (line 759).

[43]   Compare GN iii.14, pp. 163–4 and AA iii.19–23, pp. 168–76 with FC i.14, pp. 203–15. See also Edgington's comments in AA, p. 170 n. 47.

[44]   'Infinitis ergo ab eo extorsit precibus ut repugnare desisteret': GN iii.14, p. 164.

[45]   AA iii.23, pp. 174–6. Also, C. H. MacEvitt, *The Crusades and the Christian World of the East: Rough Tolerance* (Philadelphia, 2008), pp. 58–70.

The next day he charged all of the conspirators with treason and had them mutilated in various ways.[46] The only other Latin source for this story is, again, Albert of Aachen. Sometime in the winter of 1098, though not necessarily at Christmas, Baldwin learned of a conspiracy through an informant. He ordered all of the traitors to be imprisoned, but, due to his poverty, he accepted ransoms from ten of them. The two worst traitors he had blinded. Many of the lesser conspirators were similarly mutilated, 'with noses, hands, or feet cut off'.[47] Again, the details are close enough to suggest some sort of connection between the texts.

Both Guibert and Albert also describe the severe consequences faced by crusaders who violated the army's moral code. Guibert writes specifically about a monk who had joined the crusade without the permission of his abbot and who during the siege of Antioch was caught having sex with a woman. After being subjected to an ordeal by fire, the pair were stripped naked, led about the camps and whipped, much to the terror and delight of onlookers.[48] Albert similarly describes how a man, not a monk, and his lover were caught in the act of adultery. Without mentioning an ordeal, he says that they were led through the camp naked and whipped.[49] Yet again we have a shared story told in two slightly different fashions.

Sometimes the points of overlap can be quite small. On the eve of the final battle at Antioch, for example, both Guibert and Albert mention the extreme poverty of Robert of Flanders. Albert says that Robert was reduced to begging publicly among the soldiers and that, were it not for their charity, the great prince of Flanders would not even have had a horse to ride the next day.[50] Guibert says, somewhat more evocatively, that the only thing Robert could afford to eat was a camel's foot that his steward found for him. The exotic meal made him so sick that he was barely able to rise from bed on the morning of the battle.[51] Again, each writer relates the same information – in this case, Robert of Flanders, once especially rich, was now incredibly poor – but Guibert does so in a more colourful fashion.

On other occasions Guibert and Albert are the only two historians to relate precisely the same points of information. After the battle of Antioch, almost all of the chroniclers, including the author of the *Gesta Francorum*, note that the crusade princes sent Hugh of Vermandois to Constantinople and that he never returned.[52] Guibert adds that Hugh was accompanied by Baldwin of Mons and then describes how Hugh barely survived a Turkish ambush. Baldwin of Mons was never heard from again. These details also appear in Albert's *Historia*.[53] Guibert similarly adds some details about the battle for Jerusalem not found in the *Gesta Francorum*. During the final attack, the enemy attempted to destroy

---

[46]   GN iii.14, pp. 164–5.
[47]   'naribus amputantes, manibus aut pedibus': AA v.16–17, pp. 356–60.
[48]   GN iv.15, p. 196.
[49]   AA iii.57, p. 228.
[50]   AA iv.55, p. 334.
[51]   GN vi.4, pp. 236–7.
[52]   *GF*, p. 72 and FC i.23, p. 258.
[53]   GN vi.11, p. 243, and AA v.3, pp. 340–2.

the Franks' siege towers with Greek fire. The Franks, however, had taken the precaution of covering the structures in vinegar. Albert of Aachen gives the same information, adding that the Franks had learned this tactic from local Christians more familiar with the techniques of war in the east.[54]

When the Franks finally breached Jerusalem's walls, Guibert writes, the crusaders rushed into the city with a 'harmful swiftness', trampling one another as they fought through the newly opened breach. Complicating the attack, he adds, Saracens had dug pits in the city and concealed them. Several of the Franks fell into these traps and suffered injury.[55] Albert describes the same scenes, though with different emphases. In the rush to enter Jerusalem, at least sixteen men were trampled under the feet of horses, mules and men. Other crusaders, while pursuing Saracens around 'the royal cistern', fell through the openings to wells, some of them drowning. Others' necks snapped in two.[56] The so-called Temple of Solomon around which this fighting occurred, both historians stress, was not the actual Temple of Solomon whose destruction Christ had foretold. It was rather a temple built by later people – probably Christians, Albert guesses.[57]

After the capture of Jerusalem, Godfrey's election as the city's first Christian king causes Guibert to meditate on the duke's earlier heroism. For the first time he tells how Godfrey once fought an enormous bear. Godfrey had seen the bear attacking a soldier, and he courageously leapt forward to save his companion. Godfrey, after dealing the animal a mortal blow, fell in such a way that his own blade cut into his leg. The injury took several months to heal.[58] Albert tells a similar story, except that he says the bear originally attacked a peasant, not a knight. Albert also reports that Godfrey cut himself while trying to unsheathe his sword.[59]

On the eve of the battle of Ascalon, both Guibert and Albert mention – in agreement with the *Gesta Francorum* – that the Franks captured a mixed herd of camels, oxen and sheep.[60] Unlike the author of the *Gesta Francorum*, both Guibert and Albert argue that the Saracens had deliberately left these animals in the Franks' path, 'as a trick', 'according to the duplicity of the Gentiles', hoping to distract them from their battle preparations.[61] The leaders therefore proclaimed that anyone who claimed one of these animals as his personal property would be punished. According to Albert, a violator's ears and nose would be cut off. He adds that a Muslim advisor, the prefect of the city of Ramla, had warned Godfrey in advance of this stratagem, a detail that Guibert, less sympathetic to Saracens, did not include, or else he did not find it worth mentioning.[62]

---

[54] GN vii.36, p. 334, and AA vi.18, p. 426.

[55] GN vii.7, pp. 278–9.

[56] AA vi.21–2, pp. 428–30.

[57] GN vii.10, p. 283, and AA vi.25, p. 434.

[58] GN vii.12, pp. 285–6.

[59] AA iii.41, pp. 142–4.

[60] *GF*, pp. 94–5; GN vii.17, p. 296; AA vi.42, pp. 456–8.

[61] 'in dolo': AA vi.42, p. 458; 'fraude Gentilium': GN vii.17, p. 296.

[62] AA vi.42, p. 458. On Albert's attitude toward Muslims, see S. B. Edgington, 'Albert of Aachen Reappraised', in *From Clermont to Jerusalem: The Crusades and Crusader Societies, 1095–1500*, ed. A. V. Murray (International Medieval Research, 3; Turnhout, 1998), pp. 55–67.

About the subject of Godfrey's death the two writers seem to engage in a muted debate. Guibert argues that the king was poisoned. A certain nearby 'prince from neighbouring Gentiledom' sent him gifts, which Godfrey improvidently accepted. As became apparent, the Saracens had covered the gifts in poison, and Godfrey died as a result. Some people, however, reject this belief, saying that the king died of natural causes.[63] Albert of Aachen does not acknowledge these rumours, but he does say that, shortly before his death, Godfrey met the emir of Caesarea, who offered him dinner. Godfrey refused, but did accept a few cedar fruits. Shortly thereafter, upon reaching Jaffa, he fell ill and died. The possibility that the emir had poisoned Godfrey is obvious, but Albert does not address it.[64]

Finally, both Guibert and Albert describe the brief career of Gervais of Bazoches, appointed count of Tiberias in 1107.[65] One year later, in 1108, Gervais was captured and taken as prisoner to Damascus. There the emir of the city had the knight's skull cut off and turned it into a drinking vessel. The primary difference between the two versions of these events is that Guibert fashions Gervais's death so that it conforms to the conventions of martyrdom. The Saracens kill him because he refuses to renounce Christianity. Albert has Gervais executed as a prisoner of war because Baldwin I does not wish to give up control of three cities in exchange for the warlord's life.[66] In this case, because Gervais came from Soissons, nearby to Nogent, Guibert more than Albert wished to imbue his death with the sweet scent of sanctity.

We have assembled by now a fairly extensive list of instances where Guibert and Albert share information not found in other contemporary chronicles [see Table 1]. In some cases, such as their jaundiced descriptions of the holy goose, the identification of Baldwin of Mons as Hugh of Vermandois's companion on the road to Constantinople, or their accounts of Anselm of Ribemont's death, the points of overlap are nearly identical. On other occasions, they tell the same stories, but employ different images or narrative techniques. Guibert's version of Baldwin's activity in Edessa follows the general outline of Albert's but he employs different narrative strategies. In Godfrey's battle with the bear, both Guibert and Albert tell broadly similar tales – Godfrey rushing to rescue an endangered follower, Godfrey overcoming the bear, Godfrey gravely wounding himself with his own sword – but they reconstruct the scene differently. Both of them had heard about Robert of Flanders's extreme poverty, though they chose to describe it differently. Both of them knew that the crusaders accidentally trampled one another in a mad rush to enter Jerusalem, and both knew that some met their deaths falling into pits, but the numbers and explanations differ. Each of them had heard a rumour of Godfrey's poisoning but responded to it according to his own instincts.

---

[63] 'contiguae gentilitatis principe': GN vii.25, p. 317.
[64] AA vii.18, pp. 510–12. OV, v, 340 reports rumours of poison. FC i.36, pp. 348–9 does not mention these rumours.
[65] AA x.8, p. 726 and x.25, p. 742, and GN vii.46, pp. 347–8.
[66] GN vii.49, pp. 349–50 and AA x.55–7, pp. 768–70.

Table 1: Similarities between Guibert of Nogent and Albert of Aachen

Narrative Element	Location in Guibert	Location in Albert
Goose Full of Holy Spirit	vii.32	i.30
Baldwin's Arrival in Edessa	iii.14	iii.19-23
Conspiracy in Edessa Against Baldwin	iii.14	v.16-17
Punishment of Adulterers	iv.15	iii.57
Robert of Flanders's Poverty	vi.4	iv.55
Baldwin of Mons's Departure with Hugh for Constantinople	vi.11	v.3
Peter Bartholomew's Ordeal and the Crowd's Role in His Death	vi.22	v.32
Detailed Description of Anselm of Ribemont's Death	vi. 23	v.32
Use of Vinegar to Protect Siege Tower Against Greek Fire	vii.36	vi.18
Chaotic Frankish Charge into Jerusalem	vii.7	vi.21-2
Temple of Solomon Not, in Fact, Biblical Temple	vii.10	vi.25
Godfrey's Battle with the Bear	vii.12	iii.41
Herds Outside Antioch Left by Saracens as a Trap	vii.17	vi.42
Godfrey's Possible Poisoning	vii.25	vii.18
Death of Gervais of Bazoches	vii.49	x.55-7

These several points of overlap strongly indicate common influence: either Albert had read Guibert's chronicle, or else Guibert had read Albert's, or perhaps they both had been influenced by a common source. The first possibility seems the most immediately attractive. I have suggested elsewhere that Albert seems to engage in a historical debate with Guibert about Peter the Hermit.[67] But as Table 1 demonstrates, Albert places all of the details and anecdotes shared with Guibert more or less in chronological order. Guibert, on the other hand, has scattered them throughout his chronicle, wherever he could fit them in or wherever they seemed to him especially appropriate. This characteristic is all the more apparent when compared with Guibert's treatment of Fulcher, the discovery of whose chronicle led him not to scatter revisions throughout his book, but rather to add an entirely new block of material near the end of the manuscript.[68] Based on the

---

[67] Rubenstein, *Guibert of Nogent*, p. 247 n. 43.
[68] GN vii.32–45, pp. 329–47.

placement of the details shared in common with Albert, if one writer influenced the other, it would appear that Guibert discovered Albert and edited his book accordingly, not that Albert consulted Guibert.

But we should also consider the other possibility: that Guibert and Albert shared a common source or set of sources. Historians have long speculated as to whether Albert worked from a lost source, a 'Deeds of the Lotharingians', as it were.[69] If that were the case, however, it is surprising that Guibert does not mention the book, either to praise it or condemn it, especially if it really were a pro-Lotharingian text. One of Guibert's explicit historiographical intentions was to present the crusade as a uniquely Frankish achievement, not a Germanic one. He even tells us in the course of his chronicle that he once insulted an archdeacon of Mainz because, in Guibert's analysis, the Germans had contributed almost nothing to the crusade.[70] Given the zest with which he attacked Fulcher's intelligence, it would seem likely that he would leap at the opportunity to lampoon a Germanic chronicle. Albert similarly does not mention the existence of a written source, saying only that he based his work on 'what was made known through listening [*auditu*] and through the report [*relatione*] of those who were there present'.[71] Guibert likewise stresses his dependence on eyewitness sources, on 'the true narration of those speaking'.[72] Indeed, when he introduces one of the more memorable details listed above, the story of Robert of Flanders eating the camel's foot, he says, 'I heard this'.[73]

We are left then with what seem three unlikely propositions: either Guibert discovered Albert and uncharacteristically did not ridicule him, or else both Guibert and Albert consulted the same book and did not mention it, or else both of them, in the process of randomly gathering oral reports of the First Crusade, found several witnesses who passed on roughly the same fifteen or sixteen details. Barring a major archival discovery, any explanation here is necessarily speculative. With that caveat in mind, the most likely way to account for these points of overlap is the existence of two or three common sources, and probably not written ones but oral, performed sources. As Susan Edgington notes in her edition of Albert: 'There is a demonstrable but complex relationship between Albert's *Historia* and certain poetic sources'.[74] It seems plausible, based on the evidence presented here, that Albert and Guibert both heard performed one or more *chansons* about the crusade, from which Guibert gleaned a few extra details for his chronicle and upon which Albert based a significant portion of his work. Such a scenario is more likely than the idea of Guibert and Albert independently debriefing several returning crusaders and coincidentally learning from them the same several points.

---

[69] See Edgington in AA, p. xxvi and n. 12. Flori, a recent advocate for the existence of a lost chronicle, has since abandoned the idea: *Chroniqueurs et propagandistes*, p. 278.

[70] GN ii.1, pp. 108–9.

[71] 'auditu et relatione nota fierent ab hiis qui presentes affuissent': AA i.1, p. 2.

[72] 'vera dicentium narratio': GN iv pref., p. 166.

[73] 'Audivi': GN vi.4, p. 236.

[74] AA, p. xxvii.

In terms of Guibert's particular creative processes, we can now draw a few specific conclusions. He composed most of *God's Deeds through the Franks* in 1107–8, during his exile from Nogent. Shortly after his return he discovered the *Historia* of Fulcher of Chartres. It was the first recension of Fulcher's book, now lost, and it would have contained material very similar to what one reads in Bartolf of Nangis's *Gesta Francorum* and the 'L' manuscript of Fulcher. Rather than integrate Fulcher's information into his recently completed book, Guibert wrote a long rebuttal. He then gradually added a few other stories to his manuscript, perhaps as a new quire or bifolio. These chapters include the stories about Gervais of Bazoches.

At a still later date, Guibert discovered still more material, probably through *chansons* performed by one or two *jongleurs* claiming to have been veterans of the original Jerusalem campaign. Based on what he remembered of what they sang, he scattered several new details throughout his book. The process finally came to an end around 1120, when Guibert, feeling theologically cantankerous, incorporated two ideas from his polemical literature about saints' relics and the Eucharist.

God's Deeds through the Franks, in sum, was more than a simple revision of the *Gesta Francorum*, infused with a new theological sensibility and bits of overheard gossip, completed quickly by 1108. It was instead a massive historical project, one to which Guibert returned year after year, and in that sense, it was a book wholly typical of everything else that the author had written or would write, a book whose careful reading allows us to see not only how Guibert researched and assembled his materials but also how Fulcher of Chartres and Albert of Aachen worked as well.

UNDERSTANDING THE GREEK SOURCES FOR
THE FIRST CRUSADE

Peter Frankopan

In April 1081, a young general named Alexios Komnenos was crowned Emperor of the Romans in the great imperial city of Constantinople. He was the fifth man to rule the Byzantine empire in less than fifteen years. He took power from Nikephoros III Botaneiates, himself a usurper, who had been incompetent and ineffective in his three years on the throne, more keen on choosing fabric for his clothes than in dealing with affairs of state – a barb carefully chosen by an author writing later to contrast with Alexios's commitment, resolve and lack of pretence.[1] The new emperor could barely have chosen a less auspicious moment to take responsibility for the empire. Relations with the papacy were at an all-time low, to the point that no sooner had Alexios been crowned than he was excommunicated by Pope Gregory VII – just as had happened to his predecessor.[2] He was also facing a major attack on the western coast of Epirus, led by Robert Guiscard, one of the great figures of the early medieval period, who had established Norman control over southern Italy and Sicily, and was now seeking to extend his authority on the eastern side of the Ionian and Adriatic Seas.

Byzantium was in trouble elsewhere too. Its Danube frontier seemed to be porous, allowing steppe nomad raiders to cross over and plunder the Balkans with impunity. Things were no better in the east, where bands of Seljuk Turks had reached deep into the interior of Asia Minor, in some cases, ironically, as a result of being hired as mercenaries by a seemingly never-ending stream of magnates seeking support for their own bids for the throne. The result was a chronic dislocation of an empire that only a few decades earlier had been not just stable

[1] Nikephoros Bryennios, *Hyle Historias*, iv.29, ed. and trans. P. Gautier (Corpus Fontium Historiae Byzantinae, 9; Brussels, 1975), p. 299.

[2] For the excommunication of Nikephoros III, see *Sacrorum Conciliorum Nova et Amplissima Collectio*, ed. J. Mansi, 31 vols (Florence, 1759–98), xx, 507–8; *Das Register Gregors VII*, ed. E. Caspar, 2 vols (Epistolae Selectae, 2; Berlin, 1920–3), ii, 400–6. For that of Alexios, Bernold of Constance, *Die Chroniken Bertholds von Reichenau und Bernolds von Konstanz 1054–1100*, ed. I. S. Robinson (MGH Scriptores Rerum Germanicarum, n.s. 14; Hanover, 2003), pp. 479–80.

but dominant in the eastern Mediterranean, controlling not only the Balkan peninsula, Apulia and Calabria, and Asia Minor, but also stretching far into the Caucasus and northern Syria. By 1081, however, according to one source, the territory that was subject to Constantinople had shrivelled to little more than the imperial capital itself.[3] The doors of the treasury were left unlocked, says the same author, as there was nothing precious left worth keeping secure.[4] Although the numismatic evidence cannot back up this statement specifically, the fact that the empire's coinage, for centuries a beacon of stability, was debased successively and rapidly in the decade before Alexios seized power shows that the economy was under huge strain from collapsed revenues on the one hand and sharply increased expenditure on the other: an eleventh-century liquidity crisis, in other words.[5]

Alexios's coup marked a turning point in the empire's fortunes. Here, finally, was a man who could rebuild Byzantium; a man whose outstanding military track record stood him in good stead for dealing with difficult and ambitious neighbours; a man whose determination and indefatigability were sorely needed in an empire that had lost its way and was now teetering on the brink of destruction. Here was a man who was in the right place at the right time. Although Alexios's reign is of central importance in Byzantine history, it has, however, been largely overlooked by scholars. One reason for this is the problematic source material for this period. The later eleventh and twelfth centuries represent something of a golden age for Byzantine literature, where there was much experimentation with genre, form and style. It was also a period that saw a marked rise in medieval Greek narrative history-writing: works by writers such as Michael Psellos, a precocious polymath with a prodigious output, Michael Attaleiates, a lawyer and astute observer of the court, and Nikephoros Bryennios, Alexios's son-in-law, that chart the decline of the empire as it entered rough waters. Then there are histories written by figures such as John Skylitzes, John Zonaras, Michael Glykas and Constantine Manasses, the last in poem form, that have wider aims, relating a broad sweep of history spanning several centuries – in some cases back as far as republican Rome. And finally, there are accounts that cover the reigns of the Komnenian emperors John II and Manuel I by John Kinnamos, and, at the turn of the thirteenth century, by Niketas Khoniates.

The problem with all these accounts, as far as the reign of Alexios I Komnenos is concerned, is that almost none deals with the crucial period between 1081 and 1118. All either end with the accession of the usurper, or begin at the point of his death. Zonaras includes an overview of Alexios's rule that is brief but nevertheless important because of its scathing appraisal of the emperor and his reign. The same is true for Michael Glykas, whose account is dependent on Zonaras but for minor additions and corrections. But to all intents and purposes,

---

[3] *Alexias*, vi.11.iii, ed. D. Reinsch and A. Kambylis, 2 vols (Corpus Fontium Historiae Byzantinae, 40; Berlin, 2001), i, 193 [all subsequent references to the text are to volume one].

[4] *Alexias*, v.1.iv, pp. 142–3.

[5] C. Morrisson, 'La dévaluation de la monnaie byzantine au XIe siècle', *Travaux et Mémoires*, 6 (1976), 3–29; C. Kaplanis, 'The Debasement of the Dollar in the Middle Ages', *Journal of Economic History*, 63 (2003), 768–801.

contemporary historians gave the reign of Alexios a wide berth; modern historians have done much the same.

At a moment when history sparkles, then, Alexios is left in the shadows. This is ironic, for in fact, while there is a dearth of narrative sources, there is an astonishing array of primary material that relates to this period. The plentiful corpus includes speeches, tax exemptions, trade concessions, land grants, extensive collections of letters and diplomatic treaties – to say nothing of the archaeological evidence, above all that provided by coins and lead seals. Many of these are relevant, directly or indirectly, to the study of the First Crusade. None, however, appears in the volume of the *Recueil des historiens des croisades* that purports to deal with Greek sources for the First Crusade. The account of John Zonaras that includes a short section on the expedition to Jerusalem does not appear in this volume.[6] Nor does part or all of the chronicle of Theodore Skutariotes, who wrote in the early thirteenth century, which contains an important passage about how and why the Emperor Alexios called for help. The empire was in turmoil: in desperate need of help, the emperor turned to the west, using Jerusalem as bait.[7]

Since the nineteenth century, little energy has been spent on assessing the Byzantine background to the crusade, on its effect on the empire, or on its aftermath. As a whole, the Greek sources have been poorly explored and have been little used either to build up a picture of the reign of Alexios I or of the Byzantine context for the First Crusade. Even Runciman, who is widely perceived as providing a Constantinopolitan perspective on the First Crusade, in fact made little use of the abundant material that allows vital questions like the state of Asia Minor in the 1090s, or the precariousness of Alexios's position at this time, to be properly understood.[8]

The lack of focus on the east is all the more surprising given the fact that there is a narrative account that does cover the period 1081–1118 in detail, including a lengthy treatment of the First Crusade itself. The *Alexiad* of Anna Komnene is well known to crusade historians, as it is to Byzantine specialists, and is regularly cited or alluded to by modern scholars. It is also the target of consistent criticism, particularly on the part of historians of the Latin west. Although Gibbon's highly negative opinion of this work is notorious, dismissing Anna's account as betraying 'on every page the vanity of a female author', more recent historians have formed no higher a view of Anna Komnene's work.[9] Central amongst the complaints levelled at the text is that it seeks to glorify Alexios and is inherently untrustworthy. It is repeatedly branded as being biased, ill-informed and unreliable. Almost every major work on the First Crusade sweeps Anna's account to one side. It is routinely described as 'heavily coloured by hindsight', 'confused and misleading', or as having 'probably relied on the recollections of elderly people'. One recurring allegation is that the text cannot be trusted because it was written 'years later' – as

6   John Zonaras, *Epitome Historion*, in *Epitome Historiarum*, ed. M. Pinder and T. Büttner-Wobst, 3 vols (Bonn, 1841-9), iii, 740–1.
7   Theodore Skutariotes, *Synopsis Khronike*, in *Bibliotheca Graeca Medii Aevi*, ed. K. Sathas, 7 vols (Paris, 1872–94), vii, 184–5.
8   S. Runciman, *History of the Crusades*, 3 vols (Cambridge, 1952–5).
9   E. Gibbon, *Decline and Fall of the Roman Empire*, ed. J. B. Bury, 7 vols (London, 1909–14), vi, 335.

though that in itself discredits the account: this is curious given that modern historians of the medieval west seem to encounter no problem writing about events that took place 'many years earlier'. Nevertheless, for centuries up to and including today, the *Alexiad* has been routinely and unceremoniously discarded as an important source for the late eleventh and early twelfth centuries and for the expedition to Jerusalem that set off from Europe in the mid-1090s.[10] This is epitomized by the statement of one highly distinguished scholar who has recently gone so far as to imply that the text has little value since it is nothing more than a 'work written long afterwards by an old lady writing in exile'.[11]

As so often tends to happen, views like these tend to reinforce themselves. In the *Alexiad*'s case, there is no escape from truisms that the source is fatally biased and that the author's only aim is to present the emperor in the best possible light. Apart from the fact that many if not all of the other narrative accounts of the expedition to Jerusalem are highly-coloured and partial – such as the *Gesta Francorum* and the *Gesta Tancredi*, which drip with the opinions of their authors – the main problem with the prevailing view of the *Alexiad* is that it is plainly wrong. In fact, the text, which was most probably written in the 1140s and certainly no later than 1153, the year of Anna's death, is a careful and crafted work of history, rather than a slipshod work by the ill-informed daughter of the eponymous hero. For one thing, it is made up of an astonishing tapestry of sources. The author evidently had access to a major archive of official documents, if not to the imperial archives themselves. As a result, several documents are not just referred to but are cited in full. These include a grant giving executive powers to the emperor's mother in 1081, a letter sent to Henry IV in the early 1080s, and the terms of the Treaty of Devol, the humiliating settlement forced on Bohemond in 1108. In addition, the author drew on other official documents, such as trading privileges that were awarded to Venice in the first half of Alexios's reign, as well as letters written by provincial governors to inform the emperor and the government in Constantinople of developments on or immediately beyond the frontiers. The author was also evidently able to use an extensive collection of campaign notes relating to the disposition of the army on its many expeditions into the field in the 1080s and 1090s. Anna is able to identify which senior commanders took part in operations, and can record positions they took on the battlefield when engaging enemy forces.[12] Her account includes detailed itineraries of marches, noting where the army set camp and how long it remained there before continuing on.[13]

It was not only official notes that formed part of the sources that underpin the *Alexiad*. It is also possible to identify secular aristocratic histories, written in Constantinople in the late eleventh and early twelfth centuries, that are used

---

[10] T. S. Asbridge, *The First Crusade: A New History* (London, 2004), p. 104; C. J. Tyerman, *God's War: A New History of the Crusades* (London, 2006), p. 111; J. France, *Victory in the East: A Military History of the First Crusade* (Cambridge, 1993), pp. 110–11.

[11] J. S. C. Riley-Smith, 'Expedition Over Well-Trod Paths', *The Tablet*, 29 March 2012.

[12] For example, Anna records not only the names of the commanders at the battle of Lebounion in 1091 but where they deployed their men: *Alexias*, viii.5.v, p. 247.

[13] *Alexias*, vii.2.i, p. 204.

by the author. Two of these, family accounts relating to the Doukas and the Palaiologos families, have not survived, although evidence of the use of both is unmistakable in the text.[14] Another is the *Hyle Historias*, ostensibly unfinished, written by the author's husband, Nikephoros Bryennios, which has prompted some to question the role Bryennios may have played in gathering material that appears in Anna's history and the relationship between the two works.[15]

Then there are other sources that the author of the *Alexiad* made extensive use of, not least the *Gesta Roberti Wiscardi*. Written by William of Apulia, this account sets out the deeds of Robert Guiscard, and focuses considerable attention on two major attacks he made on Byzantium in 1081–3 and 1084–5. It is an important text both because it was written precisely at the time of the First Crusade, and also because it represented part of a deliberate attempt to rebuild bridges between Norman Italy, the papacy and Constantinople that was crucial in the launch of the crusade. As such it is emollient, treating Byzantium generously and sympathetically, and portraying Alexios in a favourable light. Perhaps not surprisingly, therefore, it forms the backbone of the *Alexiad*'s coverage of the Norman attacks, including several passages that are cited word for word.[16] In addition to these contemporary sources is a mosaic of borrowings from authors from classical antiquity. Homer is quoted often and liberally; so too is Galen. Allusions to Herodotus and Plutarch crop up regularly throughout the text, as do references to Aristotle and Plato. Repeated borrowings from Psellos demonstrate familiarity with this writer's work, above all the *Chronographia*, but also other compositions too, including the panegyrics and his thoughts on theology. The Bible provides another corpus of citations, cross-references and parallels that are liberally sprinkled across the *Alexiad*.[17]

Far from being the work of a naïve, foolish ingénue, disconnected from high politics and clueless about the events of the late eleventh and early twelfth centuries, the *Alexiad* was written by a scholar who was highly erudite, well read and diligent, a shrewd observer of court politics and of the empire's relations with its neighbours. Meticulously researched, and based on a wide range of materials from different sources, the text is of a high quality as a work of history and as a piece of literature, even by the lofty standards of medieval Greek literature. Not only that, but the way in which it was written likewise bears testimony to the skills of a highly sophisticated author. The language is stylized and florid; like many great works of literature, it can seem clumsy and over-elaborate to the

[14] P. Frankopan, 'Deconstructing the *Alexiad*: Identifying an Unknown Palaiologan Source in Anna Komnene's History', in *Reading in Byzantium and Beyond: Festschrift for Elizabeth and Michael Jeffreys*, ed. I. Toth and N. Gaul (Cambridge, forthcoming); For the hypothesis of a Doukas source, see L. Neville, 'A History of Caesar John Doukas in Nikephoros Bryennios's *Material for History*?' *Byzantine and Modern Greek Studies*, 32 (2008) 168–88.

[15] J. Howard-Johnston, 'Anna Komnene and the *Alexiad*', in *Alexios I Komnenos: Papers*, ed. M. Mullett and D. Smythe (Belfast Byzantine Texts and Translations, 4.1; Belfast, 1996), pp. 260–302.

[16] P. Frankopan, 'Turning Latin into Greek: Anna Komnene and the *Gesta Roberti Wiscardi*', *Journal of Medieval History*, 38 (2013), 80-99. Also see P. Brown, 'The *Gesta Roberti Wiscardi*: A "Byzantine History"', *Journal of Medieval History*, 37 (2011), 162–79.

[17] See still G. Buckler, *Anna Comnena: A Study* (Oxford, 1929), pp. 191ff; also see *Alexias*, ed. Reinsch and Kambylis, vol. ii, *Pars Altera: Indices*.

untrained eye and ear. But this was precisely the point: unlike the Latin accounts of the crusade, some of which were aimed at a wide audience and therefore have elements of the lowest common denominator in terms of language, vocabulary, symbolism and style, Anna Komnene was writing for an audience far more well versed in classical and biblical literature than we are today, far more able to understand sly references, puns and in-jokes, and far more likely to understand the nuances of the text. Unfortunately and ironically, the complexity of the *Alexiad* has proved to be its undoing in the modern era: it is a text that requires thought if it is to be understood properly.

One key area where this is of central importance concerns the issue of chronology and the sequence of events that is presented by Anna. This often proves to be highly suspect. There are occasions where this is the result of deliberate manipulation on the part of the author, where events are misplaced on purpose, such as the difficult circumstances that Robert Guiscard found himself in during the winter of 1084–5 but which Anna moves three years earlier.[18] Other mistakes, such as the positioning of the grant of trading privileges to Venice in the mid-1080s rather than 1092, are as likely to have more innocent explanations.[19] The major issue, however, stems from the fact that material is not grouped sequentially but is rather gathered by subject matter – which has caused havoc with the way in which the shape of Alexios's reign has been assessed. This has led to persistent misunderstandings about the state of Byzantium at the time of the crusade, where positive assertions about the relative strength of the empire contrast sharply with the picture of chronic collapse that can be assembled from the *Alexiad* and from the other primary sources. For many scholars, Anna's sequence of events has proved entirely distracting, though not necessarily deliberately so.

It does not help, then, that the text is seldom read in its entirety. This is particularly true when it comes to the crusade, where the approach of most historians again echoes that of the editors of the *Recueil* in the nineteenth century: the passages on the expedition are typically detached from the remainder of the text and are taken in isolation. Little thought or consideration are given as to whether the passages on the western expedition to Jerusalem are consistent with other parts of the text, or how this part of the text reads compared to the rest in terms of language and style. What are Anna's sources for this section, and does she marshal and edit her source material in the same way as she does elsewhere? What is missing from the *Alexiad*'s coverage of the crusade, and why? Was the expedition to Jerusalem the defining moment in her father's reign; or was the passage of thousands of men across imperial territory perhaps less significant for Byzantium than might be assumed?

The first misconception about the *Alexiad* that should be set straight is the assumption that the text is a eulogy, a paean to the deeds of the Emperor Alexios, providing an unashamedly rosy picture of his reign and of his achievements.

---

[18] Frankopan, 'Turning Latin into Greek', 92.

[19] P. Frankopan, 'Byzantine Trade Privileges to Venice in the Eleventh Century: The Chrysobull of 1092', *Journal of Medieval History*, 30 (2004), 135–60.

In fact, Anna Komnene's account is nothing of the sort. Time and time again, the author is at pains to stress her father's searing unpopularity. She records relentless plots against him, stemming from serious doubts amongst the Byzantine aristocracy, and even within his own family, about his leadership. The Alexios who emerges from the pages of the *Alexiad* is no epic hero who can do no wrong, but a man whose decisions often proved to have disastrous consequences. For example, Anna does not hold back from cataloguing the gossip that spread through the highways and byways in the early 1080s and threatened to develop into concrete plans to remove him from power. This was because many harboured doubts about whether the new emperor was indeed the man to save the empire,[20] perhaps not surprising given the first months of his reign: the author had little doubt that it was her father's rash move against Robert Guiscard at Dyrrakhion in the autumn of 1081 that resulted in a defeat of catastrophic proportions. Not only was the cream of the Byzantine elite slaughtered in battle, but Epirus was opened up to the invaders, enabling a demoralized Dyrrakhion, the key point on the empire's western flank, to fall a few months later. It is clear from the *Alexiad* that the emperor was personally responsible for the rash decision to seek a quick victory rather than grind the enemy into submission, and also that there were many in Constantinople who blamed Alexios for just this reason. No attempt is made to conceal this.[21]

Nor does Anna fail to record her father's shortcomings with respect to other significant leadership decisions. The appalling scenes that accompanied the Komnenoi and their supporters as they rampaged through the capital in 1081 are made all too clear, as is the fact that Alexios was forced to appear in front of a synod soon afterwards to apologize for the behaviour of his men. Although the new emperor is presented as taking his punishment seriously, insisting in addition on wearing a hair shirt for forty days and sleeping on the floor in the palace to show the sincerity of his contrition, it does not take much to recognize that he accepted that he had fallen short of what was expected of a military commander. Again, the conspicuous inclusion of episodes such as this in the *Alexiad* is striking and sits at odds with superficial blanket statements that the text is little more than a work whose aim is to glorify the author's father.[22]

The inclusion of all these cases, and many other similar episodes, says much about what the author of the *Alexiad* was trying to achieve. For in fact, Anna is conspicuously and remarkably candid about controversial and even damaging allegations levelled at the Emperor Alexios during his own lifetime. For example, the author reports how her father expropriated church treasure in 1082 to help fund efforts against the Normans. She also notes that the emperor was called to account by the clergy, and was once again censured by them for his actions and forced to make a full apology.[23] This could easily have been left out of the text

---

[20] *Alexias*, vi.7.i, p. 181.

[21] For the defeat, *Alexias*, iv.6.i–7.v, pp. 131–8; for criticism in Constantinople afterwards, vi.3.i, pp. 171–2.

[22] *Alexias*, iii.5.i–vi, pp. 97–100.

[23] *Alexias*, v.2.ii–iv, pp.144–5; V. Grumel, 'L'affaire de Léon de Chalcédoine: le Chrysobulle d'Alexis Ier sur les objets sacrés', *Revue des Etudes Byzantines*, 2 (1944), 126–33.

had the author's intention been to provide a whitewashed portrait. The fact that it was not is telling.

In fact, time and again, Anna establishes a causal link between Alexios's policies and decisions and their devastating consequences – to the point that there are occasions where the author does her father no favours. For instance, she reports the brutal treatment of Manichean heretics in the early 1080s, noting how the family of a man who had served Alexios personally and loyally fell victim to a policy that was as vicious as it was short-sighted. The result was a major insurrection by the Danube: antagonized by the new emperor's ruthless dispersal of a tight-knit community, those who managed to escape concluded that they were better off making common cause with Pecheneg steppe nomads than with the Byzantines. It was not long before raids were being launched that proved disastrous for imperial control of the Balkans. Anna makes no bones about the fact that this resulted from Alexios's handling of the dualist minority that had not only been living peacefully and unobtrusively, but had also provided important military support to the attempts to drive back the Norman attack led by Robert Guiscard.[24]

But nowhere is Anna's account more sanguine and honest than with the true pivotal moment in Alexios's reign. This did not come with the First Crusade, but with the plot of Nikephoros Diogenes, which came to a head in the summer of 1094.[25] The *Alexiad*'s account of the discovery of the conspiracy is devastating. It presents the emperor as being entirely unprepared for a massive ground-swell of resentment against his policies and his rule; it shows him, furthermore, as being detached both from the senate and the military high command, who were more or less unanimous in their agreement that Alexios's time had passed, and also from the rank and file: even the common soldier had concluded that the emperor was not going to lead Byzantium back from the brink and that it was time for another man to try to do so.[26] It is certainly true that Anna attempts to downplay the aftermath of the uprising, and conceals the identities of some of those who had lent Diogenes their support. Nevertheless, it is only a small handful of names that the author does not divulge, but which can be detected from other sources from this period. Some of the most high-profile figures who had come out against the emperor are in fact named directly. It is the identities of specific individuals, therefore, rather than the plot itself, which are protected from being revealed.[27]

In this way, far from reading the *Alexiad* as a eulogy, the right way to understand this text is as a work that does not hide from presenting the problems that scarred the period between 1081 and 1118. In some places, certainly, the author does try to take the edge off the blame that the emperor should bear. She carefully

---

[24] *Alexias*, iv.2.i–iv, pp. 170–1; vi.14.ii, pp. 199–200. For Paulician support against the Normans, iv.4.iii, pp. 126–7.

[25] P. Frankopan, 'Challenges to Imperial Authority in the Reign of Alexios I Komnenos: The Conspiracy of Nikephoros Diogenes', *Byzantinoslavica*, 64 (2006), 257–74.

[26] *Alexias*, ix.6.v, p. 272.

[27] P. Frankopan, 'Kinship and the Distribution of Power in Komnenian Byzantium', *English Historical Review*, 122 (2007), 1–34.

notes, for example, that Alexios had taken counsel with his senior officers before the disastrous defeat at Dyrrakhion in 1081, and likewise before a setback of almost equal proportions a few years later when an expedition in the Danube region went spectacularly wrong.[28] She says too that her father was diligent and tireless, often not bathing after his return to the palace because he did not have time before setting out on campaign once again – with the aim of making clear that it was not Alexios's fault that Byzantium was besieged from all sides.[29] He was prepared to work through the night to listen to the grievances of his subjects in person, and never complained about shouldering this burden.[30]

Rather than a swashbuckling figure who can do no wrong in his daughter's eyes, the emperor is in fact consistently portrayed as a man struggling to steer the empire through an ocean of worries, or a sea of troubles. Alexios is not presented as a man triumphantly and effortlessly bringing a difficult political and economic position under control, but quite the opposite, struggling to do so. He was like a helmsman desperately trying to steer the state away from the perilous rocks, doing all he could to prevent the dangers hurtling towards him and towards Byzantium from every side from delivering a lethal blow.[31] The emperor is shown barely able to comprehend the scale of opposition to his reign from within the empire, something which Anna Komnene too comments upon: how was it possible, she asks, that so many were prepared to line up against him?[32] As it was, Alexios's body and mind already bore deep scars and wounds as the price of leadership. Injuries he sustained fighting the Pechenegs in the 1080s troubled him for decades, to the point that he found moving difficult towards the end of his life.[33] Then there was the deep trauma of the Diogenes conspiracy inflicting a mental rather than physical price on the emperor.[34] Even in death, Alexios cuts a lonely figure, nursed by his daughters and a small group of doctors. In Anna's account, visitors and friends are conspicuous by their absence as he fades. This was the passing of a man, the *Alexiad* says, who had given his life for Byzantium.[35]

The image of the emperor that emerges from the text, then, is a solitary and melancholic one. Alexios and his achievements are presented as being misunderstood and unrecognized by his peers – and by his descendants.[36] This is why Anna states at the beginning of the text that her aim was to record the various successes against the empire's neighbours, so that they would not be forgotten. The fact that this was in danger of happening lies at the heart of the history. Alexios's achievements were at risk of being swept away because the world

---

[28] *Alexias*, iv.5.iii, p. 130; vii.3.iv–v, pp. 210–11.

[29] For example, *Alexias*, viii.1.i, p. 236.

[30] *Alexias*, xiv.4.iii, pp. 439–42.

[31] J. Shepard, '"Father" or "Scorpion"? Style and Substance in Alexios' Diplomacy', in *Alexios I Komnenos*, ed. Mallett and Smythe, pp. 68–9.

[32] *Alexias*, vii.3.xii, p. 214.

[33] *Alexias*, xiv.4.iv, p. 440.

[34] *Alexias*, ix.1.ii, p. 258.

[35] *Alexias*, xv.11.iii–xxiv, pp. 494–505.

[36] *Alexias*, vi.8.v, p. 185; xiv.3.ix, p. 438.

had moved on, as Anna says in the opening line of the text: 'Time, which flies irresistibly and perpetually, sweeps up and carries away with it everything that has seen the light of day and plunges it into utter darkness, whether deeds of no significance or those that are mighty and worthy of commemoration.'[37]

As it was, Alexios had stamped his character on the imperial palace right from the start of his reign, replacing the lascivious atmosphere with a rather more stern and dour environment where sacred hymns were sung in the palace to a timetable.[38] It was a period when there was little new building, no landmark architecture to mark Alexios or his achievements, no triumphal arches to commemorate victories, no columns or monumental buildings. Indeed, apart from a few exceptions, even church building, the hallmark of imperial patronage, came to an abrupt halt.[39] If this void was partly the result of strained finances in the first part of the emperor's reign, then the personal modesty and parsimony of Alexios were also responsible. Given the weight of other material testifying to his character from speeches, letters and other sources, there seems no reason to doubt the comment attributed to him by his daughter when she said that she was going to write a history of his reign: it would be better, he remarked, to mourn for him than to write about his life.[40] This is entirely in keeping with the man who was the central figure in the *Alexiad*.

The absence of narrative sources relating to Alexios's reign therefore becomes easier to understand. For one thing, after the Diogenes conspiracy, a major purge cleared out an entire generation of the elite and replaced them with a new guard. In addition, having faced down such a serious threat to his regime and to his life, Alexios began to deal with rivals decisively. Where in the first half of his reign he showed clemency to those plotting against him, in the second he chose harsher punishments. The death sentence passed on the Anemas brothers was commuted only at the very last minute; those who stepped out of line, like Gregory Taronites, were taken prisoner and held captive in solitary confinement; Bogomil heretics, meanwhile, were burned alive in the hippodrome in Constantinople. Alexios's Byzantium evolved into a place where criticisms of the emperor and his policies were not to be tolerated.[41]

Equally, Alexios had little interest in commemorating his achievements. Dismissive of so-called intellectuals and mistrustful of silver-tongued clerics, his failure to sponsor poets or authors to write about his reign hardly comes as a surprise. The emperor was much more comfortable reading the Bible with

---

[37] *Alexias*, Prologue, 1.i, p. 5; translation from *Alexiad*, trans. E. R. A. Sewter, rev. P. Frankopan (London, 2009), p. 3.

[38] *Alexias*, iii.8.ii, p. 105.

[39] One exception was the building of an orphanage, known as the Orphanotropheion, in the north-eastern corner of the capital: *Alexias*, xiv.7.iii–ix, pp. 450–4; see also J. Miller, 'The Orphanotropheion of Constantinople', in *Through the Eye of a Needle: Judeo-Christian Roots of Social Welfare*, ed. E. A. Hanawalt and C. Lindberg (Kirksville, MO, 1994), pp. 83–104. See in general L. Rodley, 'The Art and Architecture of Alexios I Komnenos', in *Alexios I Komnenos*, ed. Mullett and Smythe, pp. 339–58.

[40] *Alexias*, xv.11.i, p. 494.

[41] For Anemas, *Alexias*, xii.5.iv–6.ix, pp. 372–6; for Gregory Taronites, xii.7.i–iv, pp. 376–8; for the Bogomils, xv.8.i–10.v, pp. 485–93.

his wife late into the night than indulging in anything more light-hearted or pleasurable.[42] Perhaps he was also concerned about how his reign could be fairly portrayed: as the frequent struggles of the *Alexiad* show, there was a difficult balance to strike between showing just where the emperor's policies had led the empire to the brink and where they had saved them. The success against the Normans in 1081–5, for example, could be set against the disastrous set of decisions that had made the situation worse in the first place. Likewise, the collapse of the empire's position in Asia Minor, which accelerated rapidly to crisis point in the early 1090s, stemmed from the emperor's gamble on how to stabilize the east going badly wrong.[43] Presenting Alexios as the saviour of the empire when he was also the architect of many of its problems required a delicate touch, and one that in this case in particular did not fit easily with the model of eulogy.

Nowhere is the quandary about Alexios more acute than with the question of the First Crusade. On the one hand, the expedition to Jerusalem was a triumph from a Byzantine point of view. It led to the recovery of Nicaea, the gateway to western and central Asia Minor, and enabled the reconquest of the strategically and economically important western coast of the sub-continent, as well as the crucial Maiander valley. It secured a string of fortified locations stretching deep towards the east that offered the prospect in the future of nodes and military strong points from which Byzantium's position could be further consolidated. The problems lay both further east and also in the west. On one level, the creation of Latin states in Palestine and Syria opened up possibilities for Alexios and his successors in Constantinople that did not exist when those territories were in Muslim hands. There were bridges to be built, alliances to be made, military support to be given and economic and logistical assistance provided that offered opportunities for Byzantium to extend its influence, and in due course its authority too, into areas that had been under imperial control in the eleventh century, like Antioch and Edessa, and indeed into those that had not, like southern Syria.

But at the same time, the establishment of the crusaders in the east made life difficult for the emperor and his successors. With Antioch in the hands of ambitious, independent-minded figures like Bohemond and Tancred, who were willing to do battle with Christians and Muslims alike to protect their domains, there was the real chance that the city would serve as a base not for operations against the Turks, but against Byzantine-held Cilicia. Moreover, competition with the eastern Roman empire had repercussions that went far beyond local or even regional politics, for they were felt in France and southern Italy almost immediately. Brought along lines of communication that were quickly established in the wake of the First Crusade, the reputations of Alexios and of Byzantium were systematically dismantled in the story of the expedition to Jerusalem that emerged in the early twelfth century. The

---

[42] *Alexias*, v.9.iii, p. 165; xiv.7.ix, p. 453.

[43] For the collapse in the east, see P. Frankopan, *The First Crusade: The Call from the East* (London, 2012), pp. 57–70.

version of the crusade as told by the *Gesta Francorum* and the many sources that were heavily reliant on it gave the emperor and the empire short thrift, both portrayed as inherently untrustworthy and unreliable – and much worse.[44] How to assess the crusade, therefore, was not immediately clear to writers like Anna Komnene, just as assessing Alexios's reign as a whole was not straightforward.

What was more obvious to the author of the *Alexiad* was how to describe what actually happened in the mid to late 1090s. And here, contrary to the claims of historians of the medieval west, Anna's account is not emotional, partial or misleading. The emperor, says the author, was astonished to hear news that thousands of pilgrims were bearing down on Constantinople in the summer of 1096. 'Outnumbering the sand of the seashore or the stars of heaven, carrying palms and bearing crosses on their shoulders', this rabble was not what Alexios or Pope Urban II had expected when carefully co-ordinated appeals were made during the course of the previous winter. Indeed, the pope had made a concerted effort to ensure that only men with fighting experience took part in the expedition. Set alongside clues that point to considerable logistical arrange-ments being put in place for the large numbers of men expected from Europe, Anna's statement that the emperor was disturbed is entirely reasonable: unarmed men, women and children, the old and the infirm were not what he had been anticipating – and not several months too early at that.[45] Moreover, what else we learn from the *Alexiad* tallies closely with what the western sources say about the passage of the crusade across imperial territory. Anna says nothing that contra-dicts the western accounts, and more often than not complements them. In fact, from the point of arrival up to the battle of Dorylaion, the account dovetails neatly with the Latin sources and provides coverage of the events that is entirely credible and eminently reliable. A convincing picture is painted of the skirmishes outside Constantinople and of the arrival of the various leaders in the imperial capital.[46]

Anna's conviction that the capital was under threat from the crusaders, rarely taken seriously, finds some support in the account of Albert of Aachen, who reports that there was discussion about an assault on Constantinople over the winter of 1096–7. Even if Albert, like Anna, was swayed by what happened later on the expedition, the fact that Raymond of Aguilers also mentions that the use of force was at the forefront of the crusaders' minds as they gathered and met the emperor suggests that the fears of violence were not misplaced.[47] The great care taken by the emperor to cultivate the senior leaders of the expedition is set out in detail that is compelling and above all plausible. Little if anything jars with what we are told by the Latin chronicles. Even Anna's comment that participants of the so-called People's Crusade murdered children and impaled them and tortured

---

[44] Frankopan, *First Crusade*, pp. 186–205.
[45] *Alexias*, x.5.iv, p. 297; Frankopan, *First Crusade*, pp. 101ff.
[46] *Alexias*, x.7.i–11.x, pp. 301–21.
[47] *Alexias*, x.5.x, p. 299; AA ii.14, p. 82; Raymond of Aguilers states that Bohemond threatened to use force against the count of Toulouse in the spring of 1097: RA, p. 24.

the old may not be an exaggeration, especially set alongside the horrific acts of violence committed against Jewish populations in cities across Germany by the same individuals only a few months earlier.[48]

The reception of the leaders is related at length, particularly in the case of Bohemond, who was wined and dined in an elaborate fashion.[49] The reason for this was not only to ensure collaboration with the emperor as the crusade went on, but to set up the western leaders so that they gave oaths of loyalty to the emperor. The purpose of the oaths was twofold: first, to provide a clear understanding that all gains of territories, towns and places that had been Byzantine be restored to the empire; and second, as we can tell from the modified commitment given by Raymond of Toulouse, to undertake not to do anything to harm the emperor's life. The way that Alexios set about getting these commitments stands to reason and makes perfect sense.[50] In the wake of the Diogenes conspiracy, where dark rumours still swirled around Constantinople, such an approach was entirely understandable. Moreover, the fact that there were still whispers of discontent explains why the westerners themselves caught wind of dissatisfaction with the emperor when they reached the imperial capital. The *Alexiad* is transparent about this, and notes that at one point tension rose so high that the emperor's few remaining loyal friends came to tell him to put his armour on to face down an armed uprising.[51] Again, the attention drawn to Alexios's crushing unpopularity and the precariousness of his regime could hardly be more sanguine or candid. The account of the siege of Nicaea, too, fits neatly alongside the various Latin accounts, and, like the meetings in Constantinople, was evidently assembled from eyewitness accounts, perhaps, in this case, from material drawn from a source based on the life of Manuel Boutoumites, one of the new breed of lieutenants, whose thoughts, decisions and comments are quoted at length in the *Alexiad*.[52]

But where Anna's account of the First Crusade is most useful is with the emperor's crucial decision not to advance from Philomelion to support the beleaguered crusader army that was trapped outside Antioch. The author of the *Alexiad* carefully explains why her father did not advance: for one thing, there were reports of yet another attack on the Balkans; for another, the emperor was still nervous about being too far from the capital, given the chronic insecurity of his own position at home. Both would have been reasonable justification for not heading deeper into the interior. However, as Anna makes clear, what was decisive was the report brought by Stephen of Blois. The crusaders, he said, were on the point of annihilation when he had left Antioch; it was all but certain that

[48] *Alexias*, x.6.ii, p. 300. For the appalling scenes that accompanied the People's Crusade in Germany, see M. Gabriele, 'Against the Enemies of Christ: The Role of Count Emicho in the Anti-Jewish Violence of the First Crusade', in *Christian Attitudes towards the Jews in the Middle Ages: A Casebook*, ed. M. Frassetto (Abingdon, 2007), pp. 61–82. Also J. Rubenstein, *Armies of Heaven: The First Crusade and the Quest for Apocalypse* (New York, 2011), pp. 48–53.
[49] *Alexias*, x.11.i–x, pp. 317–21.
[50] Frankopan, *First Crusade*, pp. 133–6.
[51] *Alexias*, x.9.iv, p. 310,
[52] *Alexias*, xi.1.ii–2.x, pp. 322–9.

they had already been crushed.[53] It is tempting, of course, to think that Anna places the blame on Stephen of Blois and on his devastating report in order to absolve her father for not helping the crusaders in their hour of need. Crucially, however, we know that this is not fabricated or even twisted by the author because the *Gesta Francorum* provides a corroborating account that mirrors that of the *Alexiad* almost exactly. Even the *Gesta* states that Stephen of Blois, one of the leading figures on the expedition, left the emperor with no choice but to retreat. 'Return home while you still can', Stephen urged, 'in case the [Turks] find you and your men.' There was no point heading east: 'our men are terribly besieged, and, in all likelihood, have all been killed by now.'[54]

The section of the *Alexiad* that follows, which deals with the immediate aftermath of the crusade following the capture of Jerusalem, is convoluted and riddled with problems of chronology, as first demonstrated by Liubarskii and later by Ralph-Johannes Lilie.[55] These most naturally reflect difficulties in gathering reliable information from what was effectively a frontier region, and problems that Anna experienced with editing material from a disparate range of sources. Where Anna leaves nothing to chance, however, is with Bohemond's attack on Epirus at the start of the twelfth century, which amounted to a crusade in its own right. Apart from the lengthy account of the invasion, the author of the *Alexiad* crowns her account with the full text of the Treaty of Devol, which established the legal basis for Byzantine authority over Antioch. Although this did not translate to practical control over the city – imperial envoys were sent away by a mocking Tancred – the purpose of the document and its inclusion in the text was to provide clear and incontrovertible proof of Alexios's rights to the city.[56]

Ambivalent attitudes to the First Crusade and to Alexios I characterize the Byzantine historiography of the expedition that led to the knights of western Europe marching across Asia Minor and establishing themselves in Syria and Palestine in a series of states in Outremer. The shortage of narrative accounts of the period between 1081 and 1118 as a whole means that the information from the dominant source, the *Alexiad*, needs to be handled with considerable care. Anna Komnene's account is not always easy to unpick or understand; but it is clear that it is more nuanced and more complex than is usually presumed. The author's motivations and objectives are not always straightforward, and the way in which she presents the crusade, and indeed her father's reign as a whole, is often guarded and laced with allusions and clues that need to be spotted if her meaning is to be fully grasped.

The failure of other writers to focus on this period reflects in some part the austere vision that Alexios had for his empire, and the dour and often stark ways in which Byzantium was transformed under his leadership, especially after the cardiac arrest of the emperor's inner circle on the very eve of the crusade. This

---

[53] *Alexias*, xi.6.i–v, pp. 338–40.

[54] *GF*, p. 63; *Alexias*, xi.6.i–iv, pp. 338–9.

[55] Ia. Liubarskii, 'Zamechaniya k khronologii XI knigi "Aleksiady" Anny Komninoi', *Vizantiskii Vremennik*, 24 (1963), 47–56; R.-J. Lilie, *Byzantium and the Crusader States 1096–1204*, trans. J. Morris and J. Ridings (Oxford, 1993), pp. 259–76.

[56] *Alexias*, xiii.12.i–xxviii, pp. 413–23.

had aftershocks that were felt long afterwards, and were still being felt many years after his death, leading historians to avoid confronting the difficulty of how best to present his achievements. As time went on, this gave way to them being forgotten, and therefore to Anna Komnene feeling the need to record them in the *Alexiad*.

But there are signs, nonetheless, that the crusade was positively viewed in Constantinople from the snatches of evidence that refer to the expedition that had such a significant impact on western Europe and on the Holy Land. In a pair of poems written immediately after Alexios's death, the late emperor is portrayed as dealing with the knights with commendable and obvious success. If his heirs took the same approach, the first poem states, they too would benefit from the support that the impressive 'horsemen of the west' had given to Byzantium during Alexios's reign.[57] This owed something to wishful thinking; but it encapsulates perfectly the fact that as with Zhou Enlai's response in the 1960s to the question of how the French Revolution should be viewed, from the perspective of Constantinople several decades after the capture of Jerusalem, it was still too early to tell just what the upshot of the First Crusade would be. By 1204, things would become rather more clear.

---

[57] P. Maas, 'Die Musen des Kaisers Alexios I', *Byzantinische Zeitschrift*, 22 (1913), ll. 312–51 at pp. 357–8.

THE MONTE CASSINO TRADITION OF THE FIRST CRUSADE: FROM THE *CHRONICA MONASTERII CASINENSIS* TO THE *HYSTORIA DE VIA ET RECUPERATIONE ANTIOCHIAE ATQUE IERUSOLYMARUM*

Luigi Russo

When focusing on the analysis of texts in order to reconstruct the past, we often overlook the importance of the geography of historiographical memory. One exception, made some years ago, is the case study of the abbey of Fleury-sur-Loire by Robert-Henri Bautier in an essay whose conclusions have since been resumed and expanded.[1] Indeed, in the period between the end of the tenth century and the first decades of the twelfth, this abbey was responsible for the writing of some of the most important texts that represent the origins of 'official' French historiography in the Middle Ages, by reason of the strong organic link that it established with the Capetian dynasty as it assumed a more central role in the French political scene. It can be suggested that the case of Monte Cassino deserves similar attention in the light of its historiographical output in the period close to the events of the First Crusade. Situated on one of the most important roads that connected northern and southern Italy, and lying less than 100 kilometres from Rome, the monastery of Monte Cassino played a central role, not only in the history of western monasticism, but also in the intellectual life of the central Middle Ages, as has been demonstrated, for example, by the work of Herbert Bloch and John Cowdrey.[2]

---

[1] R.-H. Bautier, 'La place de l'abbaye de Fleury-sur-Loire dans l'historiographie française du IXe au XIIe siècle', in Études *ligériennes d'histoire et d'archéologie médiévales*, ed. R. Louis (Auxerre, 1975), pp. 25–33; *idem*, 'L'École historique de l'abbaye de Fleury d'Aymoin à Hugues de Fleury', in *Histoires de France, Historiens de la France*, ed. Y.-M. Berce and P. Contamine (Paris, 1994), pp. 59–72. The interest taken by Fleury in the First Crusade is noted by G. Rösch, 'Der "Kreuzzug" Bohemunds gegen Dyrrachion 1107–8 in der lateinischen Tradition des 12. Jahrhunderts', *Römische Historische Mitteilungen*, 26 (1984), 182–4.

[2] H. Bloch, *Monte Cassino in the Middle Ages*, 3 vols (Cambridge, Mass., 1986), i, 3–112;

Let us start by taking a step back. The strategic role of Monte Cassino as a point of contact between the west and the east is revealed by the many traces left in the Cassinese Chronicle, a text written by at least three authors in the eleventh and twelfth centuries.[3] Thanks to references in it we know, for example, of the arrival in southern Italy of precious relics from Jerusalem, which testifies to the movement of a substantial number of western pilgrims:[4] one of the most famous visitors to be mentioned is the bishop of Prague ('Sclavorum episcopus'), Adalbert, who arrived at Monte Cassino en route to his intended destination, Jerusalem, and was, in vain, petitioned by the monks to stay with them; and a venerable bishop 'de Galliarum partibus' is mentioned by the chronicle in 1023.[5] In addition, the centrality of the monastery from a historiographical point of view is attested by a text which is now available in an up-to-date edition, thanks to Michèle Guéret-Laferté: the *History of the Normans* produced by the monk Amatus of Monte Cassino.[6] The original Latin text is now lost, and we only have an early fourteenth-century translation into French – an example of the sometimes slender evidential base for the study of Norman Italy.[7] It was

---

H. E. J. Cowdrey, *The Age of Abbot Desiderius: Montecassino, the Papacy, and the Normans in the Eleventh and Early Twelfth Centuries* (Oxford, 1983). See now the papers reprinted in M. Dell'Omo, *Montecassino medievale: Genesi di un simbolo, storia di una realtà* (Montecassino, 2008).

[3] Begun by Leo of Ostia up to 1075 (Book III, c. 33), the chronicle was continued by a certain Guy (as far as Book IV, c. 95), and completed by his disciple Peter the Deacon, who revised the entire text. See the detailed introduction in *Chronica Monasterii Casinensis*, ed. H. Hoffmann (MGH SS, 34; Hanover, 1980), pp. vii–xii; see also H. Hoffmann, 'Studien zur Chronik von Montecassino', *Deutsches Archiv für Erforschung des Mittelalters*, 29 (1973), 59–162; and E. D'Angelo, *Storiografi e cronologi latini del Mezzogiorno normanno-svevo* (Naples, 2003), pp. 34–6. For the language of the *Chronica Monasterii Casinensis*, see the grammatical analysis by P. Greco, '*Accusativus cum Infinitivo*' *e subordinate completive con 'quod', 'quia' e 'quoniam' in alcune cronache latine dell'Italia*, tesi di dottorato in Filologia Moderna, XX ciclo, University of Naples (2007), pp. 245–319, 450–1. On the mysterious Guy, see Peter the Deacon, 'Liber de viris illustribus Casinensis coenobii', *PL* clxxiii, 1010.

[4] For example, see the arrival (in 990) of a 'portionem ligni dominicae crucis non parvam' with the monk Leo: *Chronica Monasterii Casinensis*, p. 189.

[5] See *Chronica Monasterii Casinensis*, pp. 200–1, 274.

[6] Amatus of Monte Cassino, *Ystoire de li Normant: Édition du manuscript BnFfr. 688*, ed. M. Guéret-Laferté (Classiques français du moyen âge, 166; Paris, 2011), which replaces *Storia de' Normanni*, ed. V. Bartholomaeis (Fonti per la storia d'Italia, 76; Rome, 1935). See also J. Dufournet, 'Autour d'Aimé du Mont-Cassin', *Le moyen âge*, 117 (2011), 363–8.

[7] See the remarks of M. Zabbia, 'La cultura storiografica dell'Italia normanna riflessa nel "Chronicon" di Romualdo Salernitano', in *Progetti di ricerca della Scuola storica nazionale: Contributi alla IV settimana di studi medievali*, ed. I. Bonincontro (Rome 2009), p. 10: 'Chi si soffermi sul panorama della cronachistica normanna non può che rimanere colpito dallo scarso numero di opere conservate, dall'esile tradizione manoscritta dei testi, e allo stesso tempo, dall'elevata qualità letteraria di alcune almeno tra le cronache giunte sino a noi.' The best overall analysis of Amatus's text is still V. D'Alessandro, *Storiografia e politica nell'Italia normanna* (Naples, 1978), pp. 51–98 [published previously in *Bullettino dell'Istituto storico italiano per il Medio evo e Archivio murato-riano*, 83 (1971), 79–130]; see also G. A. Loud, 'Amatus of Montecassino and his "History of the Normans"', in *Mediterraneo, Mezzogiorno, Europa: Studi in onore di Cosimo Damiano Fonseca*, ed. G. Andenna and H. Houben (Bari, 2004), pp. 715–26. See now also the important treatment in J. Kujawiński, 'Alla ricerca del contesto del volgarizzamento della "Historia Normannorum"

written for an unknown 'seigneur conte de Militree'.[8] In the preface to his work, the author reports that, around the years 1078–85,[9] and at the behest of Abbot Desiderius, he wrote the history of the Norman princes Richard of Capua and Robert Guiscard, as well as of the deeds of the Norman people (*le fait de li Norman*),[10] that is to say the principal players in the conquest of southern Italy.[11] For our immediate purposes, what is of most interest is the historiographical positioning of the Norman population and its leaders, after their settlement in southern Italy, that Amatus articulates. Arrivals in Italy from the north,[12] having travelled a route similar to that taken some years later by Geoffrey Malaterra, the author of a text celebrating the deeds of Roger I of Sicily,[13] these people became an integral political and cultural element in the area around Monte Cassino. As a result, Amatus's historiographical project was to recount and explain the providential appearance of the Normans, as well to account for their victories over their Arab and Byzantine opponents, forces whose power in southern Italy had hitherto long remained undisputed.

The main point to emphasize is the historiographical centrality of the monastery of Monte Cassino: all the major events that took place in southern Italy in the eleventh and twelfth centuries are reported by members of this Benedictine abbey, their efforts affording a detailed demonstration of Marjorie Chibnall's suggestion that 'monastic studies gave, inadvertently, the best historical training available in the late eleventh century',[14] while also highlighting the sustained interest taken by Monte Cassino's leadership in the history of the areas where their properties were concentrated. Indeed, Amatus's *History* concludes with praise of the generous assistance that the two Norman princes had provided in the safeguarding of the abbey's properties, with particular reference made to the actions taken by the prince of Capua right up to

---

di Amato di Montecassino: il manoscritto francese 688 della Bibliothèque nationale de France', *Bullettino dell'Istituto storico italiano per il Medio evo e Archivio muratoriano*, 112 (2010), 91–136, which analyses the whole manuscript.

[8] Amatus of Monte Cassino, *Ystoire de li Normant*, p. 233.

[9] For the dating see D'Angelo, *Storiografi e cronologi latini*, p. 21 and n. 57.

[10] Amatus of Monte Cassino, *Ystoire de li Normant*, pp. 235–6: 'Et pour ce que je voi, lo pere mien abbé molt benigne, ceste parole et toutes autres qui la sequte[nt] estrea empliez en ces II principes [*sc.* Richard and Robert], et pour ce ai je mise ma volenté et moncorage à escrivre l'ystoire lor. Et croi que non dirai je tant solement lo fait de li home, mes ce que fu concedut, par dispensation de Dieu que fust fait par li home. ... Et li fait de li Normant liquel sont digne de notre memoire ai je en VIII volume de livre distincté, et a ce que non soit fatigue de chercier a ceuz qui volissent alcune chose lire de l'ystoire, chascun volume ai je note o cert capitule'.

[11] For an excellent account, see G. A. Loud, *The Age of Robert Guiscard: Southern Italy and the Norman Conquest* (Harlow, 2000), pp. 60ff; see also J. France, 'The Occasion of the Coming of the Normans to Italy', *Journal of Medieval History*, 17 (1991), 185–205; and L. Russo, 'Convergenze e scontri: per una riconsiderazione dei rapporti greco-normanni nei secoli XI–XII', in *Fedi a confronto: Ebrei, Cristiani e Musulmani fra X e XIII secolo*, ed. S. Gensini (Florence, 2006), pp. 263–78.

[12] Amatus of Monte Cassino, *Ystoire de li Normant*, pp. 243–4.

[13] Geoffrey Malaterra, *De rebus gestis Rogerii Calabriae et Siciliae Comitis et Roberti Guiscardi Ducis fratris eius*, ed. E. Pontieri (Rerum Italicarum Scriptores, 5.1; Bologna 1927–8), pp. 7–9.

[14] M. Chibnall, *The World of Orderic Vitalis* (Oxford, 1984), p. 113.

his death to protect the monastery from all its enemies, aggressors characterized as tyrants.[15]

Closely connected to the historiographical undertaking represented by the *Chronica Monasterii Casinensis* is the reordering of the abbey's documentation that was undertaken by some of the same writers responsible for the historiographical text, first Leo of Ostia and then Peter the Deacon.[16] Like any large monastic institution in the central medieval period, Monte Cassino found itself forced to develop an archive to preserve the large numbers of documents relating to its patrimony: as two recent scholars of Monte Cassino's documentation have observed, 'en faire mémoire permet de fournir au monastère un outil de gestion'.[17] The importance attached to memory is noteworthy: the monks of Monte Cassino's need to organize a large complex of estates, the *terra Sancti Benedicti*, which stretched from Tuscany to Apulia – an area whose homogeneity and compactness have recently been questioned[18] – amounted to an intellectual operation closely linked to their historiographical activity, in that both involved an understanding of events in the outside world, remembrance of benefactors of the abbey, and criticisms of the monks' enemies for their violent depradations at the expense of St Benedict's patrimony.[19] The importance of such attention to organized memory is demonstrated by the enormous work undertaken between 1131 and 1133 by a team of scribes under the direction of Peter the Deacon to assemble a cartulary preserving more than 700 records of the donations and the privileges that the monastery had acquired all the way back to its distant origins.[20] This endeavour represented the realization of a scheme to rationalize the abbey's archival memory that had led Leo of Ostia, some years earlier, to transform the Monte Cassino Chronicle into an 'ébauche de cartulaire-chronique',[21] without at

---

[15] Amatus of Monte Cassino, *Ystoire de li Normant*, pp. 509–10. Extensive donations made by Robert were remembered in the *Chronica Monasterii Casinensis*, pp. 438–40. The monks of Monte Cassino, however, additionally criticized Norman greed: Desiderius of Monte Cassino, *Dialogi de miraculis sancti Benedicti*, ed. G. Schwartz and A. Hofmeister (MGH SS, 30:2; Hanover, 1934), p. 1124.

[16] For discussion of Peter the Deacon's *Registrum*, the following are fundamental: P. Chastang and L. Feller, 'Classer et compiler: La gestion des archives du Mont-Cassin au XIIᵉ siècle', in *Écritures de l'espace social: Mélanges d'histoire médiévale offerts à Monique Bourin*, ed. D. Boisseuil, P. Chastang, L. Feller and J. Morsel (Paris, 2010), pp. 347–70; P. Chastang, L. Feller and J.-M. Martin, 'Autour de l'édition du "Registrum Petri Diaconi": Problèmes de documentation cassinésienne: chartes, rouleaux, registre', *Mélanges de l'École Française de Rome: Moyen Âge-Temps Modernes*, 121/1 (2009), 99–135. My thanks to Professor Laurent Feller (University of Paris I) for the opportunity to consult these papers prior to publication.

[17] Chastang and Feller, 'Classer et compiler', p. 350.

[18] *Ibid.*, pp. 359–60. Professor Jean-Marie Martin (École française de Rome) is preparing a new study of this topic. See the claim in P. Toubert, 'Pour une histoire de l'environnement économique et social du Mont-Cassin (IXᵉ-XIIᵉ siècles)', *Comptes-rendus des séances de l'Académie des Inscriptions et Belles-Lettres*, 120 (1976), 698, for the 'exceptionelle homogénéité' of the *terra Sancti Benedicti*.

[19] See Chibnall, *The World of Orderic Vitalis*, pp. 109ff. See also the valuable study by L. K. Little, *Benedictine Maledictions: Liturgical Cursing in Romanesque France* (Ithaca, 1993).

[20] Chastang, Feller and Martin, 'Autour de l'édition', 99, 132–5. In some instances the preserved documentation antedates the foundation of Monte Cassino.

[21] The formulation of Chastang and Feller, 'Classer et compiler', p. 351.

that stage giving the historical material effective shape. For example, in section 79 of Book II, when narrating the short pontificate of Pope Damasus II (1048) and the early reign of his successor Leo IX (1049-54), the chronicler lingers on his telling of the story of the visit to the abbey made by the new pope, who in returning from the shrine of St Michael at Monte Gargano arrived at Monte Cassino on Palm Sunday; mention is then made of the privileges that were granted to the monks, and these are itemized.[22] It appears that the intention was to link an account of the difficult years of the late 1040s, during which there had been a remarkably rapid turnover in popes, with the confirmation of the papal privileges in favour of Monte Cassino that were kept in its archives. However, due to the text's inorganic mode of exposition, the chronicler does not succeed in providing a clear account of events.[23] This was because his primary interest was solely to peg the memory of the papal visit to the documentation issued in favour of his monastery. In other words, the monks' historiographical memory was indissolubly linked to the security and protection of the *terra Sancti Benedicti*, an illustration of the growing importance attached to writing that is attested from the eleventh century onwards.[24]

This brings us to the question of the First Crusade. Chapter XI of Book IV of the *Chronica Monasterii Casinensis* contains an interesting passage bearing on the origins and early stages of the expedition, covering the period from Pope Urban II's tour of parts of France in 1095-6 to the arrival of the pilgrims outside the walls of Antioch (October 1097).[25] There are many indications in the text to suggest that the writer[26] may have used as his starting point a version of the 'Jerusalem History' hypothesized by Jay Rubenstein in an important discussion of the relationships between the various texts that we have at our disposal concerning the events that led to the conquest of Jerusalem.[27] In this connection, mention may also be made of indications of the existence of a common source that emerge from a comparison between the anonymous *Gesta Francorum* and the Monte Cassino Chronicle:[28] a) the use of the term *motio* to indicate the

---

[22] *Chronica Monasterii Casinensis*, pp. 323–6.

[23] For Leo IX in southern Italy, see Bloch, *Monte Cassino*, i, 33–4.

[24] Similar cases in documentation from the eleventh and twelfth centuries have been analysed by S. Vanderputten, 'Monastic Literate Practices in Eleventh- and Twelfth-Century Northern France', *Journal of Medieval History*, 32 (2006), 101–26. See also the seminal work of M. T. Clanchy, *From Memory to Written Record: England, 1066–1307*, 3rd edn (Chichester, 2013).

[25] *Chronica Monasterii Casinensis*, pp. 475–81. A thorough stylistic analysis is presented by P. Greco, 'Chronica Monasterii Casinensis IV,11: un'analisi sintattica e un'ipotesi genetica', in *Auctor et Auctoritas in Latinis Medii Aevi Litteris*, ed. E. D'Angelo (Florence, forthcoming).

[26] His identity is now uncertain. This section is discussed by Hartmut Hoffmann in his Introduction to *Chronica Monasterii Casinensis*, pp. xxviii–xxx, arguing that 'Das Kapitel IV 11 nimmt in der Chronik eine Sonderstellung ein ... In dem ganzen Kapitel [IV, 11] dürfen daher den Rest von Leos *ystoria peregrinorum* sehen'.

[27] J. Rubenstein, 'What is the *Gesta Francorum*, and who was Peter Tudebode?', *Revue Mabillon*, 16 (2005), 179–204: 'There was indeed a common source, an early draft of the *Gesta Francorum*, which I shall refer to here, with deliberate imprecision, as the "Jerusalem history"': 192.

[28] This hypothesis was proposed for the first time by P. Meyvaert and P. Devos, 'Autour de Léon d'Ostie et de sa Translatio S. Clementis (Légende italique de ss. Cyrille et Méthode)', *Analecta Bollandiana*, 74 (1956), 217–23.

movement of the pilgrims;[29] b) the triple repetition of the cry by means of which the pilgrims expressed their conformity to the divine will;[30] c) the correspondences between the lists of commanders undertaking the crusade, and the division of the forces setting out for the Holy Land into three groupings;[31] d) the list of those warriors who follow Bohemond;[32] e) the scene in which the Normans siege of Amalfi is abandoned and Count Roger I of Sicily returns sadly home;[33] f) and the wording of the promise that the emperor Alexius I Comnenus makes to Bohemond.[34]

As these similarities demonstrate, the existence of a common source is clear. It is particularly noteworthy that the text that the Cassino chronicler used as a source must have been abruptly and unexpectedly interrupted at the point at which the Christian armies reach Antioch.[35] Up to that moment it seems that the author was consulting a text that had many points of contact with the version of events in the *Gesta Francorum*, even allowing for significant differences in terms of point of view, content and style. At the end of Chapter XI, however, all parallels seem to disappear. On the contrary, the narration of the events of the latter stages of the crusade, culminating in the capture of Antioch and then of the Holy City, is extremely brief: 'Eodem anno stella cometes apparuit, et urbs Antiochena a christianis capta est. Sequenti vero tempore idibus Iulii christicole civitatem

---

[29] *Chronica Monasterii Casinensis*, p. 475; *GF*, p. 1.

[30] *Chronica Monasterii Casinensis*, p. 475 ('Deus lo volt, Deus lo volt, Deus lo volt'); *GF*, p. 7 ('Deus vult, Deus vult, Deus vult!').

[31] Cf. *Chronica Monasterii Casinensis*, p. 476: 'Factis igitur tribus turmis ex omni illa, que ad id iam consenserat, multitudine una pars eorum cum duce Gotfrido et eius frater Balduino et cum comite Balduino de Monte, simul et cum quodam Petro heremita, quem sequebatur ingens turba Alemannorum, Ungariam ingressi per viam, quam olim rex Carolus statuerat, abierunt Constantinopolim'; *GF*, p. 2: 'Fecerunt denique Galli tres partes. Una pars Francorum in Hungariae intravit regionem, scilicet Petrus Heremita, et dux Godefridus, et Balduinus frater eius, et Balduinus comes de Monte. Isti potentissimi milites et alii plures quos ignoro venerunt per viam quam iamdudum Karolus Magnus mirificus rex Franciae aptari fecit usque Constantinopolim'.

[32] *Chronica Monasterii Casinensis*, pp. 476–7; *GF*, pp. 7–8. The Norman and other knights are listed in the same order. But there are two differences in the *Chronica*: the addition of the son of Count Gerard of Buonalbergo (*Robbertus filius Girardi*), and the change of Humphrey of Montescaglioso (already dead in 1096) to the name of his son Geoffrey, as already noted by E. Jamison, 'Some Notes on the *Anonymi Gesta Francorum*, with Special Reference to the Norman Contingent from South Italy and Sicily in the First Crusade', in *Studies in French Language and Medieval Literature Presented to Professor Mildred K. Pope* (Manchester 1939), p. 195.

[33] *Chronica Monasterii Casinensis*, p. 476: 'Qua fama exciti omnes Rogerii milites tam multi ad huiuscemodi confederationem subito confluxerunt, ut paucis sibi relictis predictus comes mestus ad Siciliam remeaverit'; *GF*, p. 7: 'Coepit tunc ad eum vehementer concurrere maxima pars militum qui erant in obsidione illa, a deo ut Rogerius comes pene solus remanserit, reversusque Siciliam dolebat et merebat quandoque gentem amittere suam.'

[34] *Chronica Monasterii Casinensis*, p. 478: 'insuper et Boamundo quindecim dierum terram in longitudine, octo autem in latitudine ex ista parte Antiochia daret'; *GF*, p. 12: 'Fortissimo autem viro Boamundo quem valde timebat ... quondam si libenter ei iuraret, quindecim dies eundi terre in extensione ab Antiochia retro daret, et octo in latitudine.'

[35] Cf. *Chronica Monasterii Casinensis*, p. 481. The modern editor considers the problem in the introduction to the text, pp. xxviii–xxx, arguing that this passage presents 'die stilistische Signatur' of Leo of Ostia.

Ierusalem ceperunt. Et in celo ignea via per totam noctem visa est quinto kalendas Octobris.'[36] It is as if the chronicler had at his disposal a detailed source that only took the story as far as the initial phases of the siege of Antioch; this would explain the absence of information for the remainder of the expedition and the unexplained absence of details about the conquest of Jerusalem, a topic strictly extraneous to the institutional history of the abbey of Monte Cassino but one very difficult to leave untold given the importance of the Holy City and the impact that its capture made throughout the west. This uneven pattern in the distribution of narrative details accords with the recent suggestion by Jean Flori that more than one chronicler who participated in the First Crusade wrote his account by drawing on oral information and 'des documents anterieures accessibiles dans l'armée de la croisade'.[37] If this assumption is correct, whoever completed the Monte Cassino account of the crusade had access to a poorly structured and incomplete text, perhaps a rough draft, that only recounted the first stages of the pilgrims' journey to Jerusalem. The Monte Cassino account represents a further piece of evidence to consider in recent debates about the content and form of the narrative sources for the First Crusade, texts that are often approached in a monolithic fashion without due regard to the processes that led to their assuming the forms in which they survive.[38]

Manuscript no. 300 of the abbey of Monte Cassino preserves a compilation that the recent editor of the text has restored to its original title: the *Hystoria de via et recuperatione Antiochiae atque Ierusolymarum*,[39] which previously had been known as the *Historia peregrinorum*, the title it was given by its editors for the *Recueil des historiens des croisades*.[40] Many sequences within this text reveal that it is a compilation.[41] Its principal interest resides in the manner in which it was created as an historiographical project at some point between 1130 and 1153.[42] Based on a range of sources, not all of which are now identifiable, the *Hystoria de via* is clear evidence of the interest in the First Crusade that persisted at the abbey of Monte Cassino into the second quarter of the twelfth century, to the point that someone chose to write a text that has hitherto tended to be undervalued, and which merits reconsideration in the context of Monte Cassino's global

---

[36]   *Ibid.*, p. 485.
[37]   J. Flori, *Chroniqueurs et propagandistes: Introduction critique aux sources de la Première croisade* (Hautes études médiévales et modernes, 98; Geneva, 2010), p. 85.
[38]   See Rubenstein, 'What is the *Gesta Francorum*', 179–204; and also Flori, *Chroniqueurs et propagandistes, passim*; J. France, 'The Anonymous *Gesta Francorum* and the *Historia Francorum qui ceperunt Iherusalem* of Raymond of Aguilers and the *Historia de Hierosolymitano itinere* of Peter Tudebode: An Analysis of the Textual Relationship between Primary Sources for the First Crusade', in *The Crusades and Their Sources: Essays Presented to Bernard Hamilton*, ed. J. France and W. G. Zajac (Aldershot, 1998), pp. 39–69; E. Lapina, '"Nec signis nec testis creditor ...": The Problem of Eyewitnesses in the Chronicles of the First Crusade', *Viator*, 38 (2007), 117–39.
[39]   *Hystoria de via et recuperatione Antiochiae atque Ierusolymarum*, ed. E. D'Angelo (Florence, 2009), p. xxx: the text's editor defines it as 'un' opera storiografica di compilazione'.
[40]   'Historia peregrinorum euntium Jerusolimam ad liberandum Sanctum Sepulcrum', *RHC Occ* iii, 165–229.
[41]   For further details see *Hystoria de via et recuperatione*, p. xliii.
[42]   *Ibid.*, p. xvi.

historiographical engagement with the memory of the crusade. Moreover, despite the compiled nature of the text, there is a good deal of 'original' information to be found within it, even after allowance is made for the high probability that some of its sources are no longer extant.[43] In fact, the text supplies numerous expansions upon or additions to the information contained in other sources. By way of illustration, reference may be made to some of the details to be found in the *Hystoria de via* that are not supplied elsewhere: a) the exact date, the feast of All Saints (1096), is given for the arrival of the southern Italian Norman contingent on the eastern coast of the Adriatic;[44] b) the location where Bohemond receives the hospitality of the Byzantine authorities upon reaching Constantinople is specified;[45] c) and a certain 'Paganus Longobardus' is mentioned as the first warrior to climb the walls of Antioch during the night-time assault that leads to the capture of the city.[46] To these we may add a further series of twenty-nine original episodes that are itemized in the recent edition of the text, half of which feature members of the southern Italian Norman contingent on the crusade.[47] These include details of immediate historical interest, such as the shipping to Bari, at Bohemond's command, of the defeated Muslim general Kerbogha's tent as a trophy of victory; the conversion of a Turkish prisoner who is given the baptismal name Ilario but is subsequently discovered to have faked his conversion; an omen that anticipates the premature death of the young Bohemond II; the request by Baldwin of Boulogne for a sworn declaration of loyalty from Tancred soon after Baldwin became king of Jerusalem; and a description of Bohemond's pilgrimage to the shrine of St Leonard at Noblat in central France, and the ensuing recruitment campaign for Bohemond's expedition against the Byzantine empire.[48] It is evident that the *Hystoria de via* supplies precious details on various aspects of the crusade, most of them attributable to eyewitness testimony, that are absent from our other sources.[49] There are good grounds for supposing that many of these elements originated with returning pilgrims who had belonged to the southern Italian Norman contingent; while the remaining addenda represent, for the most part, information in the public domain to which many informants could have had ready access, such as the embassy sent to the Fatimid court at the suggestion of the Byzantine emperor, or the discussions among the various crusade princes before the election of Godfrey of Bouillon as ruler of Jerusalem.[50]

---

[43] *Ibid.*, p. l: 'È dunque possibile che una parte delle sezioni originali dell'HAI derivino da una fonte scritta attualmente perduta'.

[44] *Ibid.*, p. 20.

[45] *Ibid.*, p. 23: 'extra civitatem in Sancto Argenteo'.

[46] *Ibid.*, p. 64.

[47] See *Hystoria de via et recuperatione*, pp. xl–xli.

[48] See *Hystoria de via et recuperatione*, pp. 48–9, 89, 111–12; 133–4, 135. For Bohemond's campaign of recruitment against Byzantium, see L. Russo, 'Il viaggio di Boemondo d'Altavilla in Francia (1106): un riesame', *Archivio Storico Italiano*, 163 (2005), 3–42.

[49] For further discussion see *Hystoria de via et recuperatione*, pp. liv–lix.

[50] See *Hystoria de via et recuperatione*, pp. 28, 128–9. For Godfrey's election, see L. Ferrier, 'La couronne refusée de Godefroy de Bouillon: eschatologie et humiliation de la mayesté aux premiers temps du royaume latin de Jérusalem', in *Le concile de Clermont de 1095 et l'appel à la croisade*, ed. A. Vauchez (Collection de l'École Française de Rome, 236; Rome, 1997), pp. 245–65.

To conclude this necessarily brief survey: the study and analysis of the sources we have at our disposal can sometimes run the risk of undervaluing the role of institutional factors in the shaping and sedimentation of memory. In order to preserve a memory over the long term it is essential that there exists an institutional framework equipped with the intellectual capital – resources and trained people – that can be mobilized in the collection, selection and drafting of what to narrate and what not.[51] A few decades after the events of the First Crusade, the need was felt at Monte Cassino to create an account of the events that had led to the conquest of Jerusalem. The first stage in this process was made by the author of Chapter XI of Book IV of the *Chronica Monasterii Casinensis*, resulting in an initial and still partial telling of the events that had led to the departure of southern Italian Norman knights for the Holy Land under Bohemond and the first stages of the expedition.[52] Nevertheless, this solution was not considered satisfactory, especially in view of the growing interest in the Holy Land that is evident in the twelfth century – an interest demonstrated, for instance, by a short treatise on the Holy Places penned by Peter the Deacon at the behest of Abbot Wibald.[53] The need was felt for someone to supply a complete narration of the events of the crusade; an anonymous chronicler duly assumed this responsibility, producing what we know today as the *Hystoria de via et recuperatione Antiochiae atque Ierusolymarum*, which combined information available from written sources, some now lost, and material obtained from eyewitnesses. Though fragmentary, Monte Cassino's historiographical output in the twelfth century, much of it tied to the question of the abbey's patrimony, points towards a more complex and layered interplay of memory and narrative than the surviving evidence permits us to see. We sometimes need to put to one side the legitimate project of reconstructing events in order to focus upon the work done by authors writing at Monte Cassino in the decades following the fall of Jerusalem in order to craft narratives describing and explaining the deeds of the triumphant crusaders. The texts explored in this paper represent important evidence for the progressively shifting and refined focus that the monks of Monte Cassino brought to bear upon events such as the

---

[51]   In fact, Monte Cassino took an active role in such operations, as noted by F. Newton, '"Expolitio" per l'Umanesimo: la formazione classica dei monaci cassinesi nell'XI secolo', in *Il monaco il libro la biblioteca*, ed. O. Pecere (Montecassino, 2003), pp. 169–79.

[52]   For an analysis see L. Russo, 'I Normanni e il movimento crociato: Una revisione', in *Il papato e i Normanni: Temporale e spirituale in età normanna*, ed. E. D'Angelo and C. Leonardi (Florence, 2011), pp. 163–74.

[53]   See Petrus Diaconus, 'Liber de locis sanctis', *PL* clxxiii, 1115–34. The author says (col. 1118) that his abbot Wibald had come by first-hand information concerning the Holy Land from several pilgrims, as well as from various written sources: 'Nec novi vos et incogniti hactenus aliquid in hoc itinerario ediscituros, sed ea quae jam viva voce illis referentibus qui ad sepulcrum Domini perrexerunt edidicistis, vel ea quae per volumina diversa librorum legistis, nos hic noveritis collegisse.' Nevertheless, it should be noted that Wibald was abbot of Monte Cassino for just one month, which problematizes the attribution: for further discussion, see H. Hoffmann, 'Die älteren Abtslisten von Montecassino', *Quellen und Forschungen aus italienischen Archiven und Bibliotheken*, 48 (1967), 334–5.

First Crusade.[54] In sum, we must always recognize that the sources we work with today in order to reconstruct the events of the crusade are the partial and fragmentary results of a cumulative intellectual enterprise that spanned several decades.

---

[54] Cf. C. J. Tyerman, *The Debate on the Crusades* (Manchester, 2011), pp. 19–20: 'Certain networks of transmission are obvious, such as the northern French Benedictine abbeys that produced the major histories of the First Crusade. The chain of Cistercian houses provided similar likely channels of transmission as members of the order led successive preaching campaigns from the Second to the Fifth Crusade, a role that passed to the friars in the thirteenth century.'

NOVA PEREGRINATIO: THE FIRST CRUSADE AS A PILGRIMAGE IN CONTEMPORARY LATIN NARRATIVES

Léan Ní Chléirigh

Despite a considerable historiography on the crusades, there are still flickers of division among historians as to the definition of a crusade, or rather, divisions as to when all the features of a crusade became established. The First Crusade suffers the most from this tendency. Although it was the first campaign of its kind which historians agree to be definable as a 'crusade', the campaign of 1096–9, like many 'firsts', did not have all of the features of a crusade in a fully developed form.[1] For example, the indulgence, which became a defining characteristic of the crusades, was in all likelihood not legally established or universal until almost fifty years after its origins were mooted at the Council of Clermont.[2] Some of this tension arises because modern terms to define a crusade come with accumulated inferences and meanings which are anachronistic when applied retrospectively. The term 'pilgrimage' is such a contentious term, given its implications of an unarmed endeavour, and it is often qualified. The crusade was, therefore, an 'armed pilgrimage' or a 'crusade-pilgrimage'; the crusaders were 'warrior pilgrims'.[3] Although a seemingly contradictory impulse, the term 'pilgrimage' became associated with the crusade because the Latin *peregrinatio* was frequently used by contemporaries for these expeditions. The crusades also shared a number of features with pilgrimages; participants often took a vow before setting off; each was considered an act of penance which would count against the individual's

---

[1]   Rousset's suggestion that the First Crusade was the only 'véritable et typique' instantiation of the crusades is no longer held to be true: P. Rousset, 'L'idée de croisade chez le chroniqueurs d'Occident', in *Relazioni del X Congresso Internazionale di Scienze Storiche, Roma 1955, III: Storia del Medioevo* (Florence, 1955), p. 547.

[2]   J. A. Brundage, *Medieval Canon Law and the Crusader* (Madison, 1969), pp. 149–52; C. J. Tyerman, *The Invention of the Crusades* (London, 1998), p. 9; H. E. Mayer, *The Crusades*, trans. J. Gillingham, 2nd edn (Oxford, 1988), pp. 30–3.

[3]   N. J. Housley, *Contesting the Crusades* (Oxford, 2006), p. 15; J. S. C. Riley-Smith, *The First Crusade and the Idea of Crusading*, rev. edn (London, 2009), pp. 22–5.

sins in the soul's reckoning after death; canon law protected the property and position of both crusaders and pilgrims during their absence from home. Thus by inductive reasoning as well as similarities in terminology, the crusades were deemed to be pilgrimages, albeit a specific type of pilgrimage.[4]

Recently, however, some more reductive analysis has challenged this interpretation. Although often used to denote a pilgrimage, *peregrinatio* could also be applied more normally to any journey and *peregrinus* to any traveller.[5] Evidence for the shared characteristics of pilgrims and crusaders exists from the late twelfth century only. There is very little indication that these features were present in the earliest incarnation of the crusade. Even if they were, it is argued that this does not make the two endeavours analogous, merely parallel. These factors have led to the suggestion that the First Crusade was not envisaged as a pilgrimage by its primary instigator, Pope Urban II, but that the features of pilgrimage and crusade fused towards the end of the twelfth century, if indeed they fused at all. Proponents of this argument place the development of the crusade idea within the evolution of holy war or penitential warfare.[6]

Three principal bodies of evidence can be accessed in order to approach the question whether the First Crusade was envisaged by contemporaries as a pilgrimage. The preaching of the primary instigator of the expedition, Pope Urban II, has been exploited by those historians on both sides of the issue. The surviving letters of the pope do not explicitly link crusade with pilgrimage, however; due to the destruction of the register of Pope Urban II, historians are in possession of an extremely small number of letters from this pope, only three of which can be linked to the crusade.[7] Similarly, no 'official' record survives of the canons of the Council of Clermont, where the pope first preached the crusade.[8] With such a small body of surviving evidence, it is dangerous to attempt to draw any conclusions as to the pope's notion of the expeditions. Conversely, there is an abundance of sources in the second category of evidence consulted by historians: the charters which departing crusaders contracted with local religious institutions. Although these sources will not demonstrate what message Urban preached, they may show what the eventual participants in the crusade understood by his message. Many of these charters characterize the crusade in terms of pilgrimage in their stated reasons for the departure

---

[4]   Rousset, 'L'idée', p. 550; Riley-Smith, *First Crusade*, pp. 19–25; M. G. Bull, *Knightly Piety and the Lay Response to the First Crusade: The Limousin and Gascony c.970–c.1130* (Oxford, 1993), p. 19; Mayer, *Crusades*, pp. 28–30.

[5]   *Mediae Latinitatis Lexicon Minus*, ed. J. F. Niermeyer and C. van de Kieft, 2nd edn (Leiden, 2002), p. 1026.

[6]   J. M. Jensen, '*Peregrinatio sive expeditio*: Why the First Crusade was Not a Pilgrimage', *Al-Masāq: Islam and the Medieval Mediterranean*, 15 (2003), 126–8; A. Becker, *Papst Urban II. (1088–1099)*, 2 vols (MGH Schriften, 19; Stuttgart, 1964–88), ii, 396–8.

[7]   *Epistulae et chartae ad historiam primi belli sacri spectantes: Die Kreuzzugsbriefe aus den Jahren 1088–1100*, ed. H. Hagenmeyer (Innsbruck, 1901), pp. 136, 137; *Papsturkunden in Spanien: i. Katalanien*, ed. P. Kehr (Abhandlungen der Gesellschaft der Wissenschaften zu Göttingen, Philologisch-Historische Klasse, n.s. 18:2; Berlin, 1926) pp. 286–8.

[8]   *The Councils of Urban II, I: Decreta Claremontensia*, ed. R. Somerville (Annuarium Historiae Conciliorum Supplementum, 1; Amsterdam, 1972), p. 74.

of the participants and use similar terms in their description of the journey.[9] While this body of evidence has the added attraction of seeming to access the concerns of the laity, a rare feature in medieval records, its value in this instance is also disputed by historians. Critics of the approach point to the fact that diplomatic conventions tended to demand a very specific structure to charters which rested on centuries of tradition and would not respond quickly to a new form of expedition. This, they argue, led inevitably to the couching of the crusade in terms of pre-existing ideals, hence the use of pilgrimage imagery and terminology. Charters were also written almost exclusively by the monastic house or church with which the charter was contracted and did not therefore always reflect the notions of the laymen but rather the monks or clerics involved.[10] While Bull has argued that developments in eleventh-century diplomatic resulted in more fluidity in charter production and consequently more responsiveness in the texts to the feelings of the layman concerned, similarities between charters emanating from particular houses caution that the monastic author's input was still paramount.[11]

The third avenue for the historian to explore for evidence of parallels between crusade and pilgrimage is a return to the Latin narrative sources of the early twelfth century. It is with these narratives that some responsibility lies for the initial recognition of the parallels between pilgrimage and crusade, as the authors used the term *peregrinatio* and *peregrini* widely in their description of the crusade. Some have dismissed these terms as merely meaning 'journey' or 'expedition', or, at the least, lacking sufficient specificity to denote pilgrimage as a discrete practice. Until now, however, detailed analysis of the terms in the narrative sources, as well as the context in which they appear, has not been undertaken. Such an analysis reveals that in some cases the authors were demonstrably referring to a pilgrimage or pilgrims when they used the terms *peregrini* and *peregrinatio*. That these terms were then used to denote armed crusaders demonstrates that bearing arms did not disqualify one from being a *peregrinus*. It is also clear that on many occasions their use can be shown to reflect an opinion among the authors that the crusaders were to be considered pilgrims in the existing traditional sense. That is to say, what is reflected in the narratives is not a new use of the term but the acceptance of a new group into an older category. The use of these terms alongside features associated with pilgrimage such as fasting or praying also suggests that on the expedition itself the participants consciously replicated the behaviour of pilgrims and identified themselves as such.

---

[9]   J. S. C. Riley-Smith, 'The Idea of Crusading in the Charters of Early Crusaders, 1095–1102', in *Le Concile de Clermont de 1095 et l'appel à la croisade,* ed. A. Vauchez (Collection de l'École Française de Rome, 236; Paris, 1997), p. 157.

[10]   J. Flori, 'Ideology and Motivations in the First Crusade', in *Palgrave Advances in the Crusades,* ed. H. J. Nicholson (Basingstoke, 2005), pp. 22–3; C. Kostick, *The Social Structure of the First Crusade* (The Medieval Mediterranean, 76; Leiden, 2008), pp. 293–4.

[11]   M. G. Bull, 'The Diplomatic of the First Crusade', in *The First Crusade: Origins and Impact,* ed. J. P. Phillips (Manchester, 1997), pp. 36–8; *idem, Knightly Piety,* pp. 15–16, 179–81. Bull also notes that the charters pertaining to the most valuable grants made to a house tended to have the most elaborate *arengae,* distorting the evidence towards the wealthier donors: *Knightly Piety,* p. 180.

The textual interactions between the Latin narratives of the First Crusade are extremely complex, and while there is much consensus as to the broad strokes of the relationships between various texts, there are still some outstanding details to be resolved.[12] A large proportion of the texts were reliant either directly or indirectly on the anonymous *Gesta Francorum et aliorum Hierosolimitanorum*. Most of these texts contain information which their authors obtained independently, however, and all of the authors recast the narrative structure which they found in the *Gesta Francorum* to suit their own understanding of the crusade phenomenon. Much of the terminology, therefore, is reflective of the author's own understanding of the crusade, not merely a replication of the usage in his *fons formalis*.[13]

In many cases, the use of the term *peregrini* or *peregrinatio* in the narrative is somewhat ambiguous and can be interpreted as either 'pilgrim' or 'traveller'. In many other cases, however, there is no ambiguity and a translation as 'pilgrim' is appropriate.[14] The clearest examples of this occur when the person referred to is a pilgrim in the traditional sense, that is, an unarmed person journeying to a holy place as an act of piety, often as a penitential act. Traditional pilgrims appear frequently in the narratives, particularly when the authors described attacks on unarmed *peregrini* by the Muslims of the east. In his account of the speech of Urban at Clermont, Baldric of Bourgueil reported that the pope mourned the fate of pilgrims come to worship at the Holy Places at the hands of the Muslim governors of Jerusalem: 'that which the *peregrini* had brought, [the Muslims] swindled utterly.'[15] Albert of Aachen attributed the inception of the idea of crusade to Peter the Hermit, the charismatic leader of the so-called 'People's Crusade'. In his description of Peter's visit to Jerusalem, he reported that the hermit saw and lamented the ill-treatment of the pilgrims to the Holy Sepulchre, including the exaction of tribute: 'The Turks ... had invaded the city some time before and taken possession for a long time and used to exact heavy tributes from Saracens as well as Christ's *peregrini* and the local faithful.'[16] In the same passage

---

[12] The scholarship on this subject is considerable and the introductions to the forthcoming editions of many of the texts will provide much information. Three key treatments of the question are J. France, 'The Anonymous *Gesta Francorum* and the *Historia Francorum qui ceperunt Iherusalem* of Raymond of Aguilers and the *Historia de Hierosolymitano Itinere* of Peter Tudebode', in *The Crusades and their Sources: Essays Presented to Bernard Hamilton*, ed. J. France and W. G. Zajac (Aldershot, 1998), pp. 39–69; J. France, 'The Use of the Anonymous *Gesta Francorum* in the Early Twelfth-Century Sources for the First Crusade', in *From Clermont to Jerusalem: The Crusades and Crusader Societies, 1095–1500*, ed. A. V. Murray (International Medieval Research, 3; Turnhout, 1998), pp. 29–42; J. Rubenstein, 'What was the *Gesta Francorum* and who was Peter Tudebode?', *Revue Mabillon*, 16 (2005), 179–204.

[13] In this paper, examples where a term is a direct appropriation from another source have been omitted, except where otherwise stated.

[14] Ekkehard of Aura, Caffaro di Caschifelone and Ralph of Caen used the terms *peregrini* and *peregrinatio* on occasion; however, no author's use is elaborate or frequent enough to determine whether they considered the crusade to exhibit the features of a pilgrimage or not, and for this reason these works have been omitted from this study.

[15] BB i.2, p. 12: 'peregrinos funditus emungebant'.

[16] AA vi.31, p. 442: 'paulo ante hanc invadentes, multo tempore obtinuerunt, et gravia tributa tam a Sarracenis quam a peregrinis Christi et indigenis fidelibus exigebant'.

Albert further described how, since the time of Suqmān ibn Artuq, no pilgrims had been admitted to the city until its capture by the crusaders in 1099: 'With every sort of defence of weapons and strength of soldiers he [Suqman] could devise he denied entry to the city to *peregrini*.'[17]

During the siege of Antioch, Raymond of Aguilers reported, there arrived legates from the Fatimids of Egypt. These legates, we are told, offered the friendship of the 'king of Babylon' to the crusaders and pointed to the generosity of the king towards Egyptian Christians and *peregrini*: 'This embassy promised to us grace and benevolence from their king and besides referred to the many kindnesses of the king towards Egyptian Christians and our *peregrini*.'[18] This appears to refer to pilgrims who travelled to the Holy Land through Egypt following the capture of much of Asia Minor and Syria by the Turks. When describing the crusaders' arrival at Jerusalem, Baldric of Bourgueil paused to lament the torments which the city had undergone, in particular that her rightful sons and pilgrims had long been exiled from her: 'Indeed behold, she had no sons in her, who could govern her solicitously; but she lately suffered exiled lords and *peregrini*.'[19] In the description of the final assault on Jerusalem in the *Gesta Francorum*, a reference to the gate of the city at which the *peregrini* had been accustomed to pay tribute represents the only use of the term in this work to denote traditional pilgrims as opposed to crusaders.[20] When the city was captured by the crusaders, Raymond of Aguilers related that the new patriarch of the city, Arnulf of Chocques, began to search for the lost relic of the True Cross, which had been one of the objectives of pilgrims travelling to Jerusalem, 'which the *peregrini* had been accustomed to adore before the capture of Jerusalem'.[21] Albert of Aachen's account continues to describe the kingdom of Jerusalem until 1119, and in the later sections of his work, references are made to *peregrini*, most likely traditional pilgrims, come to worship in the Holy Land. In 1113, a group of *peregrini* asked King Baldwin I of Jerusalem to escort them past the city of Tyre. This request for an armed escort suggests that these *peregrini* were unarmed.[22] Another group of *peregrini* stayed in Jerusalem at Easter in 1119 and were travelling down to the River Jordan when they were attacked by Saracens from Ascalon and Tyre. That these were almost certainly traditional pilgrims can be seen by Albert's comment that they were unable to resist their attackers due to their physical weakness from having fasted 'in the name of Jesus'.[23]

Initial investigations thus suggest that the term *peregrini* was well known to the authors of the Latin narratives of the First Crusade to denote pilgrims in the

---

[17] AA vi.32, p. 444: 'nam urbis introitum peregrinis negavit omni armorum defensione et militum virtute qua potuit'.

[18] RA, p. 58: 'Hii autem legati graciam et benevolentiam apud regem suum nobis promittebant. Praeterea plura beneficia regis, in christianos Egyptios et peregrinos nostros referebant.'

[19] BB iv.9, p. 97: 'Ecce enim nullos in se habebat filios, qui ei consulentes principarentur; sed modo patiebatur dominos extorres et peregrinos, discolas et impuros, qui ei captivae jugo abusivo dominabantur.'

[20] GF, p. 91 See n. 29 for a discussion of the payment of tribute by pilgrims to the rulers of Jerusalem prior to the crusade. See also GN vii.8, p. 280; and BB iv.14, p. 102.

[21] RA, p. 154: 'quam peregrini ante captam Iherusalem adorare consueverant'.

[22] AA xii.10, p. 838.

[23] AA xii.33, p. 880: 'pro nomine Iesu'.

older, more traditional sense. In these instances, therefore, 'traveller' will not suffice as a translation of *peregrini*. Whether the members of the crusade army were also referred to as *peregrini* must now also be assessed. In doing this, it must be acknowledged that this 'army' had an unusual demographic. While many medieval fighting forces contained large numbers of non-combatants, the figures of the unarmed in the First Crusade were extremely high, indeed remarkably so.[24] Should the term *peregrini* be applied only to those not taking part in the battles, it would be clear that, while contemporary commentators used the term *peregrini* to denote traditional unarmed pilgrims, they did not accept this new armed expedition as a *peregrinatio*. If it applied equally to warriors and camp followers, however, it will be shown that armed persons were not disqualified from being *peregrini*.

In some cases, it is clear that the term *peregrini* was applied specifically to unarmed persons. In 1098 the Byzantine emperor, Alexios I Komnenos, campaigned in Asia Minor with an army consisting of some Latins who had followed the crusade, some of his own men and some non-combatants. When he heard that the crusade army had been besieged within Antioch by the forces of Kerbogha, atabeg of Mosul, he retreated again. The *Gesta Francorum* reported that this retreat was so hasty that many pilgrims (*peregrini*) who were unable to keep pace with the army (*militia*) died on the journey to Constantinople.[25] It is likely that this use of *peregrini* refers to unarmed crusaders or camp followers. Albert of Aachen also used the term to denote non-combatants in his description of how Godfrey of Bouillon saved a *peregrinus* from a bear attack. This *peregrinus*, who was described as 'helpless' (*inops*), was collecting firewood and both the description of him as vulnerable and the menial task which he was undertaking suggest that he was unarmed.[26] Elsewhere, Albert described the massacre of 'poor and ill *peregrini*' by the Seljuk sultan Kilij Arslan while they bathed in hot springs near Philomelion. These *peregrini* were also likely to have been unarmed.[27]

For the most part, however, the word *peregrini* was used as a collective term for the entire crusade army, similar to the use of *Franci* or *Christiani*. As the crusade leaders passed through Constantinople on their way to the east in 1097, Alexios Komnenos attempted to get them to swear oaths of loyalty to him and to undertake to return all lands conquered by them which had previously belonged to the Byzantine Empire. According to a number of reports, the emperor in turn swore to aid the crusade logistically and militarily. In the account of Robert the Monk, the emperor swore not to harm the *peregrini Sancti Sepulchri*, clearly

---

[24] J. France, *Victory in the East: A Military History of the First Crusade* (Cambridge, 1994), pp. 125–7. The high proportion of non-combatants is another reason to suppose that the expedition held distinct echoes of a pilgrimage.

[25] *GF*, pp. 55, 81: 'Voluissent noluissent nostri reversi sunt retrorsum, dolentes amarissime usque ad mortem; fueruntque mortui multi ex peregrinis languentes nec valentes fortiter militiam sequi; remanebantque morientes in via.'

[26] AA iii.4, p. 142.

[27] AA iii.54, p. 224; v.11, p. 352.

denoting the whole crusade.[28] Albert of Aachen used the term *peregrini* as a synonym for *Christiani* and *fideles* for the entire crusade host during the sieges of Jerusalem and Antioch.[29] During the siege of Antioch, the *Gesta Francorum* reported that Turks in the service of Kerbogha of Mosul confiscated the weapons of some *Franci*, who were described as *pauperes peregrini*, yet their bearing of arms clearly indicated that they were active members of the army.[30]

As well as being used to denote obviously active members of the crusade army, the term *peregrini* was often paired with military terms to describe a person or persons. Albert of Aachen described a group of crusaders in the following of Peter the Hermit, who were besieged in a castle by the Turks, as *peregrini milites* or 'pilgrim-knights'.[31] During a skirmish between a group of crusaders and some of Kerbogha's army outside Antioch, a particular crusader was described as a 'knight' (*miles*), a 'pilgrim' (*peregrinus*) and a 'pilgrim-knight' (*miles peregrinus*).[32] When Bohemond of Taranto left his troops to confer with the emperor at Constantinople in April 1097, the anonymous author of the *Gesta Francorum* related how Tancred was left at the head of the 'knighthood of Christ' (*militia Christi*), who were then immediately referred to as *peregrini*.[33]

It is not the case, therefore, that only traditional pilgrims and unarmed crusaders were labelled *peregrini* by the commentators; active fighting members of the army were too and the term was often interchanged or coupled with military terminology. This does not prove that the term held connotations of pilgrimage, however, or that the crusaders were considered to have the status of pilgrims. In fact, such indiscriminate use of the term might even support a generic definition of 'traveller', rather than the more specific 'pilgrim'. Where it becomes clear that the term *peregrini* still held the meaning of 'pilgrims' while being applied to those who were armed is in the instances where characteristic features of pilgrimage were applied to crusaders. If the crusaders performed acts and rituals traditionally associated with pilgrimage, were credited with the status of pilgrims, and were accorded the rewards associated with pilgrimage, all while being termed *peregrini*, then it is clear that the expedition was considered to be a pilgrimage from the outset.

After the costly siege of Ma'arrat al-Nu'mān in November–December 1098, Raymond of St Gilles, whose insistence on maintaining the siege had cost him much support in the army, continued his march to Jerusalem barefoot. For Baldric of Bourgueil these bare feet were a sign of Raymond's status as a *peregrinus*: 'He (Raymond) left Ma'arrat on the Ides of January, in bare feet,

---

[28]   RM ii.19, p. 749: 'Ego Alexius imperator juro Hugoni Magno et Godefrido duci, ceterisque qui hic astant Francorum principibus, quod nunquam in vita mea injuriabor ullum peregrinum Sancti Sepulcri, aut permittam injuriari.'

[29]   See e.g. AA iv.23, p. 284; iv.30, p. 292; iv.31, p. 294; iv.32, p. 296; iv.35, p. 300; iv.40, p. 312; v.4, p. 342; v.23, p. 366; v.25, p. 368; v.43, p. 398; vi.8, p. 414; vi.12, p. 418; vi.18, p. 426; vi.42, p. 458.

[30]   GF, p. 51.

[31]   AA i.22, p. 44.

[32]   AA iv.42, p. 314.

[33]   GF, p. 11: 'Tancredus remansit caput militiae Christi, vidensque peregrinos cibos emere, ait intra se quod exiret extra viam, et hunc populum conduceret ubi feliciter viveret.'

and he voluntarily joined with the other *peregrini homines*; by taking this sign, the count exhibited the humility of *peregrinatio*.[34] Orderic Vitalis asserted that Robert, duke of Normandy, went on crusade as penance for his sins, sins which he felt were so great that they were reflected in the disorder inherent in the duchy of Normandy: and he journeyed *[pergere]* to Jerusalem, taking up the cross in order that God may be satisfied for his sins'.[35]

On two occasions Guibert of Nogent discussed the benefits of the crusade for the souls of those who took part, provided that they did so following confession and with sincere penance: 'We consider how much those who devoutly undertook the *peregrinatio*, after confession and sincere repentance, profited'.[36] Following an anecdote in which a crusader who initially submitted to the devil and his temptations then resisted them by confessing his sins, Guibert commented that if the *peregrinatio* could benefit such a sinner, then the rewards meted out to the pure at heart must have been immense: 'By this example we can understand how valuable the *peregrinatio* must have been for the pure in heart, since it offered so much defence and support for the impure'.[37] The crusade, like a pilgrimage, benefited those who had cleansed themselves through confession and penitence before departing, more than those who had not. Similarly it was necessary for those on the crusade to continue to behave according to Christian morals. This point was expressed by Fulcher of Chartres. In a well-known passage, he marvelled at the vast number of different nationalities represented on the expedition. Indeed, he noted, language was often a barrier to communication. This did not hinder the crusade, however, as they were all of one mind and one goal and the behaviour of the crusaders towards each other was fitting to the holy purpose of those who travelled as *peregrini*: 'For instance, if anyone should have lost any of his things, for many days it was kept carefully by he who had found it until the sought-after loser was found and the found item was returned to him, for this befitted those who righteously *peregrinantur*'.[38]

Orderic Vitalis reported that Urban II had excused the crusaders from the obligation to fast or otherwise mortify the flesh because of the physical harm inherent in the journey, which would count as penance in the same measure. This implies that, as pilgrims, the crusaders would be expected to expose themselves to bodily rigours on their journey, but that the traditional means of fasting and mortification would be replaced by the danger and exertion of the journey.[39] As the Norman followers of Bohemond moved through Byzantine territory, they were attacked by the imperial army. Following the defeat of the emperor's men by the crusaders, their leaders were brought before Bohemond, who asked them why they attacked Christians who bore them and their emperor no ill will. In his

---

[34] BB iv.1, p. 89.

[35] OV, v, 26.

[36] GN vii.29, p. 323: 'quantum pure peccata confessis et sincere penitentibus profuerit istius peregrinationis devota susceptio'.

[37] GN vii.30, p. 327: 'Ecce pia ista peregrinatio pensemus quantum valuerit puris, quae tantum attulerit tutelae ac securitatis impuris.'

[38] FC i.13, p. 203.

[39] OV, v, 18.

angry remonstrations with the emperor's men, Orderic reported Bohemond as saying, 'We have foresaken our riches and voluntarily set out on *peregrinatio*.'[40] In the same way as they abandoned physical comforts, so the crusaders also gave up many of their possessions before setting out.

Raymond of Aguilers mingled his uses of *peregrini* with other phrases reminiscent of pilgrimage. For example, when the crusaders were at Tripoli, a visionary called Peter Desiderius was commanded in a vision to go to the church of St Leontius and to take the relics of four saints there. When he and others arrived at the church, according to Raymond, they prayed to God to commend the relics to the crusaders so that the saints to whom they belonged would not despise the 'fellowship of *peregrini* and exiles of God' (*peregrinorum et exulum pro Deo ... consorcium*), but rather be bound to them and bind them to God.[41] The invocation of the notion of exile alongside the mention of *peregrini* demonstrates a clear understanding of pilgrimage as a self-imposed exile, in line with a long tradition in western European thought. Elsewhere, Raymond commented that the defeat of the Muslim leader Kerbogha outside Antioch occurred on the vigil of SS Peter and Paul, which, he stated, was fitting as it was through the intercession of these Apostles that Jesus had granted victory to the *peregrina ecclesia Francorum*.[42] This appears to be an allusion to the Augustinian idea of *ecclesia peregrinans* applied to the crusade.[43] Although not elaborated on elsewhere in the *Historia*, Raymond's use of *exules Dei* and *peregrina ecclesia* seems to demonstrate a conception of the crusade as righteous exile for Christ. After describing the capture of Jerusalem in July 1099, Raymond described his pleasure at seeing the *peregrini ante sepulcrum Domini*.[44] Again the sense of traditional pilgrimage was associated with the worship at the Holy Sepulchre, which would have been the climax of a pilgrimage to Jerusalem. When the anonymous author of the *Gesta Francorum* reported the worship at the Holy Sepulchre by *nostri*, he described it thus: 'and they rendered to him [God] the principal duty'.[45]

Robert the Monk likewise discussed the features of the *peregrinatio* in such terms so as to demonstrate that a pilgrimage was being referred to specifically, rather than a simple journey or expedition. In his discussion of the preparations for the crusade, he noted that laymen were to undertake the journey only with the permission of their priest.[46] In the description of how Bohemond of Taranto came to know about the crusade, both Robert and Guibert embellished the narrative found in their source, the *Gesta Francorum*, to label the

---

[40] OV, v, 22.
[41] RA, p. 132: 'Obtulimus candelas et vota Deo et sanctis eiusdem ecclesie, ut Deus omnipotens qui eos sanctificaverat nobis eos consortes et coadiutores donaret. Et illi sancti peregrinorum et exulum pro Deo non spernerent consorcium, sed magis ex caritate nobis coniungerentur, et nos Deo coniungerent.'
[42] RA, p. 83.
[43] Augustine, *De Civitate Dei*, x.17, ed. B. Dombart and A. Kalb, 1 vol. in 2 (Corpus Christianorum, Series Latina, 47–8; Turnhout, 1955), p. 291.
[44] RA, p. 151.
[45] GF, p. 92: 'et reddiderent ei capitale debitum'.
[46] RM i.2, p. 729: 'Quippe nec laicis expedit peregrinari, nisi cum sui benedictione sacerdotis.'

expedition a *peregrinatio*. Robert reported that the Norman prince asked of the messengers who brought word of the crusade what sign or badge of *peregrinatio* the participants wore: 'Asking what sign [*signum*] of pilgrimage they wore, he was told that they bore the Holy Cross either on their forehead or their right shoulders.'[47] When the crusaders arrived at Rome on their journey through Europe to the Byzantine Empire, Robert described how they visited many of the city's holy sites – sites which would have been on the itinerary of pilgrims: 'They remained there several days and visited the holy sites on the usual route of the *peregrini*.'[48] As the crusade army left Constantinople and journeyed to Nicaea, the roads became too narrow for the army to pass. Godfrey of Bouillon caused men to journey ahead and widen the road with picks and axes. According to Robert, the men then marked the route with crosses, which was a fitting signal for such an endeavour: 'they erected wooden crosses on the bends as a symbol so that everyone would know that this was a road of *peregrinatio*.'[49]

A number of authors recognized that the crusade was an atypical form of *peregrinatio*, particularly due to the arms carried by the crusaders. This discomfort with the term is the most compelling evidence that the term *peregrini* was clearly understood by contemporaries as pilgrimage. When describing Bohemond's questioning of the crusade upon first hearing of it, Guibert reported that the Norman asked 'if they were carrying arms or packs, and what sign of this new *peregrinatio* they were wearing, and finally, what war cries they carried into battle.'[50] Here Guibert reflects unease among some that this new type of pilgrimage needed some clarification such as whether the participants would be armed or not. The apparent dichotomy between unarmed pilgrims and armed crusaders was acknowledged by a number of authors. Before the crusade was even considered, Guibert related that Godfrey of Bouillon had often contemplated a journey to Jerusalem and spoke of it to his mother. He did not want to go 'simply', however, as other pilgrims did, but rather at the head of an army: 'For he said that he wanted to go to Jerusalem, not simply [*simpliciter*] as the others, but forcefully, with a large army if he could raise one.'[51] Describing the journey of the crusaders through the Byzantine Empire, Robert the Monk commented that the crusaders bought their supplies, like unarmed pilgrims, despite their weapons: 'Yet despite being protected by all those weapons and armour, they still bought their provisions like unarmed *peregrini*.'[52]

---

[47] RM ii.3, p. 741.

[48] RM ii.3, p. 740: 'Ibi aliquot diebus commorantes, loca sancta peregrina consuetudine perambulaverunt.'

[49] RM iii.1, p. 755: 'posueruntque cruces ligneas per reflexus viarum, in testimonium, ut cunctis notum fieret quod via illa erat peregrinantium.'

[50] GN iii.1, p. 136: 'At ille interrogat an arma deferant, utrum peras, an aliqua hujus novae peregrinationis insignia praeferant, quae ad ultimum in bellis signa conclament.'

[51] GN ii.12, p. 129: 'Dicebat namque se desiderare proficisci Iherosolimam, et hoc non simpliciter ut alii, sed cum violentia exercitus, si sibi copia suppeteret, magni.'

[52] RM ii.3, p. 741: 'Et quum sic telis et armis accingantur, tamen, ut inermes peregrini, necessaria sibi mercantur.'

The status of armed crusaders as pilgrims drew comment from a number of authors. While the army of the southern Italian Normans travelled through Byzantine territories, the *Gesta Francorum* reported that the local population feared that they would attack them, not recognizing that they were *peregrini*: 'not supposing us to be *peregrini*, but those wishing to plunder their lands and kill them'.[53] Guibert of Nogent said of the same incident that the Byzantines mistook the crusaders for 'warriors' rather than *peregrini*.[54] In his description of the incident noted above in which Byzantine troops attacked and were defeated by the followers of Bohemond, Robert the Monk reported that the envoys declared that their emperor refused to believe that the crusaders were on a pilgrimage.[55] Nor, according to Robert, was Alexios alone in doubting that the crusaders were *peregrini*. During the siege of Antioch, the crusaders received an embassy from the Fatimids of Egypt attempting to negotiate with them. These envoys allegedly demanded to know why the crusaders were carrying arms, since this was forbidden to *peregrini*: 'They are amazed that you should seek the Sepulchre of your Lord as armed men, exterminating their people from their long-held lands, indeed butchering them at the point of a sword, something which is wicked for *peregrini*.'[56] This discomfort with the term *peregrini* to denote the crusaders among some authors is very revealing. It suggests that the term was not appropriated by the authors of their own volition, but rather that it was in general use and that they had to grapple with it, albeit perhaps unwillingly at first.

For the majority of the authors of Latin narratives of the First Crusade, the crusaders were *peregrini* and the crusade a *peregrinatio*. This applied to the armed as well as the unarmed. That the terms were not used generically as meaning 'travellers' or 'journey' is clear from the context of their use. Traditional pilgrims were *peregrini*; the crusaders were termed *peregrini* while performing rituals long associated with pilgrimage. The rewards historically associated with pilgrimage were also received by these crusader-pilgrims. Most strikingly, the inherent conflict between the status of a *peregrinus* and the armed crusaders was highlighted. This tension would not have been felt if the term *peregrini* held the innocuous meaning of 'traveller'.

It is true that corroboration between a number of sources is not a guarantee of fact. Nevertheless it is must be acknowledged that a large number of the narrative histories of the First Crusade use the term *peregrini* for the crusaders. While the Latin historical narratives of the First Crusade bear much of the responsibility for the genesis of the idea that the crusades were armed pilgrimages, they have

---

[53] *GF*, p. 8: 'non putantes nos esse peregrinos, sed velle populari terram et occidere illos'.

[54] GN iii.2, p. 139: 'sed ipsi noluerunt eis praebere consensum eo scilicet quod vererentur eos, militares illos aestimantes, non peregrinos, et quia vellent exterminio terram tradere ac perimere illos'.

[55] RM ii.14, p. 746: 'Imperator noster magis perhorescit agmina vestra quam coeli fulmina, quia plus intelligit vos velle eum regno suo privare quam velle peregrinari; et ideo non cessat malum erga vos machinari. Sed pro Deo, cujus peregrini et milites estis, dignemini nostri miserere'.

[56] RM v.1, p. 791: 'Mirantur enim ut quid sic armati quaeritis Domini vestri Sepulcrum, gentem suam a finibus diu possessis exterminantes, immo, quod nefarium est peregrinis, in ore gladii trucidantes'.

latterly been neglected by both sides of the argument for and against the presence of a pilgrimage dimension within crusading. This is partly because they seem remote from the experience of the crusade and 'tainted' by the results of the expedition. In a recent article, Jensen has argued that the terms *peregrini* and *peregrinatio* could not be used to demonstrate that the crusade was considered a pilgrimage as the terms could relate to any journey or expedition. It is clear, however, that the terms *peregrini* and *peregrinatio* were not used casually as bywords for travellers but with full cognisance of the implications of pilgrimage. The authors of these narratives understood the crusade to be a new kind of pilgrimage and, despite their arms, the crusaders were a new kind of pilgrim. The geographical diversity of the authors and their multiple levels of experience of the crusade – some were participants, some wrote apparently from gathered eyewitness testimony, others embellished pre-existing narratives, while most employed permutations of these types of evidence-gathering – suggest that their ideas of the nature of the crusade were not principally influenced by each other. For many of them, the discussion of the crusaders as *peregrini* was based on events on the journey, such as Raymond of St Gilles travelling barefoot. This suggests that the authors are not independently refining the events to place them in their own understanding of the world, an understanding which they all coincidentally share. Instead, it is likely that they are reflecting a widely held view that the expedition launched by Urban II in November 1095 was a new kind of pilgrimage, in which arms could be employed to regain the Holy Places for Christianity. Although we are still not directly informed of Urban's own theory of crusade, nor are we likely to be without further evidence coming to light, we are considerably closer to the first crusaders' understanding of their actions than if we were to focus only on the canon law of the late twelfth century. We are also, perhaps, closer to understanding how so many people joined such a supposedly new and unknown enterprise. If the crusade was in fact a 'new pilgrimage', then its appeal, particularly to the poor, is not so mysterious.

WHAT REALLY HAPPENED TO EURVIN DE CRÉEL'S DONKEY? ANECDOTES IN SOURCES FOR THE FIRST CRUSADE[1]

Carol Sweetenham

Just before the climactic battle in the *Chanson d'Antioche*, the author breaks off into a hundred-line account about a donkey.[2] The animal belongs to Eurvin de Créel. One morning Eurvin goes off to Mass. His best friend Pierre Postel is watching narrowly. He has several squires to feed and nothing to give them. End of the road for the donkey, which is turned into kebabs. Eurvin returns to find no donkey and a smell of roasting meat. There is a quarrel with Pierre followed by a tearful reconciliation. The two go into the battle as best friends and we hear nothing more of them.

This is a particularly striking example of the anecdotes contained in crusade sources, where a particular episode and/or character stands out for a moment against the collectivized heroism of the crusade.[3] Anecdotes are found from the earliest sources for the crusade through to its depiction in the Old French Crusade Cycle in the early years of the thirteenth century. It is hard to tie these anecdotes down to any one source, and it is tempting to assign them to a loosely defined category known as 'personal anecdote and tradition'.[4] This paper offers

---

[1]   I am most grateful to Simon John of Swansea University for his helpful suggestions on an earlier draft of this paper and for a number of references. Susan Edgington was also kind enough to read a draft. My thanks go to both.

[2]   *La Chanson d'Antioche*, ed. S. Duparc-Quioc, 2 vols (Documents relatifs à l'histoire des croisades, 11; Paris, 1976–8) [hereafter *Antioche*]; trans. S. B. Edgington and C. E. Sweetenham, *The Chanson d'Antioche: An Old French Account of the First Crusade* (Crusade Texts in Translation, 22; Farnham, 2011); see also *La Chanson d'Antioche: chanson de geste du dernier quart du XIIe siècle*, ed. and trans. B. Guidot (Classiques du moyen âge, 33; Paris, 2011). The anecdote about Eurvin's donkey is at ll. 7576–642.

[3]   Cf. F. Suard, 'Héros et action épiques dans la *Chanson d'Antioche*', in *Filologia romanza e cultura medievale: Studie in onore di Elio Melli*, ed. A. Fasso, L. Formisano and M. Mancini, 2 vols (Alessandria, 1998), ii, 763.

[4]   A description which goes back at least to Heinrich von Sybel: 'one great tradition, current throughout the whole of the West': H. von Sybel, *The History and Literature of the Crusades*, trans. L. Duff Gordon (London 1861), p. 237.

some thoughts on what anecdotes are and how valuable or otherwise they are to our understanding of the events and perceptions of the First Crusade. There are three parts. The first offers a definition of anecdotes and sets out a typology of their use in First Crusade sources. The second offers some observations on their role in the sources. The third explores briefly how such anecdotes might have originated and developed over time. The conclusion considers how far we can believe them and what they tell us about the reality and perceived reality of the crusade.

In narrative theory an anecdote can be defined as 'the literary form that uniquely lets history happen by virtue of the way it introduces an opening into the teleological, and therefore timeless, narration of beginning, middle and end... it produces the effect of the real, the occurrence of contingency, by establishing an event as an event within and yet without the framing context of historical successivity, i.e. it does so only in so far as its narrative both comprises and refracts the narrative it reports.'[5] This definition suggests four key features:

- differentiation: the story is clearly marked out from the surrounding text; it focuses on a figure or an event which is out of the ordinary in some way, for example grotesque, comic, heroic.
- narrative self-containment: the anecdote is a self-contained story with a clear beginning, middle and end, which sits within the surrounding narrative.
- authenticity: the story aims to give the effect of the real. It may be asserted to be true, its source may be specified and it may be given realism by precise detail.
- purpose: the anecdote is linked to and given validity by the surrounding narrative, existing to illuminate a particular aspect. It is told for a purpose, whether amusement, edification, illustration or other.

The anecdote about Eurvin's donkey demonstrates these features. It is differentiated from the rest of the text by its *fabliau*-like tone and the status of the main characters, *vavasors* rather than knights.[6] It has a clear narrative parabola: starvation leads to theft, a quarrel and ultimate reconciliation. Authenticity is implied by vivid detail about the starving squires, the cooking of the donkey and the subsequent confession of Pierre. And it has a clear purpose in the text. Placed as it is just before the battle of Antioch, it crystallizes two key themes. Firstly, hunger: after a siege of three weeks the crusaders were literally starving, to a point where the only option was to steal and eat a friend's donkey. And this in turn mattered because it underlined the miraculous nature of the victory at Antioch: the crusaders won despite being famished with hunger, demonstrating

---

5 J. Fineman, 'The History of the Anecdote: Fiction and Fiction', in *The New Historicism*, ed. H. A. Veeser (New York, 1989), p. 61.
6 See *Fabliaux du Moyen Age*, ed. and trans. J. Dufournet (Paris, 1998). *Fabliaux* are short stories written in octosyllabics 'qui relatent, sur un ton trivial, une aventure digne d'être racontée parce que plaisante ou (et) exemplaire' (Dufournet, Introduction, p. 9); they are realistic and often humorous.

the divine rightness of their cause.[7] Secondly, the tearful reconciliation demonstrates the spirit of Christian unity with which the crusaders marched into battle, commented on elsewhere in the text:[8] Eurvin forgives Pierre the theft of the only valuable – or edible – thing he still possessed.

We find similar features to a greater or lesser degree in anecdotes in the Latin chronicles about the crusades. They stand out from the surrounding text, and authors often, though not always, mark their start and finish. They tell a story whether in a few words or in more elaborate detail, often evoked vividly. And they illuminate themes in the surrounding text. An example is the account in the *Gesta Francorum* of the attempted flight and recapture of William the Carpenter.[9] The basic narrative describes how William and Peter the Hermit flee the siege of Antioch. Tancred pursues them and brings them back ignominiously. William spends the night on the floor in Bohemond's tent 'uti mala res'. The following morning he receives an excoriating scolding from Bohemond: 'O infelix et infamia totius Franciae, dedecus et scelus Gallorum'. He is forced to take an oath not to flee, although subsequently he does. The author is at pains to point out that he had done so earlier in Spain. There is a clear narrative structure and use of direct speech which both give clarity for an audience. The anecdote is at the centre of Book VI, which has a classic ring structure. The Christians flee a Turkish attack and have to be rallied by Bohemond. Food prices soar as the Armenians and Syrians profiteer. William flees on account of hunger and is retrieved. Food shortage remains as Tatikios fails to return with provisions. The Turks attack again and this time Bohemond is victorious. William's flight from hunger thus becomes emblematic of the whole: many might have fled like William, and like him they would not have succeeded. And his flight becomes a symbol of the wider trials faced by the crusaders: 'hanc paupertatem et miseriam pro nostris delictis concessit nos habere Deus.' We do not know whether these incidents actually happened. In a way that does not matter: like the anecdotal tale of Peter Mandelson and the mushy peas he allegedly took for guacamole, an anecdote is a story which is too good not to have happened.[10] What may or may not have been a true event is reimagined in a way which dramatizes and heightens the events of the crusade and which may over time take on a greater degree of fantasy.

For these purposes therefore my definition of an anecdote is an episode about an individual or individuals which is distinct from the surrounding text,

---

[7] See for example RM vii.18, pp. 835–6: the Saracens remaining in Antioch are convinced to be baptized by seeing the celestial forces fighting at Antioch and realizing that God is on the side of the Christians; RM vi.14, pp. 814–15 for hunger in Antioch.

[8] See *Antioche*, ll. 7236–8, 7527–48.

[9] *GF*, pp. 33–4.

[10] 'My rivals for the nomination were understandably keen to paint me as an outsider, out of touch both politically and socially with the working-class constituency I wanted to represent. They especially delighted in dragging up, and embellishing, a media myth about me from a by-election campaign a few years earlier. In its final form it had me strutting into a Hartlepool fish and chip shop and mistaking mushy peas for guacamole. For the record, I have never mixed up the two. And I quite like mushy peas. In fact it was an American intern working for Jack Straw who had made the error': P. Mandelson, *The Third Man* (London, 2010), p. 122.

constituting a story in its own right. It gives the appearance of authenticity. And it illuminates and is linked to the surrounding narrative. In practice the lines between anecdote and narrative can be blurred. Some anecdotes are so fleeting as to be hardly distinguishable from the surrounding text, with a character or action coming into focus for a brief moment: for example in the *Gesta Francorum* we get a vivid glimpse of Everard the Hunter blowing a trumpet atop a siege tower at Ma'arrat al-Nu'mān but no details as to his actions.[11] In others actions are recounted in terms of conventional heroism, making it hard to know what might or might not have happened, for example in descriptions of single combat.[12] Some anecdotes provide a moment of pause and illumination in the text: others are integral to the narrative. All however share a key feature: they focus on an individual or individuals as a way of carrying the story forward.

Anecdotes in First Crusade sources fall into four basic types: heroism and exemplary behaviour; criticism; apparently realistic episodes; and tall stories. They tend, predictably, to be about the leaders and major figures of the crusade. However, we also find anecdotes about less well known minor figures who come into sharp focus for a moment and disappear again, apart from perhaps a fleeting mention, as is the case with Raimbold Croton or Gontier of Aire.[13] There are also some anecdotes about anonymous figures: for example Guibert describes the punishment inflicted on a monk found committing lecherous acts.[14]

The first category is heroism and exemplary behaviour. Ralph of Caen, for example, describes how Tancred skewered three Turks in single combat, modestly swearing his arms-bearer to silence.[15] The anecdote is full of classical comparisons which point up Tancred's heroism. Raymond of Aguilers describes how Godfrey fights off 150 Turks with only twelve knights, killing thirty, capturing a further thirty and coming back with a crop of severed heads.[16] It immediately precedes the debate over who should have Antioch and who should lead the army to Jerusalem: the implications of focusing on Godfrey's heroism at this precise point are clear.

The second category is critical anecdotes. There are relatively few of these compared to heroism, and criticism is not always direct. Some is: for example Orderic Vitalis criticizes Godfrey directly for refusing to co-operate with Raymond of St Gilles in taking Ascalon after the battle.[17] Other criticism is more nuanced: Albert of Aachen, for example, is ambivalent about Godfrey's actions over a gift from a local ruler stolen and given to Bohemond.[18] The *Gesta*

[11] *GF*, p. 78.
[12] See for example RM vii.11, pp. 830–1, where Hugh of Vermandois is first into battle at Antioch in classic *chanson de geste* style. We cannot say whether Hugh did or did not do this. But it provides a symbolic start to the battle, and bolsters Hugh's heroic credentials.
[13] Respectively *Antioche*, ll. 3815–93; *Antioche*, ll. 3058–115; and PT, pp. 79–80.
[14] GN iv.15, p. 196.
[15] RC, c. 52, p. 645.
[16] RA, pp. 92–3.
[17] OV, v, 184–6.
[18] AA v.14, pp. 354–6.

Francorum questions the leaders' judgement over the oath to Alexios whilst suggesting they had no other option.[19]

The third are apparently realistic and often vivid episodes. Raymond of Aguilers describes how Count Raymond captures and mutilates six captives to frighten others during the passage across Sclavonia: the anecdote illustrates how Raymond carried out God's will as shown by the safe passage.[20] A particularly striking example is found in Ralph of Caen, who describes how Tancred was overcome by dysentery during the siege of Jerusalem, when the crusaders were desperate for wood to build siege engines. Whilst looking for a quiet corner Tancred finds a store of wood.[21] There is a clear narrative line: Tancred makes four attempts to find somewhere suitable, and there is a contrast between his search for privacy and the public rejoicing when the wood is found. The wider symbolism and importance of the episode are suggested by the comment that the wood had been used by the Fatimids when they took Jerusalem in 1098. The following chapter starts with Robert of Flanders gathering wood, creating a link back into the text.

The fourth category might be called tall stories: they recount episodes with exaggerated heroism, exoticism and the miraculous. Godfrey, famously, cuts a Turk in half, a feat referred to in a number of sources and rather vividly described in Orderic Vitalis as 'quasi tenerum porrum'.[22] Guibert of Nogent's treatment of this anecdote is interesting. He introduces it with the words 'ut testimonio veraci probabile id de ipso preclari facinoris cantitetur'. One heroic deed makes Guibert think of another, and he tells the story of Godfrey fighting a bear. Bears start a further chain of association and Guibert tells a third story, this time about Baldwin suffering from a wound which is slow to heal and having a bear killed and autopsied rather than a Saracen.[23] These stories occur in the context of the taking of Jerusalem, and refer to the first two rulers. By the time we get to the *Antioche* a century later the anecdote has become a full schlock-fest with half the Turk left on the saddle and the terrified horse galloping round Antioch spraying blood everywhere.[24]

We find similar categories of anecdotes for other participants in the crusade. They are almost always knights, established or aspiring. There are few if any episodes of mundane realism, by definition: an anecdote has to be worth telling, and these figures survive in the narratives only because they did something out of the ordinary, whether heroic, anti-heroic or exceptional. And, whilst the anecdote may be found in several sources, it is rare for a character to appear more than once: their sole claim to fame is in one episode. Gouffier of Lastours is an example of heroism. He is mentioned in several sources as being the first into

[19] *GF*, p. 12.
[20] RA, pp. 36–7.
[21] RC, c. 120, pp. 689–90.
[22] See e.g. PT, p. 75; RM iv.20, pp. 786–7; AA iii.65, p. 244; OV, v, 84.
[23] 'According to reliable accurate testimony, the following story is told about a remarkable deed he did': GN vii.11, pp. 284–5; trans. R. Levine, *The Deeds of God through the Franks* (Woodbridge, 1997), p. 133.
[24] *Antioche*, ll. 3681–719.

Ma'arrat al-Nu'mān. Robert the Monk elaborates on his feat by describing him as so weighed down by arrows that he can barely lift his shield. Nearly defeated, he finds a second wind and fights on successfully: the boundary between heroism and tall tale becomes blurred.[25] We find a similar blurring of boundaries in the stories about Raimbold Croton. In several sources he is mentioned as being first into Jerusalem; in Ralph of Caen he suffers terrible injuries to his hands and has to be rescued; and in the *Antioche* he becomes the hero of a different episode, swimming a river in full armour and killing hundreds of Saracens single-handedly as they attempt to cross the bridge outside Antioch.[26] The boundaries between categories can be blurred and different chroniclers report episodes in different ways. In the incident referred to above where Godfrey fights off 150 Turks, Raymond of Aguilers compares the twelve knights who help him to the twelve Apostles and Godfrey to God's vicar. The same anecdote in Albert of Aachen is far more matter of fact: Godfrey interrupts a picnic breakfast to counter a planned Turkish ambush.[27]

The use and elaboration of anecdotes vary across the sources. Fulcher of Chartres's account has very few. The *Gesta Francorum* has some: the sources based on it all add further anecdotes, with particular profusion in Guibert.[28] Ralph of Caen's and Raymond of Aguilers's anecdotes tend to be developed in more detail and carefully linked into the narrative with a quasi-exemplary function. Albert of Aachen has relatively few. Anecdotes are found in particular profusion and detail in the *Antioche*. Many concern Engelrand and Hugh of Saint-Pol, who were present on the crusade but here are the stars of the show, credited with some of the key achievements such as finding the ford over the Orontes and being given their own column at the battle of Antioch.[29] There are also extended anecdotes which are found nowhere else (although other sources contain references to Rainald and Raimbold): the death of Gosselin, the capture of the Saracen horse Faburs by Gontier of Aire, the martyrdom of Rainald Porchet and the heroism of Raimbold Croton on the bridge over the Orontes.[30] All are minor nobility (most are *ber* although it is explicitly stated that Gontier was still a squire). Their feats are on the fantastic end of reality: thus Raimbold swims the Orontes in full armour with lance and sword, climbs up a bridge and, clinging onto a platform with one hand, dispatches 200 Saracens single-handedly with the other. All are rewarded, whether through material recognition

---

[25] *GF*, p. 79; PT, p. 123; RA, pp. 97–8; OV, v, 138; in more detail in RM viii.6–7, pp. 847–8, and in *HVH* viii.188–211, pp. 208–10.

[26] RC, c. 119, pp. 688–9 for heroism at Jerusalem; *Antioche*, ll. 3815–93.

[27] RA, p. 93; AA v.27, pp. 370–2.

[28] Robert the Monk, for example, adds a long episode on the death of Walo the Constable (RM v.6–7, pp. 794–6) and the death of Gerard of Melun (RM vii.15, pp. 833–4); Peter Tudebode adds material on Rainald Porchet (PT, pp. 79–81); Guibert of Nogent adds numerous anecdotes, often of dubious relevance such as that involving the archbishop of Caesarea who cut a cross into his forehead (GN iv.17, pp. 197–8) and a knight who lost his brother and was tormented by a devil (GN vii.30, pp. 323–7).

[29] See introduction to *The Chanson d'Antioche*, trans. Edgington and Sweetenham, pp. 20–4.

[30] Gosselin ll. 2525–48; Gontier ll. 3058–15; Raimbold ll.3815–93; Rainald ll. 3766–79, 3902–4038, 4208–441; Eurvin and Peter ll. 7576–642.

(Raimbold, Gontier) or spiritual (Rainald, Gontier). Eurvin's donkey is unique in that it concerns relatively low-status participants (*vavasor*) and deals with mundanity rather than heroism.

Anecdotes supply few clues about textual relationships. They may be found in one or in several sources, and the details may be the same or different. Many of Ralph of Caen's anecdotes about Tancred or Raymond of Aguilers's anecdotes about Count Raymond are unique to those particular texts, hardly surprising in a text explicitly devoted to their deeds. Chroniclers might insert incidents known to them personally, such as Tudebode's reference to the death of his brother or Guibert of Nogent's to the martyrdom of his childhood friend Matthew.[31] Some anecdotes are found only in one group of texts: thus the death of Hugh the Berserker is found only in the *Gesta Francorum* and its derivatives.[32] Other anecdotes are found across a range of textual traditions with similar details: thus the death of Roger of Barneville in a Saracen ambush is found in Robert the Monk, and also in Gilo of Paris, Albert of Aachen and the second letter of Anselm of Ribemont to Manasses of Reims, although with varying levels of detail.[33] Others again are found across a range of sources but with different details such as the death of Anselm of Ribemont.[34]

Anecdotes evolve over time. Thus the death of Rainald Porchet is described in Peter Tudebode, who describes him being brought onto the battlements, refusing to apostasize, being decapitated and taken to heaven as a martyr. In the *Antioche* a century later his capture and torture are described; he warns the Christians not to exchange him for a Saracen prisoner. His refusal to apostasize remains; but we do not learn his ultimate fate. In the mid-thirteenth-century account given by Stephen of Bourbon as a sermon illustration, Rainald's severed head laughs when picked up by Adhemar.[35]

Anecdotes are thus found throughout the twelfth-century sources for the crusade. They play a role which reflects the basic function of the anecdote: to highlight an incident or character in a stylized way which presents reality from a particular angle to make a particular point. As such they have particular functions in the text. The first is the simplest: they make a good story. They

[31] PT, p. 97; GN iv.18, pp. 198–9.
[32] GF, p. 61; GN v.20, p. 223; PT, p. 102; BB iv.10, p. 68. RM vii.4, p. 824 has the same episode but does not give the name.
[33] RM vi.8, pp. 808–9; RA, p. 66; AA iv.27, pp. 286–8; Anselm of Ribemont to Archbishop Manasses of Reims, in *Epistulae et chartae ad historiam primi belli sacri spectantes: Die Kreuzzugsbriefe aus den Jahren 1088–1100*, ed. H. Hagenmeyer (Innsbruck, 1901), p. 159.
[34] RA, pp. 108–9, who describes in detail Anselm's vision of Enguerrand of Saint-Pol and his edifying end; GN vi.23, pp. 264–5, who is clear that Anselm died a martyr's death; RC, c. 106, pp. 680–1, who says he had a vision of saints in heaven and was advised by Arnulf to put his affairs in order; AA v.31, pp. 376–8; shorter references at GF, p. 85; RM viii.18, p. 857.
[35] PT, pp. 79–80; *Antioche*, ll. 3766–79, 3902–4038, 4208–441; Stephen of Bourbon, *Tractatus de diversis materiis praedicabilibus*, ed. J. Berlioz and J-L. Eichenlaub, 3 vols (Corpus Christianorum, Continuatio Mediaeualis, 124; Turnhout, 2002–6), iii, 228–9, 503–4 (vi.469–82). There may be a garbled echo in Arnold of Lübeck, 'Chronica Slavorum', *MGH SS* xxi, 123, where a crusader is brought onto the walls of Nicaea to appeal to the crusaders camped outside. A single combat reminiscent of a *chanson de geste* follows. I am grateful to Simon John for this reference.

humanize and break up the flow of the narrative: 'these events are real not because they occurred but because, first, they were remembered and, second, they are capable of finding a place in a chronologically ordered sequence'[36] None of the actions they describe is crucial to the narrative of the success of the crusade. But they emphasize and crystallize themes already present in the text: the combined cruelty and incompetence of the Saracens, the bravery of the Christians and the divine support for the crusade. Raimbold for example does not merely swim the river but does so in full armour with a lance and sword; he kills 200 Saracens single-handed; he is saved from drowning by St Michael and ninety-four lifeguards and nursed back to health by Godfrey's doctors. Gouffier at Maʿarrat al-Nuʿmān does not just fight single-handed: his shield is so full of arrows that he can barely lift it.[37] They thus depict a vivid episode which draws the listener imaginatively into the text and provides human interest and light relief. 'Medieval narrators provided the sorts of esthetic and affective experiences appropriate to their public … a public to whom they spoke and whom they wished to move and delight.'[38] Such use of anecdote and *exemplum* was a technique well known in sermons: Caesarius of Heisterbach describes how an audience snapped awake when promised a story about Arthur.[39]

Crusade sources are narratives which conform to narrative convention. So this too shapes the use of anecdote. The dominant vernacular influence is the *chanson de geste*. In the *Antioche* the crusaders are repeatedly portrayed as epic heroes. *Chanson de geste* convention demands, for example, that the first attack in a battle should be a distinguishing moment and that battle itself should consist of a series of single combats before disintegrating into a mêlée. The leaders of the crusade could hardly avoid being cast in this mould. So Hugh of Vermandois is duly given the honour of first slaughter, which is described in standard *chanson de geste* terms.[40] The story of Eurvin's donkey reflects a similar use of *fabliau* conventions.[41] Topoi from Latin literature are also used. Thus in Robert the Monk the death of Walo of Chaumont becomes the opportunity for an Ovidian lament from his wife.[42] Ralph of Caen compares Tancred and Bohemond to the stories of Herod, Sodom and Orpheus when they refuse to return to the Byzantine emperor.[43] These are more than simple literary parallels. They bring to the episode described a set of reminiscences beyond the here and now. And

---

[36] H. White, *The Content of the Form: Narrative Discourse and Historical Representation* (Baltimore, 1987), p. 20.

[37] *Antioche*, ll. 3815–93; RM viii.6–7, pp. 847–9.

[38] E. Birge Vitz, *Medieval Narrative and Modern Narratology: Subjects and Objects of Desire* (New York, 1989), p. 220.

[39] Caesarius of Heisterbach, *Dialogus Miraculorum: Dialog über die Wunder*, iv. 36, ed. H. Schneider and N. Nösges, 5 vols (Fontes Christiani, 86; Turnhout, 2009), ii, 760–2.

[40] *Antioche*, ll. 8637–46.

[41] The anecdote shares the *fabliaux*' emphasis on humour, apparent realism and formulaic characters: *Fabliaux*, ed. Dufournet, pp. 9–12.

[42] RM v.6–7, pp. 794–6; cf. Ovid's description of Niobe: *Metamorphoses*, vi.303–12, ed. D. E. Hill, 4 vols (Warminster, 1985–2000), ii, 50–1; and see C. W. Grocock, 'Ovid the Crusader', in *Ovid Renewed*, ed. C. Martindale (Cambridge, 1988), pp. 55–69 for reminiscences of the *Heroides*.

[43] RC, c. 19, p. 620.

the role of the anecdote becomes in turn to act as a vehicle for setting the crusade against a wider cultural landscape: 'one sometimes gets the impression that a medieval person ... could do nothing ... without rehearsing a whole series of exemplary stories.'[44]

It is a short step from this to seeing anecdotes as having an important exemplary function akin to their use in sermons. Sermons had a key function in dissemination of information; and *exempla* were essential to sermons if they were to be understood and acted on by lay people.[45] An *exemplum* might be defined as 'un récit bref donné comme véridique et destine à être inséré dans un discours ... pour convaincre un auditoire par une leçon salutaire.'[46] This could equally well apply to an anecdote. *Exempla* are linked into the main themes of the sermon: they are not ornaments. They may provide both good examples to emulate, and examples of behaviour not to follow. They provide a formalization against which conduct can be measured. All this applies equally to *exempla* in crusade sources. It is no coincidence that collections of sermon *exempla* such as that by Stephen of Bourbon include material in common with crusade sources.

By and large crusade source anecdotes have a straightforward function: they give examples of behaviour to be emulated or shunned. Many are secular, polarized around spectacular heroism or cowardice. There is a preponderance of good *exempla* to follow, such as Tancred helping an old woman cross a river or the heroism of Raymond Pilet and Raymond of Turenne at Tortosa.[47] But there are also examples of how not to behave, such as William the Carpenter's flight in the *Gesta Francorum*.[48] Some anecdotes take the focus on heroism a stage further, using it as the catalyst for spiritual *exempla*: heroism is shown as rewarded with martyrdom. The deaths of Rainald Porchet, Guibert's childhood friend Matthew and the prefect of Tiberias Gervais of Bazoches are all described in terms of martyrdom for refusal to apostasize, all three meeting a gruesome end befitting a martyr.[49] Anselm of Ribemont is not faced with that choice but is shown ascending into heaven as a reward for death on crusade.[50] These are clear examples of the spiritual reward promised on crusade. The *Antioche*, a century after the crusade, has a rather more materialistic variant of the exemplary theme. The text specifically exhorts its listeners to go on crusade

---

[44] M. J. Carruthers, *The Book of Memory: A Study of Memory in Medieval Culture* (Cambridge, 1990), p. 180: see also her discussion of Heloise casting her behaviour in terms of Cornelia's actions in Lucan's *Pharsalia*, pp. 179–82. For use of classical comparisons in William of Tyre, see P. W. Edbury and J. G. Rowe, *William of Tyre: Historian of the Latin East* (Cambridge, 1988) pp. 32–8.

[45] Carruthers, *Book of Memory*, p. 159; H. Pflaum, 'A Strange Crusaders' Song', *Speculum*, 10 (1935), 337–9 describing a poem setting out how not to be swept up by a crusade sermon. On *exempla* generally, see C. Brémond, J. Le Goff and J.-C. Schmidt, *L'exemplum* (Typologie des sources du moyen âge occidental, 40; Turnhout, 1982), esp. pp. 149–52 for the importance of *exempla* in communicating to a lay audience.

[46] Brémond *et al.*, *L'exemplum*, pp. 37–8.

[47] RC, c. 3, p. 607; *GF*, pp. 83–4.

[48] *GF*, pp. 33–4.

[49] PT, pp. 79–81; GN iv.18, pp. 198–9; vii.49, pp. 349–50.

[50] RC, c. 106, pp. 680–1.

(probably the Fourth Crusade or its aftermath),[51] and hence is particularly keen to insert anecdotes showing second-rank knights materially rewarded for heroism (Gontier, Raimbold Croton). The exemplary message acquires a human face and thereby a convincing reality: listeners could imagine that they too could be rewarded for heroic achievements.

In this context we might see Stephen of Blois as the *exemplum* to end them all. Most famously, hardly a source has a good word to say for the unfortunate Stephen.[52] Stephen's failure can be seen as a series of mirror images of crusaders who did reach Jerusalem. His failure as a leader contrasts with the heroism of the other leaders (Hugh of Vermandois's failure to reach Jerusalem being passed over with little comment), several sources observing that he was chosen as leader before Antioch.[53] He not only fails to fulfil his vow but convinces Alexios that there is no point coming to the crusaders' assistance, thus removing their last temporal hope. His discouragement of the emperor is contrasted in the *Gesta Francorum* and the *Antioche* with the honourable behaviour of Guy. Where other crusaders are brave and resilient, he is presented as a coward fit only for mockery, most strikingly in the *Antioche*. Orderic Vitalis presents him as a hen-pecked and uninspiring figure implicitly contrasted with William IX of Aquitaine: 200,000 soldiers follow the latter whilst Stephen struggles to attract followers. The actual fact that he died on the crusade of 1101–2 is elided into near-insignificance.[54] He thus becomes an anti-*exemplum*, providing both a contrast and an illustration of what not to do. And paradoxically he does have a crucial role. Without his intervention with Alexios, the Christians might have been in less desperate straits and less reliant on a miracle to win at Antioch. So like a traditional *exemplum* Stephen becomes the instrument of the divine will, although not in a way he would have relished. In terms of narrative balance he provides a contrast with the others who did fulfil their vows, and whose success is thrown into sharper relief by his failure.

Anecdotes by definition start life as oral accounts. The debate around what constitutes oral history and how it made its way into written history is fundamental in crusade historiography. I do not here attempt to summarize that debate or provide an in-depth analysis, but offer a few pointers for debate. Even if anecdotes were written down almost immediately, they all began as gossip: someone told somebody about something in some way which caught their imagination. People had to talk about something during those long evenings round the

---

[51]   See *The* Chanson d'Antioche, trans. Edgington and Sweetenham, pp. 21–4.

[52]   *GF*, p. 63 for criticism; RM vi.15, pp. 815–16 accepts the illness as genuine but depicts him as a coward; AA iv.13, pp. 266–8 mentions him in passing; RC, c. 53, p. 646 comments favourably on his prowess outside Antioch; OV, v, 324 depicts him as mercilessly hen-pecked by his wife Adela. The *Antioche* heaps him with ridicule, repeatedly portraying him as a coward (e.g. ll. 1527–39) and showing him finally leaving Antioch in a litter carried by some rank and file, waiting until he is out of sight of the army, then leaping out and running away, forcing his bearers to jog along with him (ll. 5600–44). See J. A. Brundage, 'An Errant Crusader: Stephen of Blois', *Traditio*, 16 (1960), 380–95.

[53]   e.g. *GF*, p. 63; RM vi.15, p. 815 comments on his status, 'qui inter alios principes videbatur magnus'; RA, p. 77: 'pro dictatore alii principes elegerant'.

[54]   OV, v, 346–50.

campfire outside the walls of Antioch, be it speculating about the doings of their leaders, sharing what had happened that day or reliving shared experiences. The events of the crusade were likely to be deeply seared into personal memory: and the forced communal living of three years on the march must over time have engendered a strong social memory.[55] Actual incidents would have grown and been transformed in the telling: 'to be remembered and transmitted at all, the facts must be transformed into images, arranged in stories'.[56] We cannot capture lost conversations of nearly one thousand years ago, but we can see their traces from early on. The question is how these stories moved from chatter to chapter.

Some traces of this campfire gossip can be discerned in the first-hand sources for the crusade. It is clear from the *Gesta Francorum*, for example, that the deeds of leaders were widely known and commented on: the text's comments on Bohemond's negotiations with Alexios suggest that there was a degree of knowledge in the ranks of key events and a great deal of speculation. Raymond of Aguilers gives a vivid flavour of how rumour spread – 'rumor etiam exercitum imperatoris venire nunciavit' – and of the debates in the host post-Antioch: 'cepit dicere quisque ad socium suum et ad vicinum deinde palam omnibus'. He describes how *vulgares cantus* did the rounds at Arnulf's appointment as patriarch.[57] Tales would change and improve in the telling: Godfrey's fight with a bear starts in Albert of Aachen with faintly comic overtones when Godfrey trips over his own sword and wounds his thigh; in Guibert of Nogent there is more emphasis on Godfrey's heroism in trying to save the bear's victim; and by the time we reach William of Tyre Godfrey's clumsiness has become heroism with the wound inflicted by the bear rather than his own sword.[58] The crusade created unimaginable hardships for its participants and put them into an unfamiliar world. The only way to deal with such experience was to cast it into a familiar frame of reference: 'images can be transmitted socially only if they are conventionalized and simplified.'[59] This might be supernatural, with, for example, victory against all the odds at Antioch ascribed to divine aid and defeat ascribed to fornication.[60] It might be reflected in retaining social norms familiar from previous existence such as national stereotyping.[61] It might also be reflected by adopting literary and cultural conventions, particularly about Saracens. Tudebode, for example, describes the Turks using Christians as target practice, selling and giving them away like animals and sending them to Khorosan, Antioch and Aleppo:[62] they may well have done these things but the description

---

[55] See C. Wickham, 'Gossip and Resistance among the Medieval Peasantry', *Past and Present*, 160 (1998), 3–23; *GF*, p. xvi.

[56] J. Fentress and C. Wickham, *Social Memory* (Oxford, 1992), p. 73.

[57] RA, pp. 55: 'an unconfirmed story spread that the army of the emperor was approaching'; 93–4: 'the people … began to suggest privately and later publicly'; 154.

[58] AA iii.4, pp. 142–4; GN vii.12, pp. 285–7; WT iii.18, pp. 219–20. See the forthcoming article by Natasha Hodgson on animal references in crusade sources.

[59] Fentress and Wickham, *Social Memory*, p. 47.

[60] T. Asbridge, *The First Crusade: A New History* (London, 2004), pp. 176-7.

[61] See, famously, RC, c. 61, p. 651 on national stereotypes.

[62] PT, p. 19.

is also consistent with stereotypes about Saracen cruelty and taking of Christian captives.[63] The salient point in all this is that from early on there is a blending of reality and myth, which is after all exactly what an anecdote is.

In the early years after the crusade anecdotes made their way back to Europe in a variety of ways. Letters were sent. At court and dynastic level a range of accounts was written. As might be expected many of these concern the leaders of the crusade. Some, notably Tancred, had accounts produced by their own chroniclers; Ralph of Caen comments how Tancred and Bohemond 'specialiter in me ... saepius visi sunt oculos retorquere, ac si innuerent: "Tibi loquimur, in te confidimus".[64] Reputation mattered in an age of limited literacy. We do not need to take at face value the often-quoted complaint by Lambert of Ardres that a jongleur had omitted to mention the great-grandfather of Lambert's patron because he refused him a pair of scarlet shoes.[65] What is striking is the subtext. Lambert, writing a century after the crusade on behalf of his patron, feels acutely the absence of any recognition of Arnold's role in the crusade. He therefore invents or retails an anecdote designed to explain the absence of anecdote.

Monasteries provided a fertile environment for the capture and retelling of anecdotes. Returning crusaders told stories of their own. According to Orderic Vitalis, for example, Ilger Bigod paid a visit to Arnold of Tilleul at Chartres to give him some hairs of the Virgin, and news of this event then made its way to Orderic.[66] Monasteries would preserve accounts of the bravery of their advocate: this is implied in Robert the Monk's reference to Anselm of Ribemont as a tireless defender of the monastery of Anchin.[67] Some of the accounts of pious deaths accompanied by the agonies of martyrdom suggest that a number of local *passio*-type stories may have existed: the *Passio Raginaldi* of c. 1200, which similarly places stress on the agonies undergone by Rainald of Châtillon may give some clue as to their existence and nature.[68]

Anecdotes might equally be preserved in a family and secular context. Alongside direct memories of parents and grandparents, families could preserve stories of ancestors stretching back over generations. Van Houts describes accounts of the Norman Conquest still current in the reign of Henry II and

[63] Cf. the lurid atrocities in Robert the Monk's account of Urban's speech at Clermont: RM i.1, pp. 727–8. The whole of the *Chanson des Chétifs* concerns Christians held captive by Saracens: *Les Chétifs*, ed. G. M. Myers (The Old French Crusade Cycle, 5; Tuscaloosa, 1980).

[64] RC, *praefatio*, p. 603: 'they often turned their eyes toward me ... as if to say "we are speaking to you, we trust you".

[65] Lambert of Ardres, *Chronique de Guines et d'Ardres*, ed. D.-C. Godefroy-Ménilglaise (Paris, 1855), pp. 311–13; trans. L. Shopkow, *The History of the Counts of Guines and Lords of Ardres* (Philadelphia, 2001), pp. 164–6.

[66] OV, v, 170.

[67] RM viii.18, p. 857: 'Aquicingensis coenobii indefesses adjutor'.

[68] Peter of Blois, *Tractatus duo: Passio Raginaldi principis Antiochie; Conquestio de dilatione vie Ierosolimitane*, ed. R. B. C. Huygens (Corpus Christianorum, Continuatio Mediaeualis, 94; Turnhout, 2002), pp. 63–4 gives an exaggerated description of his torture by the Saracens to make the point that he is a martyr.

suggests that such tales had an oral shelflife of about one hundred years.[69] Over time these memories were written down. An intriguing document survives about none other than Gouffier of Lastours in the form of points to be remembered as a sermon *exemplum* by the family priest, which talks in detail about Gouffier's role on the crusade and later legends.[70] We do not know what we do not know. Highly localized accounts could be produced which might survive in only a restricted area, and focus on the participation of a small group.[71] Ralph of Caen's account survives in only one manuscript. So the anecdotes which do survive are likely to be the remnants of a much richer tradition.

What is striking is how quickly these anecdotes start to develop into myth and legend, blurring the borders of reality with literary convention. Ralph of Caen has an intriguing description of Bohemond cutting a candle in half at supper while it was still burning, symbolizing the extinction of his line.[72] William of Malmesbury and Henry of Huntingdon preserve anecdotal material casting Robert of Normandy as a hero of the crusade and explaining his downfall at Tinchebrai as a punishment for him refusing to take the crown of Jerusalem.[73] The depiction of characters might be sharply at odds with the reality: Raimbold Croton is depicted as an unmitigated hero despite having fourteen years' penance imposed on him within a year or so of his return from crusade.[74] It is striking that these stories started to make their way into accounts within a few years of the event, in the lifetime of witnesses and in some cases whilst the actual participant was still alive. Arguably this indicates the amount of interest and weight attached to stories of the crusade. Whether or not they were realistic was of secondary importance.[75]

There were thus a number of ways in which such anecdotes might be preserved and make their way into sources. This did not mean that they were transmitted unchanged. Tales grew in the telling, as witness Godfrey's transformation into one of the Nine Worthies; the legendary and the realistic became hopelessly confused in the Second Crusade Cycle, with Corbaran's mother variously ending her days in a nunnery and marrying a Christian.[76] So the survival of an anecdote is no guarantee against later alteration. Indeed over time the distinction between truth and fiction blurred completely: Olivier de la Marche describes a

[69] E. van Houts, *Memory and Gender in Medieval Europe 900-1200* (Basingstoke, 1999), p. 6.

[70] A. Thomas, 'Le roman de Goufier de Las Tours', *Romania*, 34 (1905), 55–65.

[71] See N. Paul, 'Crusade, Memory and Regional Politics in Twelfth-Century Amboise', *Journal of Medieval History*, 31 (2005), 127–41.

[72] RC, c. 71, pp. 657–8.

[73] William of Malmesbury, *Gesta Regum Anglorum*, ed. and trans. R. A. B. Mynors, R. M. Thomas and M. Winterbottom, 2 vols (Oxford, 1998–9), iv.389, vol. i, 702; Henry of Huntingdon, *Historia Anglorum: The History of the English People*, ed. and trans. D. Greenway (Oxford, 1996), p. 442.

[74] For Raimbold's activities post-crusade see J. S. C. Riley-Smith, *The First Crusaders, 1095-1131* (Cambridge, 1997), pp. 155–6.

[75] On the differences between medieval and modern understandings of the boundaries between the real and the imaginary, see P. J. Geary, *Phantoms of Remembrance: Memory and Oblivion at the End of the First Millennium* (Princeton, 1994), pp. 158–76.

[76] See *The* Chanson d'Antioche, trans. Edgington and Sweetenham, pp. 42–3.

banquet held by Philippe le Bon in 1453 where the Chevalier au Cygne put in an appearance to encourage the participants to go on crusade.[77]

No matter how vivid some of the anecdotes seem and how vehement the claims of authenticity, the watchword is caution. We need to allow for the process of transformation and mythologization over the years: events were exaggerated, conflated with others and portrayed in line with contemporary preoccupations far removed from their origins. Sources chose to include the heroism of some and not others; a leader praised in one source would be criticized in another; the deeds of particular families would be emphasized. There is no such thing as neutral history. And crusade anecdotes were further shaped by the need to portray spiritual as well as political events. The constraints of literary composition and the simple need to please an audience also dictate the way in which anecdotes are told and the way they are used. Apparently vivid realism can be deceptive.[78]

All this means, unsurprisingly, that we should take these anecdotes with a large pinch of salt. But we should not dismiss them entirely. They give us an insight not only into what may have happened but into what people thought had happened and was important. Apparent realism is no guide. But the importance attached to memory and record means that we should not ignore their testimony entirely, whilst accepting that it may have mutated far beyond the original event.

So did Eurvin's donkey really get eaten? Of all the anecdotes in the *Antioche* this is the hardest to tie down to a specific source. It could have happened at any siege when food was short, and there is no reason for any chronicler to have preserved such a mundane story. It has the hallmarks of a *fabliau* rather than a piece of testimony. But maybe – just maybe – we have the echoes of an episode here which formed a welcome bit of amusing gossip in an otherwise grim siege nearly one thousand years ago.

---

[77] Olivier de la Marche, *Mémoires*, ed. H. Beaune and J. d'Arbaumont, 4 vols (Paris 1884–8), ii, 340–5. See also P. R. Grillo, 'Note sur le Cycle de la Croisade du MS BN fr. 12569: les reliques de Lens', *Romania*, 94 (1973), 258–67 arguing that Robert of Artois (brother of Louis IX) was inspired in 1247 by a story concerning Godfrey which actually originated in the Jerusalem continuations.

[78] Whilst not strictly speaking an anecdote, the *Antioche* contains a list of prices for food during the famine outside the walls of Antioch which sounds impressively authentic. In practice this is a topos which recurs in other sources for the crusade, each giving different commodities and prices, not a reliable twelfth-century RPI. See for example RA, p. 76; GF, p. 33; RM iv.11, p. 781.

PORTA CLAUSA: TRIAL AND TRIUMPH AT THE GATES OF JERUSALEM[1]

Nicholas L. Paul

To cross the threshold is to unite oneself with a new world.
Arnold Van Gennep, *The Rites of Passage* (London, 1960), p. 20

As the sites which welcomed the prince, defied the enemy and regulated the passage of the merchant and traveller, the gateways and entrances (*portae*) of the eleventh-century west were markers and thresholds of community, power and sanctity. For the inhabitants of this gated world who took to the roads with the First Crusade, the portals of the cities and fortresses of the Near East represented important and recurring features in the landscape that they traversed. The gates that the crusaders encountered at the old Roman and Byzantine cities of Constantinople, Nicaea and Antioch were part of an urban architecture rendered on a scale few had ever experienced, evocative symbols of ancient authority and sacrality still bearing the marks of the triumphal military rulership of late antiquity by which they had originally been shaped.[2] Nowhere, however, could the sight of gates have been as significant, and as eagerly anticipated, as at the holy city of Jerusalem itself.[3]

Jerusalem and its sites were the central focus of Latin Christian devotion, and the city's urban geography was retraced in the imagination of believers as

[1] I would like to thank the organizers and participants in the Liverpool crusade narrative conference for their helpful comments. Particular thanks are due to Steven Biddlecombe for allowing me to consult his new edition of Baldric of Bourgueil, to William Purkis for his valuable feedback, and to Gail McMurray Gibson for first introducing me to medieval 'closed-gate' motifs.

[2] M. McCormick, *Eternal Victory: Triumphal Rulership in Late Antiquity, Byzantium, and the Early Medieval West* (Cambridge, 1986).

[3] See D. Bahat, 'The Physical Infrastructure', in *The History of Jerusalem: The Early Muslim Period, 638–1099*, ed. J. Prawer and H. Ben-Shammai (Jerusalem, 1996), pp. 46–9. For references to the gates in pilgrimage narratives before the First Crusade see the 'Gazetteer' in J. Wilkinson, *Jerusalem Pilgrimage Before the Crusades* (Warminster, 2002), pp. 314–16. See also S. Schein, *Gateway to the Heavenly City: Crusader Jerusalem and the Catholic West* (Aldershot, 2005), pp. 63–90.

episodes from the life of Christ and the history of the Israelites were recited over the course of the liturgical year. The gates of Jerusalem and of its Temple are among the most common images in the Old Testament prophets and the Psalms In the Gospels it was through the city gates of Jerusalem (specifically, according to medieval tradition, the eastern, 'Golden' or 'Beautiful' gate) that Christ himself had ridden into the city astride a donkey as crowds sang *Blessed is he who comes in the name of the Lord* [Ps. 118:25–6] and laid palm branches down before Him.[4] The Palm Sunday liturgical processions that commemorated this scene also re-enacted it, turning the western portals of churches and even the gates of towns into the entry-ways to the Holy City.[5]

Christ's entry in triumphal humility was annually echoed and liturgically redoubled not only on Palm Sunday, but also at the Feast of the Exaltation of the Cross (14 September), which celebrated the return of the True Cross to Jerusalem in 629 by the emperor Heraclius after its capture by the Persians. In the Heraclius legend, the definitive version of which was written by Hrabanus Maurus in the ninth century, the gates of the city played a central role. Following Heraclius's defeat of the Persians and his conquest of Jerusalem, the emperor attempted to return the True Cross relic to the city in glorious triumph. According to the legend, as he prepared to enter, the gates of the city miraculously closed before him, only opening again when he returned to the city in penitent humility.[6]

Heraclius was not the only medieval emperor associated with Jerusalem and its city gates. Well before the First Crusade, a body of legends had already evolved which imagined the western emperor Charlemagne on a pilgrimage to the east.[7] Featured prominently in these stories were images of the emperor received in a ceremony of *adventus* at the gates of Constantinople and at Jerusalem.[8] Jay Rubenstein and Matthew Gabriele have argued that when read in the light of certain eleventh-century apocalyptic and prophetic texts, which described how the Last Emperor would be crowned in Constantinople and Jerusalem (the gates of the latter city opening to him as they had to Christ on Palm Sunday), these stories could carry with them powerful eschatological implications.[9]

---

[4] For gates in the Old and New Testaments see the entry for 'Gates' in *The Dictionary of Biblical Imagery*, ed. L. Ryken, J. C. Wilhoit, and T. Longman III (Downers Grove, IL, 1998), pp. 321–2; and E. Otto, 'ša'ar', in *The Theological Dictionary of the Old Testament: Volume 15*, ed. H. Ringgren and H.-J. Fabry (Grand Rapids, 2006), pp. 359–405. For the eastern gate and Palm Sunday see *Peregrinationes tres*, ed. R. B. C. Huygens (Corpus Christianorum, Continuatio Mediaeualis, 139; Turnhout, 1994), pp. 95–6.

[5] C. Wright, 'The Palm Sunday Procession in Medieval Chartres', in *The Divine Office in the Latin Middle Ages: Methodology and Source Studies, Regional Developments, Hagiography: Written in Honor of Professor Ruth Steiner*, ed. R. A. Baltzer and M. E. Fassler (New York, 2000), pp. 344–71.

[6] Hrabanus Maurus, 'Homiliae', *PL* cx, 133–4.

[7] M. Gabriele, *Empire of Memory: The Legend of Charlemagne and the Franks Before the First Crusade* (Oxford, 2011), pp. 41–70.

[8] Gabriele, *Empire of Memory*, p. 45.

[9] J. Rubenstein, 'Godfrey of Bouillon versus Raymond of Saint-Gilles: How Carolingian Kingship Trumped Millenarianism at the End of the First Crusade', in *The Legend of Charlemagne in the Middle Ages: Power, Faith, and Crusade*, ed. M. Gabriele and J. Stuckey (New York, 2008), p. 63; Gabriele, *Empire of Memory*, p. 115. Gabriele (p. 118) also points out how the 'blocked gate' in Jerusalem became part of this eschatological mythos.

Both traditions of imperial reception had potential points of resonance with the First Crusade, and associations were made between Heraclius, Charlemagne and the crusaders in various accounts of the crusade expedition.[10] As the title of the Old French translation of the crusade narrative of William of Tyre (*Estoire d'Eracles l'empereur*) suggests, Heraclius was the figure whose achievements most clearly paralleled those of the crusaders. The crusaders were, after all, also bearers of the cross and they believed that they, like Heraclius, had recovered the relic from pagan hands. The pilgrim Saewulf, who wrote a description of his visit to Jerusalem in the immediate aftermath of the crusade, repeated the Heraclius story in his discussion of the eastern gate of the city.[11]

Given the importance of the gates of Jerusalem in liturgy and legend, it is hardly surprising to hear the crusaders themselves, in the course of the expedition, longing to see the gates of the city open before them. When the princes who commanded the expedition wrote to Pope Urban II on 11 September 1098 announcing their capture of the city of Antioch and the death of the papal legate Adhemar of Le Puy and asking the pope to join them as the leader of the crusade, they imagined the gates that awaited them:

> And thus you will finish with us the pilgrimage of Jesus Christ undertaken by us and proclaimed by you; and you will open to us the gates of the one and the other Jerusalem and will liberate the Sepulchre of our Lord and exalt the Christian name above all.[12]

Two gated cities, one earthly and one heavenly, awaited the crusaders. The one was the gateway to the other. Whether the opening of the gates of 'the other' Jerusalem meant the opportunity for personal salvation of pilgrim travellers or a more apocalyptic sense of the triumph of Christianity over the world, the wording of the 1098 letter would lead us to believe that upon reaching Jerusalem on 7 June 1099, the crusaders would look eagerly at the ways to go in.

Despite the rich symbolic significance of the portal to the sacred history of the city which the crusaders had conquered, however, the gates of Jerusalem did not occupy a central place in the earliest written narratives of the expedition. Many of the narratives, including two of those written by participants in the crusade, assign to the gates only the simplest of functions, painting them as targets of attack from outside the walls and markers of locale from within them. The crusaders' siege warfare was directed toward walls that could be breached and surmounted and towers captured, and it was usually by way of these features that crusaders first saw the interior of the cities they besieged. Such was the case at Jerusalem, where gates were only used by the attacking crusaders once many

---

[10] GN vii.26, pp. 320–1; RM i.1, p. 728 ; WT i.1, p. 105 and i.3, p. 108.

[11] *Peregrinationes tres*, p. 68.

[12] *Epistulae et chartae ad historiam primi belli sacri spectantes: Die Kreuzzugsbriefe aus den Jahren 1088–1100*, ed. H. Hagenmeyer (Innsbruck, 1901), pp. 164–5; trans. F. R. Ryan, in Fulcher of Chartres, *A History of the Expedition to Jerusalem, 1095–1127*, ed. H. S. Fink (Knoxville, 1969), p. 111.

of their number, in a much more dramatic and famous scene, had overcome the defenders on the walls and towers.[13]

As the process of shaping the crusade narrative continued over the first decades of the twelfth century, however, the gates of Jerusalem began to achieve greater significance. While their place in the story of the conquest of Jerusalem remained marginal, the gates achieved added prominence through the addition of stories to the crusade narratives relating the experiences of Christian pilgrims to the city before its conquest by the Franks. By 1110, writers describing such scenes had adopted a common narrative motif, categorized by folklorists as 'hero must suffer humiliation to enter by city gate'.[14] For medieval audiences, this closed-gate motif carried with it a variety of associations. These included the story of Heraclius and the cross as well as the hagiographical tradition of St Mary of Egypt, who was also stopped at the threshold of a church in Jerusalem by a mysterious force or, in one Old French version, by a vision of nasty-looking soldiers carrying spears.[15] Theologians frequently associated the Virgin's chastity with the image of a 'closed gate' (*porta clausa*) mentioned in the book of Ezekiel (44:1–3), and by the later Middle Ages it was Joseph who remained barred outside the gate which only the Holy Spirit could enter.[16]

In the context of the crusade narratives, the closed-gate motif rendered the pilgrims to Jerusalem before 1099 as an earlier generation of heroes, halted at the closed city gates and unable to venerate the Holy Sepulchre that would be liberated by the crusaders. Over time, the motif became increasingly prominent, and while it never became a central or recurring element in any particular narrative text, it is clear that over the course of the twelfth century it played a major role in defining the achievements and significance of the crusade expedition. It was also part of a narrative mechanism of interlace which connected the crusade to a broader historical narrative that included Heraclius and Christ. The identification of this motif in narratives of the crusade not only highlights the existence of this broader narrative, one that lived across, between and partly outside the textual traditions, it also helps us to understand the continual process of narrative cyclification through which western medieval communities rendered the past intelligible and meaningful. Although this process was not linear, and cannot be traced entirely through relationships between texts, I will begin by locating the earliest references to the closed-gate motif in crusade narratives and

---

[13] For reconstructions based on the narrative evidence see J. France, *Victory in the East: A Military History of the First Crusade* (Cambridge, 1994), pp. 350–6; C. Kostick, *The Siege of Jerusalem: Crusade and Conquest in 1099* (London, 2009), pp. 120–3.

[14] S. Thompson, *Motif-Index of Folk-Literature: A Classification of Narrative Elements in Folktales, Ballads, Myths, Fables, Mediaeval Romances, Exempla, Fabliaux, Jest-Books, and Local Legends*, rev. edn (Copenhagen, 1955–8), p. 509 g. H1553.3; A. Guerreau-Jalalbert, *Index des motifs narratifs dans les romans arthuriens français en vers: XIIe–XIIIe siècles* (Geneva, 1992), p. 109.

[15] *La Vie de Sainte-Marie l'Égyptienne: versions en ancien et en moyen français*, ed. P. F. Dembowski (Geneva, 1977), pp. 41–2 (for the *chevalier*), 212–13, 265, 271.

[16] G. M. Gibson, "'*Porta haec clausa erit*': Comedy, Conception, and Ezekiel's Closed Door in the *Ludus Coventriae* Play of Joseph's Return", *Journal of Medieval and Renaissance Studies*, 8 (1978), 137–56.

tracing its development and use before turning to its appearance in texts focused primarily on a group of noble dynasties.

In the years immediately following the conquest of Jerusalem by the crusaders, two men who had served as household clerics to princely commanders of the expedition, Raymond of Aguilers and Fulcher of Chartres, composed narratives of the expedition. Neither chronicler assigned any narrative significance to the gates of the city of Jerusalem or its holy buildings. In fact, neither mentions the city gates at all in their respective descriptions of the siege of Jerusalem and its aftermath. This was, in both cases, a striking omission. On the one hand, both men must have been very familiar with the potential symbolic importance of gates within reception or *adventus* ceremonies in which their princely lords were greeted at the thresholds of towns, churches and monasteries. As writers, both were also concerned about claims to political power made at Jerusalem in the aftermath of the crusade, claims which Jay Rubenstein has suggested may have involved the invocation of Charlemagne and eschatological interpretations of what the crusade had achieved.[17] As the later writer Albert of Aachen deftly demonstrated, such claims could be subtly undergirded with dramatic entrances through the city gates.[18]

Raymond neglected to mention the entrance of his lord, Count Raymond IV of Toulouse, and his men (among whom he presumably numbered) into the city via the western gate (the 'David' or 'Jaffa' gate) near the Tower of David when the Tower, which the count would later claim as his headquarters in the city, was surrendered to him.[19] This was a scene celebrated in other accounts, and Raymond's silence is so strange that, in addition to leading one medieval redactor of his work to rewrite his account of the city's fall entirely, it has led modern commentators to speculate that he was ashamed of his people's poor performance at the siege.[20] Raymond's chronicle also ends abruptly with the battle of Ascalon, and does not describe the return of the crusaders to Jerusalem, an event which, as we will see, provided other writers with another opportunity to focus on the city gates.[21]

The absence of the gates is perhaps even more striking in the first book of Fulcher's work, which is both deeply exegetical in style and concerned with the topography of the Holy Land. Fulcher also carried his narrative forward, in a series of redactions and continuations, as a political history of the early kingdom of Jerusalem and its rulers. Although he was not present at the siege of Jerusalem,

---

[17] Rubenstein, 'Godfrey of Bouillon versus Raymond of Saint-Gilles'.

[18] AA vi. 26, pp. 436–8.

[19] RA, p. 151.

[20] For the added conclusion to Raymond's work see J. France, 'The Text of the Account of the Capture of Jerusalem in the Ripoll Manuscript, Bibliotheque Nationale (Latin) 5132', *English Historical Review*, 103 (1988), 640–57; *idem, Victory in the East*, p. 354.

[21] Although some thirteenth-century manuscripts of Raymond's account contain continuations describing the 'joyous' return of the crusaders to Jerusalem following their victory over the Egyptian vizier al-Afdal at the battle of Ascalon, they do not describe their triumphal entrance through the city gates: see *RHC Occ* iii, 307.

Fulcher did give an account of its fall in which the gates do not feature.[22] He also described with great emotion his own arrival at the city in December 1099, invoking Psalm 131:7 ('We will adore in the place where his feet stood'), but he did not relate his arrival to the physical geography or architecture of the city. The writer of the redaction of Fulcher's work known as 'Codex L' was so dissatisfied with this description that he added (continuing, of course, in Fulcher's first-person narrative voice) the more vivid rendering of the reception:

> When we had reached the gate, the brothers of Baldwin – Duke Godfrey and his brother Eustace – together with all of the people, went out to meet us. The priests led the way with crosses and with burning candles, exalting God in song and leading us to the church of the Holy Sepulchre.[23]

This was how western narrators wanted to imagine the newly-conquered city of Jerusalem: as a site of triumph where Christian pilgrims could be happily received at the open gates and conducted into the city. It was a scene that Fulcher himself would witness, for instance in August 1119, when the True Cross returned to Jerusalem after a victory in battle,[24] or when King Baldwin II of Jerusalem returned from captivity in 1125.[25] They were not scenes, however, that Fulcher ever associated with the crusade narrative in the first book of his history. Even when he cleverly enumerated the precious stones taken after the battle of Ascalon in 1099 – the list an exact match for the stones used in the foundations of the new Jerusalem in Revelation 21:19–20 – he stopped one verse, and one precious stone, short of invoking the gates.[26] The gates were neither in the narrative, nor in exegetical allusions, nor in the brief descriptions of the city found in various manuscripts of Fulcher's work.[27]

The seed that would eventually lead to the emergence of a narrative motif surrounding the gates of Jerusalem was first planted in an unlikely place. Lacking the sophisticated Latinity and theological rhetoric of his fellow crusade chroniclers, the author of the *Gesta Francorum et aliorum Hierosolimitanorum*, an anonymous account of the crusade apparently composed by a participant, is not usually associated with clever narrative strategy. Indeed, some have wondered whether the *Gesta* was a coherent narrative at all.[28] While the *Gesta* provides little in the way of framing for the narrative of the crusade, near the end of the text, in the maelstrom of action as the crusaders force their way into Jerusalem, we are provided with a small detail not present in the works of the learned chaplains Fulcher and Raymond: 'the amir who held the Tower of David surrendered to

---

[22] FC i.27, pp. 291–301.

[23] FC i.33, p. 332 n. 43. See also *RHC Occ* iii, 366 n. 9. See N. L. Paul, 'A Warlord's Wisdom: Literacy and Propaganda at the Time of the First Crusade', *Speculum*, 85 (2010), 534–66, esp. 540, 554–6.

[24] FC iii.19, pp. 668–9.

[25] FC iii.40, pp. 756–7.

[26] FC i.31, p. 317.

[27] FC i.26, pp. 281–92. For the variants see *RHC Occ* iii, 355–7.

[28] J. Rubenstein, 'What is the *Gesta Francorum* and who was Peter Tudebode?', *Revue Mabillon*, 16 (2005), 179–204.

the count [Raymond IV] and opened for him the gate where the pilgrims used to pay taxes'.[29]

This simple statement had the potential profoundly to reshape the narrative of the expedition. At the moment of Jerusalem's fall to the crusaders, the spatial and evenemental focus of the narrative was shifted from the walls and the towers down to ground level, and the city's western gate which stood near the fortress of the Tower of David. The reference to taxes paid by pilgrims before the crusade, and the tacit suggestion that they had been abolished after the conquest of the city, might be seen as both a pretext for the expedition and one of its major accomplishments. By suggesting the final end to a long-standing injustice at the moment when the crusaders achieve the object of their military campaign, the detail helps to bring closure to the narrative.[30] Moreover, the link between the crusade and a wider, otherwise unreferenced, historical understanding about the treatment of pilgrims in the past was to have profound implications for the development of the narrative of the crusade.

In the first decades of the twelfth century, the *Gesta Francorum* or a tradition very closely related to it was used as the source for a second wave of crusade narratives, including those of the crusader Peter Tudebode, the poet Gilo of Paris, the monks Robert the Monk, Guibert of Nogent, Baldric of Bourgueil and an anonymous author or authors of the *Historia Belli Sacri* at the abbey of Monte Cassino.[31] In the works of these later writers, even the smallest details in the *Gesta Francorum* – like the opening of the gates of Jerusalem – could take on much greater significance because they served as the foundations upon which these much more theologically sophisticated and thoroughly narrativized accounts of the expedition were constructed.

All writers who followed the *Gesta Francorum* tradition included a reference to the opening of the gates of the city at the moment of its conquest.[32] All except one, the *Historia Belli Sacri*, also referred to the exaction of money from pilgrims to Jerusalem before the crusade.[33] In Guibert, Baldric and most notably in Robert, we find significant and distinctive amplifications of the scene. What in the *Gesta Francorum* were simply 'taxes' (*tributa*) became, in Baldric and Guibert, frightening incidences of violence and detention. Baldric described the gate where 'the pilgrims, in order that they might enter, had been violently cheated out of their money. There they had been accustomed to pay the

---

[29]   *GF*, p. 91.
[30]   For the concept of narrative 'closure', as distinct from a narrative's 'ending', see E. Segal, 'The "Tel Aviv School": A Rhetorical-Functional Approach to Narrative', in *Current Trends in Narratology*, ed. G. Olson (Berlin, 2011), pp. 305–11.
[31]   For an overview see S. B. Edgington, 'The First Crusade: Reviewing the Evidence', in *The First Crusade: Origins and Impact*, ed. J. P. Phillips (Manchester, 1997), pp. 57–77. For the relationship between the narratives, with a more cautious reading of that relationship, see Rubenstein, 'What is the *Gesta Francorum*'. See also J. Flori, *Chroniqueurs et propagandistes: Introduction critique aux sources de la Première croisade* (Hautes études médiévales et modernes, 98; Geneva, 2010); but for Flori's claims of a 'propaganda' campaign cf. Paul, 'A Warlord's Wisdom'.
[32]   PT, p. 141; RM ix.24, p. 880; BB iv.14, p. 102; GN vii.8, p. 280; *HBS*, p. 221; *HVH* ix.300–1, p. 246.
[33]   *HBS*, p. 221. A virtually identical construction is found in Ralph of Caen: RC, c. 127, p. 694.

taxes. Otherwise, they had been unmercifully constrained from the gates.'[34] In Guibert's work, these taxes assumed a name: *musellae*, which the pilgrims were 'cruelly and unfairly compelled to pay'.[35]

It was, however, Robert the Monk who gave the gate scene in the *Gesta Francorum* its most subtle, extensive and creative exposition. Crucially, Robert did not refer to the gates or the experiences of pilgrims to Jerusalem in the era before the crusade in his description of the city's conquest. Instead, his evocation of these matters came at a later moment, when the crusaders return to Jerusalem from their victory at the battle of Ascalon (12 August 1099). The scene is not, therefore, one of violent conquest, but of peaceful triumph. In a chapter built around three verses from Isaiah, Robert adopted first auditory and then architectural imagery. The chapter begins with the sound of the returning crusaders' horns echoing back from the land, the literal fulfilment of the prophet's words: *the mountains and the hills shall break forth before you into singing* (Isaiah 55:12). When they reached the gates of the city, the sound of the victorious army was matched by the joyful song of the people singing praises to God. With the scene set for the army's triumphal entry, Robert paused to compare their entry with the travails of earlier generations of pilgrims:

And God was rightly praised because now his pilgrims were received with open arms and praises, whereas before they had been received only with great difficulty, with lots of insults and sometimes only by making gifts. Isaiah says of these pilgrims and gates: *therefore the gates shall be open continually; they shall not be shut day nor night* [Isaiah 60:11]. This prophecy was fulfilled in our time, because now the gates of Jerusalem were opened *to the sons of pilgrims* [Isaiah 61:5] which used to be closed in their faces day and night.[36]

At the gates of Jerusalem, Robert skilfully wove together the past time of the struggling pilgrims with the present triumph of the crusaders and the eternal future promised in prophecy. Inspired perhaps by the *Gesta Francorum*'s identification of the gates opened to the crusaders under Raymond of St Gilles as the very same gates where the pilgrims had been taxed, Robert went one step further, associating these gates with Isaiah's symbolic gates of heaven.

As neither the *Gesta Francorum* itself, nor the two other learned monks who rewrote it, nor in fact the verse narrative of Gilo of Paris, whose work closely parallels Robert's, had introduced this exegetical reading, it seems clear that the interpretation was Robert's own.[37] Given the popularity of Robert's text, his innovative exegesis would seem to open up the potential for associations between the gates of Jerusalem in 1099 and virtually any of the hundreds of references to gates in Old Testament prophecy. Robert's choice of Scripture is especially signif-

[34] BB iv.14, p. 102.
[35] GN vii.8, p. 280.
[36] RM ix.24, p. 880; trans. C. Sweetenham, *Robert the Monk's History of the First Crusade* (Aldershot, 2005), p. 232.
[37] HVH ix.300–1, p. 246.

icant, however, because in adopting Isaiah 61:5 he clearly defined the relationship between the crusaders who conquered Jerusalem and the pilgrims who struggled before its gates. The pilgrims were not just forerunners of the crusaders, they were in fact their fore*fathers*.[38] As we will see, this is especially significant given where the closed-gate motif ultimately manifested itself.

Robert's use of the gate motif in his chapter about the triumphal return to Jerusalem also served an important narrative purpose, showing how the crusaders had finally achieved something that had long been awaited and desired by all Christians. Evelyn Birge Vitz has argued that, as opposed to a chronicle, a 'story' (*récit*) must feature not just any transition but 'an *awaited* (or desired) transformation'. As such, the motif contributes to Robert's construction of the crusade as a story, and helps his audience to understand that the story of the crusade, in addition to his chronicle of its events, has reached its conclusion.[39] This is true even if, as is the case with all crusade narratives written in this period, the audience had not been made aware of the closed gate at an earlier stage in the text. In other accounts of the crusade, the establishment of an objective for the crusade (the liberation of Jerusalem) and a narrative tension or 'suspense' associated with this objective (the oppression of eastern Christians in Jerusalem and elsewhere) is established by beginning the narrative with the speech of Urban II at the Council of Clermont on 27 November 1095 rehearsing in detail the wrongs committed by Jerusalem's Muslim overlords. Something more closely resembling prolepsis, or literal foreshadowing, was created in the narratives through the use of prophecy. Guibert of Nogent, for instance, cited a prophecy made in Jerusalem to Count Robert I of Flanders, the father of the crusade commander Count Robert II, that the city would shortly be conquered by the Franks.[40] The vernacular crusade epic *Chanson d'Antioche* begins with a prophecy made by Christ, hanging on the cross, to the two thieves who hung beside him that 'the race is not born yet who will come to revenge Me for these sharp spear thrusts ... the Franks will liberate the whole land'.[41]

The importance of Robert's decision to dedicate an entire chapter of his work to the opening of the pilgrims' gate is underlined by the fact that he was not the only writer to have conceived of the open gate as the symbol of the crusade's accomplishment or to have used it as a mechanism of closure. Albert, canon of the cathedral church of Aachen, who may have been writing at about the same time as Robert, began his *Historia Ierosolimitana* by promising to tell how the 'triumphant legions killed a thousand times a thousand Turks and Saracens in a bold attack; how they laid open the entrance and approach

---

[38] Here, more resonance between Robert and Gilo can be detected, as Gilo refers to the pilgrims who had to pay money to enter Jerusalem as the 'ancestors' (*maiores*) of the crusaders: HVH ix.301, p. 246.

[39] E. Birge Vitz, *Medieval Narrative and Modern Narratology: Subjects and Objects of Desire* (New York, 1989), p. 108.

[40] GN vii.27, pp. 319–20.

[41] *La Chanson d'Antioche*, ed. S. Duparc-Quioc, 2 vols (Documents relatifs à l'histoire des croisades, 11; Paris, 1976-8), i, 26–7, ll. 170–3, 209; trans. S. B. Edgington and C. Sweetenham, *The* Chanson d'Antioche: *An Old French Account of the First Crusade* (Farnham, 2012), pp. 106–7.

[*introitum et accessum*] to the Holy Sepulchre of our Lord Jesus Christ and completely remitted the taxes and tributes of the pilgrims wishing to enter there.[42] Later, in the sixth book of his history, Albert also mentioned that, at the moment of Jerusalem's fall to the crusaders, Godfrey of Bouillon departed from the army, circumambulated the city, and entered, like Heraclius, in pious humility to pray at the Holy Sepulchre.[43] This image of Godfrey carried with it a potent mixture of political and eschatological associations and served to advance Albert's argument for Godfrey as the expedition's central figure; and as Albert went on to explain, his entry into Jerusalem, 'the gate of the heavenly homeland', was the fulfilment of the prophetic visions of a member of his household.[44]

While it provided narrative closure to the duke's own crusade, the story of Godfrey's entry was not related to Albert's earlier invocation of the difficulties of pilgrims. In Albert's account, one of those who had suffered, or more precisely 'saw' the suffering of other pilgrims who tried to reach Jerusalem before 1099, was Peter the Hermit, leader of the so-called People's Crusade of 1096 and the man to whom Albert, William of Tyre and the *Chanson d'Antioche* attributed the genesis of the entire crusading enterprise.[45] Peter was not the only individual who was said to have been to Jerusalem before the crusade. Another tradition, appearing in the works of Caffaro of Genoa and Guy of Bazoches, held that the traveller/witness was the crusading prince and first ruler of Jerusalem, Godfrey of Bouillon himself.[46] The most completely developed account of the crusader as protocrusade pilgrim appears in the thirteenth-century Spanish vernacular narrative *Gran Conquista de Ultramar*, where it is tied clearly to the closed-gate motif. In the *Gran Conquista*, the crusaders Achard of Montmerle, Raymond Pilet, and Galdemar Carpinel, all notable figures in other accounts of the expedition, journeyed to Jerusalem before the First Crusade. Having been robbed, they encounter grave difficulties gaining access to the Holy Sepulchre. One of the group, Achard of Montmerle, only does so after receiving a blow from the doorkeeper. The crusade itself becomes a vehicle for Achard's vengeance as well as, of course, removing the obstructions that had prevented pilgrims from venerating the Sepulchre.[47]

---

[42]   AA i.1, p. 2.

[43]   AA vi.25, p. 436.

[44]   AA vi.27, p. 438.

[45]   AA i.2, pp. 2–4; WT i.11–12, pp. 124–7. The story is developed most completely in the cyclical version of *La Chanson d'Antioche*, ed. J. A. Nelson (The Old French Crusade Cycle, 4; Tuscaloosa, 2003), pp. 56–9, ll. 261–374.

[46]   Caffaro, 'De liberatione civitatum orientis', in *Annali Genovesi di Caffaro e de'suoi continuatori dai MXCIX al MCCXCIIII*, ed. L. Belgrano (Genoa, 1929), pp. 99–101. Guy of Bazoches's version can be found in 'Chronica Alberici monachum trium fontium', ed. P. Scheffer-Boichorst, *MGH SS* xxiii, 803.

[47]   *La Gran Conquista de Ultramar*, ed. L. Cooper, 4 vols (Publicaciones del Instituto Caro y Cuervo, 51–4; Bogotá, 1979), i, 186–8. For a discussion of this story-element in the *Gran Conquista*, see C. Sweetenham and L. M. Paterson, *The Canso d'Antioca: An Occitan Epic Chronicle of the First Crusade* (Aldershot, 2003), pp. 41–2. Sweetenham and Paterson conclude that the story probably did not form part of the *Canso d'Antioca*, as supposed by earlier scholars.

These stories about Peter, Godfrey and the three crusading knights reveal that as the narrative of the First Crusade was transmitted and rewritten over the course of the twelfth century, new episodes relating to the people and places in the history of the expedition were being generated or collected and then interposed and interlaced into the broader story. In this way, the First Crusade demonstrated the same characteristics as other narratives of tremendous mythic power and cultural significance in the Middle Ages: it became the core story in a narrative cycle. Like other resonant narratives, the First Crusade had the capacity, in the words of Peter Happé, to 'generate other material which reflects back upon it', material which 'functions as a means of enhancing the central matter, however indirectly'.[48]

The clearest manifestation of the cyclical force of the crusade narrative is of course the great epic cycle that grew up around the *Chanson d'Antioche*, entitled by its American editors the Old French Crusade Cycle. With almost magnetic force, by the late twelfth century the song drew in related materials that were rendered into new branches, affixed to one another by specially-tailored bridging episodes and through interlace.[49] While earlier material (*Les Chétifs* and *Chanson de Jérusalem*) elaborated and continued the story of the expedition itself and its participants, it was not long before the crusade cycle, like all such projects, became concerned with ancestry. In the early thirteenth century other songs (*Le Chevalier au Cygne* and *Enfances Godefroi*) were also incorporated relating the youth and legendary ancestry of Godfrey of Bouillon, and before 1218 these seem to have included five branches of ancestral material.[50] But if a full cycle of narratives was only born at this late date and in vernacular works, it is important to remember that the process was already underway in Albert, Caffaro and Guibert, who hinted at an *Enfances Pierre* and perhaps an earlier branch based on the experiences of Robert I of Flanders.

For the *remanieurs* who worked to stitch together the thousands of verses of the Old French Crusade Cycle, the closed-gate motif provided a critical opportunity to interlace characters and episodes within the ancestral branches of the cycle while at the same time reaffirming the relationship between this material and the later songs about the conquest of Jerusalem. *La Fin d'Elias*, a work which bridged the songs about Godfrey of Bouillon's crusade with those concerning

---

[48] P. Happé, *Cyclic Form and the English Mystery Plays: A Comparative Study of the English Biblical Cycles and their Continental Iconographic Counterparts* (Amsterdam, 2004), p. 16.

[49] For the process of 'cyclification' see *Transtextualities: Of Cycles and Cyclicity in Medieval French Literature*, ed. S. Sturm-Maddox and D. Maddox (Binghamton, 1996); M. Delbouille, 'Dans un atelier de copistes: En regardant de plus près les manuscrits B1 et B2 du cycle épique de *Garin de Monglane*', *Cahiers de civilisation médiévale*, 3 (1960), 14–22; see also M. Tyssens, *La geste de Guillaume d'Orange dans les manuscrits cycliques* (Paris, 1967); L. Sunderland, *Old French Narrative Cycles: Heroism between Ethics and Morality* (Cambridge, 2010).

[50] G. M. Meyers, 'The Manuscripts of the Cycle', in *La Naissance du Chevalier au Cygne and Beatrix*, ed. E. M. Mickel and J. A. Nelson (The Old French Crusade Cycle, 1; Tuscaloosa, 1977), p. xv. For the dating of the genealogical branches, see *La Chanson d'Antioche*, ed. Nelson, p. 29. For cyclification and the crusade narrative, see D. Trotter, *Medieval French Literature and The Crusades (1100–1300)* (Geneva, 1988), p. 131; *Le Chevalier au Cygne et La Fin d'Elias*, ed. J. A. Nelson (The Old French Crusade Cycle, 2; Tuscaloosa, 1985), pp. xxvi–xxviii.

his ancestry, describes a pilgrimage undertaken to Jerusalem by Pons, provost
of the Ardennes, and Gerart of Sainteron, contemporaries of Godfrey's mythical
grandfather Helyas, the Swan Knight. Upon reaching Jerusalem, the pilgrims are
stopped at the Golden Gate by sixty Bedouin, who promise that 'nevermore will
[the pilgrims] see their relatives, that today they would be killed if at the end
to their journey they could not pay two hundred ounces of fine gold and all of
the silk that one pack horse could carry'.[51] The pilgrims, who are also told that
they will be tied to the al-Aqsa mosque and used as archery targets, eventually
gain access to the city, allowing them, and the reader, to be introduced to key
figures appearing later in the cycle. Just as important, the scene before the gates
establishes the captive state of Jerusalem and the dangers posed to pilgrims,
all of which will be undone when their successor, the hero Godfrey and his
companions conquer the city in a later part of the cycle.

With its vivid description of the Bedouin gatekeepers and their threats to
harm, capture or kill the pilgrims who could not pay the toll, thirteenth-century
vernacular texts such as *La Fin d'Elias* and the *Gran Conquista de Ultramar*
appear finally to provide all of the elements of the scene alluded to by authors of
crusading narratives from the time of the *Gesta Francorum* and the first books
of Albert of Aachen's *Historia Ierosolimitana*. The ubiquity of the stories of
violence and threats toward pilgrims, and their appearance in the very earliest
crusade narratives, force us to consider whether they might be echoes, however
indistinct, of the lived experience of eleventh-century pilgrims. Was the closed-
gate motif a narrative device, or a memory of real traumatic experiences deeply
embedded in the social memory of Latin Christians?

Pilgrims must have been accustomed to pay tolls, especially when passing
through non-Christian territories where their status might not be recognized.
It is not surprising, therefore, that returning pilgrims or crusaders would bring
home the name of these duties: *musellae*, probably a Latinization of the Arabic
maṣlaḥa. Tellingly, no references can be found to the exaction of particularly
harsh tolls at the gates of Jerusalem in texts written before the First Crusade.
Maṣlaḥa is a term referring to public welfare, and was used in Mamluk administrative documents to refer to taxes in cash and in kind associated with social
stability and just administration.[52]

While eleventh-century pilgrims faced dangers in their travels to the east,
reports written before the First Crusade suggest that these were the dangers of
the road, and did not refer to the physical punishment or exclusion of pilgrims at
Jerusalem. Pilgrims from Germany in 1064-5 famously encountered bandits and
resistance from some of the governors of towns they passed by.[53] Their journey

[51] *Le Chevalier au Cygne and La Fin d'Elias*, p. 391, ll. 1295-324.
[52] In a memorandum sent to Amir Kitbugha from the Mamluk sultan Qalawun in 1281 *maṣlaḥa* was
defined as 'social benefits like the collection of taxes in cash and kind'. See 'Memorandum to Amir
Kitbugha', in S. Tsugitaka, *State and Rural Society in Medieval Islam: Sultans, Muqta's and Fallahun*
(Leiden, 1997), p. 113.
[53] E. Joranson, 'The Great German Pilgrimage of 1064-1065', in *The Crusades and Other Historical
Essays Presented to Dana C. Munro by His Former Students*, ed. L. J. Paetow (New York, 1928),
pp. 3-56.

became easier, however, once they had travelled far enough south to fall under the protection of the Fatimid caliph.[54] As the annalist at Niederaltaich, who gives us an account of the German pilgrimage, pointed out, it was counterintuitive for the rulers of Jerusalem to allow any harm to come to pilgrims for 'no one after this would come through that land for the purpose of prayer, and thereafter a grave injury would be incurred for him and to his people'.[55] When Peter Damian (d. 1072) heard that the Marquis Rainier of Monte Santa Maria was planning to undertake a journey to Jerusalem, he composed a letter detailing the experiences of several of his fellow monks who had recently made the journey.[56] Peter's message was that pilgrimage to Jerusalem was fraught with dangers, as it would continue to be for decades after 1099, but in none of his anecdotes did he mention harsh tolls, and his brethren had encountered no difficulties at Jerusalem itself.

Although the stories about the suffering experienced by pilgrims to Jerusalem before the First Crusade may have been widely accepted as truth by the readers of twelfth- and thirteenth-century crusade narratives, the closed-gate motif and its attendant stories of pilgrim torment should be seen mainly as mechanisms that helped to shape the story of the First Crusade in written narrative and social memory. In crusade narratives ranging from the *Gesta Francorum* to the *Gran Conquista de Ultramar* and the Old French Crusade Cycle the mechanism functioned principally to complete the story-arc of the crusade expedition, giving closure to the narrative and reinforcing the crusade's purpose and significance. In Robert's work, uniquely, the motif took on an exegetical and perhaps also eschatological meaning: that the gates of Jerusalem mentioned by King David in his songs had definitively been opened.

The effectiveness of the motif as a narrative device foreshadowing the coming of the crusaders and linking together the triumphal entry of 1099 with past (and possibly also future) events from Christian history also explains its inclusion in a second group of narratives which were not directly related to the narratives of the crusade. As I have shown elsewhere, the closed-gate motif also appears prominently in several dynastic historical narratives written for the princely houses of Anjou, Normandy and Flanders.[57] The authors of dynastic narratives (*gesta principum*) had similar training, occupied similar positions and had similar didactic goals to the authors of crusade narratives (*gesta Francorum*).[58] Family

---

[54] 'Annales Altahenses maiores', ed. W. Giesebrecht and E. L. B. Oefele, *MGH SS* xx, 815–17.

[55] 'Annales Altahenses maiores', p. 816.

[56] *Die Briefe des Petrus Damiani*, ed. K. Reindel, 4 vols (MGH Briefe der deutchen Kaiserzeit, 4; Munich, 1983–93), iv, 1–5.

[57] See N. L. Paul, *To Follow in Their Footsteps: The Crusades and Family Memory in the High Middle Ages* (Ithaca, 2012), pp. 171–99. The place of the motif in the relevant areas follows: for Anjou: *Chroniques des comtes d'Anjou et des seigneurs d'Amboise*, ed. L. Halphen and R. Poupardin (Paris, 1913), p. 50; for Normandy: 'The *Brevis relatio de Guillelmo nobilissimo comite Normannorum*, Written by a Monk of Battle Abbey', ed. E. M. C. van Houts, in *Chronology, Conquest, and Conflict in Medieval England* (Camden Miscellany, 34 [5th series, 10]; London, 1997), p. 26; and Wace, *Roman de Rou*, ed. A. J. Holden, trans. G. S. Burgess, with notes by Burgess and E. M. C. van Houts (St. Helier, 2002), pp. 172–3, ll. 3151–66; for Flanders: 'Flandria generosa', in 'Genealogiae comitum Flandriae', ed. L. C. Bethmann, *MGH SS* ix, 323 n. 23.

[58] Paul, *To Follow in Their Footsteps*, pp. 77–80.

historians openly responded to what they read in crusade chronicles, and in at least one case a family's claims about the deeds of their ancestor were incorporated into a later rescension of a crusade narrative.[59]

The writers and audiences of twelfth century dynastic histories may well have believed that, as some early crusade narratives told them, Christian pilgrims were denied access to Jerusalem and the Holy Sepulchre before the First Crusade. But when they included episodes in dynastic histories concerning the experiences of pilgrims who were ancestors of early crusaders, they did so, like the crusade chroniclers, for reasons relating to their aims as storytellers. Dynastic history presented its own particular narrative challenges. Like the crusade chroniclers, the dynastic narrators, too, had to tell successful stories with satisfying arcs, but these arcs could not just be linked, as was the familiar pattern in medieval chronicle writing, like rings in a chain.[60] The powerful idea of lineage, which not only bound each succeeding story but also connected all the subjects in the entire narrative, and the implications of a moral or didactic mode of storytelling that would benefit the listener by showing good and bad examples from their ancestry, meant that the same qualities manifested in epic cycles, such as interlace and foreshadowing, occurred in dynastic narratives. The use of the closed-gate motif in this context not only helped to bring coherence to the whole family history, but also to bind that history with the narratives of the crusade.

For the princely families of Flanders, Anjou and Normandy, imagining their ancestor before the gates placed them at the centre of the stories about the genesis and significance of the First Crusade. The storytellers that entertained and educated these families were able to foreground the crusading feats of later generations within a landscape already filled with tension; an earlier generation barred, insulted and abused looked forward to the vengeance and triumph of their descendants. The image of a prince before city gates, moreover, was especially resonant within these families. The triumphs and consular processions of the ancient world had long afterlives, manifesting their ritual power in ceremonies of reception and *adventus* in which eleventh- and twelfth-century nobles, especially the territorial princes, participated as they moved around their domains.[61] The anxiety that an image such as the one presented here would engender – that the gates might not open – would therefore have been very great for a princely audience.

But following the innovative reading of Robert the Monk, these were not just any gates, and what lay beyond them was not merely the promise of political approbation. The extraordinary popularity of Robert the Monk's history in the second half of the twelfth century may suggest that his exegetical reading of Old Testament gates as the gates opened by the crusaders prepared the way for other

59 N. L. Paul, 'Crusade, Memory, and Regional Politics in Twelfth-Century Amboise', *Journal of Medieval History*, 31 (2005), 127–41.
60 Birge Vitz, *Medieval Narrative*, p. 109.
61 P. Willmes, *Der herrscher Adventus im Kloster des Frühmittelalters* (Munich, 1972); D. A. Warner, 'Ritual and Memory in the Ottonian Reich: The Ceremony of *Adventus*', *Speculum*, 76 (2001), 255–83; G. Koziol, *Begging Pardon and Favor: Ritual and Political Order in Early Medieval France* (Ithaca, 1992), p. 92.

scriptural interpretations. Here it is worth noting that the Vulgate and its glosses favoured images (not present in the Hebrew or Greek translations) of earthly *principes* and a divine *Princeps* opening and closing the gates either of the Temple or the Heavenly City. For instance, the gates which in Ezekiel 44:1–3 are closed to all, including (in the common medieval misreading of the beginning of verse 3) 'the [earthly, territorial] prince', will only be open to 'the Prince [of heaven]'.[62] Psalm 23 exhorts the 'princes' to 'Lift up your gates', so that the 'King of Glory', 'the Lord who is strong and mighty in battle' may enter in.[63] To be among the princes who open these gates, following the Psalmist, was to be among the army of the righteous with Christ. It was to follow the example of Heraclius, in humility, and others, such as Heraclius and Mary of Egypt, in penitence. Most importantly for the nobility, it anticipated the opening of those gates by the First Crusade.

At some point in the first half of the twelfth century, scribes working at the abbey of Santa Maria de Ripoll in Catalonia used the remaining folios in the final quire of a manuscript of the crusade narrative of Raymond of Aguilers to copy a series of additional texts.[64] Among these texts were a dynastic history of the counts of Barcelona, the *Gesta comitum Barcinonenium*, and liturgical materials for the celebration of the Feast of the Liberation of Jerusalem by the crusaders on 15 July. One section, addressed to the knights who had taken part in the expedition, sums up the accomplishments of the crusade:

> Look! No enemies guard the gate of Jerusalem! No one closes what has been opened through Christ's labours! None of the faithful is required to pay any tribute to enter! Oh happy month of July, that on its sixteenth day entrance was given by the Son of Light to that city where the sun of justice shone out everywhere and the power of the darkness vanished ...[65]

In anticipating the deeds of the crusaders, the motif of the pilgrim at the gates brought closure to the narrative of the crusade. It provided a neat visual metaphor, already very common from Old Testament prophecy and other legends, which highlighted the crusaders' accomplishments. The presence of the motif in dynastic histories joined the narrative of the family with that of the crusade in a way that enhanced the coherence of dynastic storytelling and suggested the place of the crusaders in a long and honourable 'lineage' of pilgrims to Jerusalem, including their ancestors, kings and emperors, and ultimately Christ.

---

[62] See Jerome, 'Commentariorum in Ezechielem', *PL* xxv, 427–30; Hugh of Saint-Cher, *In Libros Prophetarum Ezechielis, Danielis, Oseae, Joelis, Amos, Abdiae, Jonae, Michae, Nahum, Habacuc, Sophoniae, Aggaei, Zachariae, Malachae, et Machabaeuorum I* (Venice, 1754), v, 136–7; and *Bibliorum Sacrorum cum Glossa Ordinaria*, 6 vols (Venice, 1603), v, 1435.

[63] For the medieval interpretation of Psalm 23, which differs considerably from the Greek, see *Bibliorum Sacrorum cum Glossa Ordinaria*, iii, 593–4.

[64] For this section of the manuscript, see France, 'Text of the Account', 640–3. For the manuscript more generally see Paul, *To Follow in Their Footsteps*, pp. 285–94 and appendix 3.

[65] France, 'Text of the Account', 653–4.

When writers invoked the closed gate in their narratives, they introduced an image which held a wide range of potential resonances. While for noble princes, that gate may have been a reminder of the power and danger of ritualized authority, for theologians it may have held eschatological significance. But the popularity of the narrative device stemmed from the fact that, once introduced, the closed-gate motif set off a cascade of similar story-arcs that all ended in the same place. Like the gun which, once introduced to the audience, always goes off in the third act, the closed gates of Jerusalem would always ultimately be thrown open again in triumph.

THE *HISTORIA IHEROSOLIMITANA* OF ROBERT THE MONK AND THE CORONATION OF LOUIS VI

James Naus

The First Crusade captured the medieval imagination on an unprecedented scale. In addition to several letters composed by participants while still on the expedition, four eyewitness narrative accounts were circulating throughout western Europe by c. 1110. These, in turn, inspired the production of a number of 'second generation' chronicles and vernacular histories in the first half of the twelfth century.[1] It is difficult to think of another event in the Middle Ages that piqued this level of literary interest. As a result, historians have long sought to understand the relationship between the sources, in particular the process of narrative transmission from the eyewitness accounts to their offspring. A bulk of attention has focused on the *Gesta Francorum*, the most famous eyewitness account, and the three chronicles based on it: those of Robert the Monk, Baldric of Bourgueil and Guibert of Nogent. Since all three men were Benedictine monks writing in close temporal and geographic proximity, the prevailing consensus is to combine them together into a genre of monastic crusading chronicles.[2] Scholars have concentrated their efforts on understanding the various ways in which these three monks, taken as a set, reworked and refined the vulgar language of the *Gesta Francorum* to fit better within a western religious framework.[3]

---

[1] S. B. Edgington, 'The First Crusade: Reviewing the Evidence', in *The First Crusade: Origins and Impact*, ed. J. P Phillips (Manchester, 1997), pp. 57–77; C. J. Tyerman, *The Debate on the Crusades* (Manchester, 2011), pp. 7–12; Y. N. Harari, 'Eyewitnessing in Accounts of the First Crusade: The *Gesta Francorum* and Other Contemporary Narratives', *Crusades*, 3 (2004), 77–99.

[2] Christopher Tyerman has recently called the group the 'northern French Benedictine mafia': Tyerman, *Debate on the Crusades*, p. 9.

[3] Cf. J. France, 'The Use of the Anonymous *Gesta Francorum* in the Early Twelfth-Century Sources for the First Crusade', in *From Clermont to Jerusalem: The Crusades and Crusader Societies, 1095–1500*, ed. A. V. Murray (International Medieval Research, 3; Turnhout, 1998), pp. 29–42; J. Rubenstein, 'What is the *Gesta Francorum*, and who was Peter Tudebode?', *Revue Mabillon*, 16 (2005), 179–204; J. France, 'The Anonymous *Gesta Francorum* and the *Historia Francorum qui ceperunt Iherusalem* of Raymond of Aguilers and the *Historia de Hierosolymitano itinere* of Peter Tudebode: An Analysis of the Textual Relationship between Primary Sources for the First

The shared theological motive of these authors is plain. And yet, these texts also differ in their treatment of crucial (if sometimes minute) details. By approaching them only as a group, historians risk flattening the individual aims and contributions of each author and his respective text. For this reason, it may be useful to put aside temporarily the 'genre model' and consider these chronicles within the context of the milieu in which each was written; that is, as independent cultural artefacts produced at a specific historical moment. Indeed, the fact that all three chronicles were adapted from a common source allows for a glimpse into the worlds of authorial intention, textual composition and, as we will see, monastic competition. While this approach has its limits – we must, for instance, be careful not to swing too far in the other direction and underestimate the collective contribution of the First Crusade sources – it also has the distinct virtue of allowing for a fuller understanding of the First Crusade's impact on western culture. The value of such a methodological pitch is demonstrated by a number of recent works on the importance of family genealogies, crusader identity and historical memory.[4] While study of such topics is still in its early stages, it is clear that historians of the crusades have begun to pay closer attention to the broader place of their subject within European cultural history.

Constraints of space preclude an exhaustive consideration of all three Benedictine texts, but Robert the Monk's *Historia Iherosolimitana* presents an excellent case study. Not only was it the most popular crusading chronicle, surviving in over eighty medieval manuscripts, but it was also written by a monk from Reims, a city with a strong historical connection to the French kings that had reached a point of political disequilibrium when Robert was writing around 1108–10.[5] Thus, it is reasonable to expect evidence of the external factors influencing Robert to be clearly manifested in the text. And indeed, considered in this way, we will see that the *Historia Iherosolimitana* is not only a 'theological refinement' of the *Gesta Francorum*, as scholars have long proposed, but also an instrument of reflective commentary and reasoned response to the strained relationship between Reims and the French royal court.

Since historians have often noted the shared attributes of the three Benedictine chronicles, a useful point of departure will be to consider the unique features that separate the *Historia Iherosolimitana* from the work of Baldric and Guibert. One notable element of Robert's text, and in general one only remarked upon

Crusade', in *The Crusades and their Sources: Essays Presented to Bernard Hamilton*, ed. J. France and W. G. Zajac (Aldershot, 1998), pp. 39–70; J. S. C. Riley-Smith, *The First Crusade and the Idea of Crusading* (London, 1986), pp. 135–52. For an alternative approach see J. Flori, *Chroniqueurs et propagandistes: Introduction critique aux sources de la Première croisade* (Hautes études médiévales et modernes, 98; Geneva, 2010).

4   Cf. P. A. Adair, 'Flemish Comital Family and the Crusades', in *The Crusades: Other Experiences, Alternative Perspectives*, ed. K. I. Semaan (Binghamton, 2003), pp. 101–12; N. L. Paul, *To Follow in Their Footsteps: The Crusades and Family Memory in the High Middle Ages* (Ithaca, 2012); M. C. Gaposchkin, *The Making of Saint Louis: Kingship, Sanctity, and Crusade in the Later Middle Ages* (Ithaca, 2008).

5   For Reims generally see J. Le Goff, 'Reims, City of Coronation', in *Realms of Memory: The Construction of the French Past*, ed. P. Nora, ed. L. D. Kritzman, trans. A. Goldhammer, 3 vols (New York, 1996), iii, 193–249.

in passing, is his clear attempt to sanitize the crusading careers of various members of the royal court who behaved shamefully in the east. Featuring most prominently in this effort is Hugh of Vermandois, the younger brother of King Philip I and the only member of the royal family to have joined the First Crusade.[6] Philip could not go himself since he was excommunicated in 1094 for carrying off Bertrada of Montfort, the wife of one of his vassals.[7] Yet, one must not confuse inability with disinterest; there is good reason to believe that Philip was keenly interested in the crusade. From a practical point of view, he wanted to keep track of his vassals while they were gone from France, and for this reason it was important to him to have a close family representative on the expedition.[8] Thus, the king lobbied for official recognition of Hugh's position as the royal representative, even securing a papal banner for his brother by announcing his acceptance of the crusading vow to Pope Urban II at the Council of Nîmes in July 1096.[9] This was a move designed to situate Hugh above the other crusader leaders on the basis of his royal status.

This is an important point because despite Philip's efforts and best hopes, Hugh's crusading career was stained with shame. Shortly after the battle of Antioch in June 1098, Hugh and Baldwin of Mons travelled to Constantinople as envoys to meet Emperor Alexios I. At some point during their journey Turkish or Turkopole marauders attacked them, killing Baldwin. While Hugh managed to arrive safely in Constantinople, the experience, perhaps coupled with the dire situation at Antioch, had frayed his nerves to their limit and he decided to return home to France. The spectre of the resulting shame ultimately prompted his return to the east to fulfil his vow as part of the ill-fated crusade of 1101, on which he died in 1102.

The eyewitness accounts all included the story of Hugh's departure: he was, after all, something of a celebrity and his abandonment of the expedition served well to demonstrate the horrific conditions the crusaders faced (even a member of the French royal family dealt with these conditions, the sources seem to say). Given this point, the extent to which Robert altered the original narrative of

---

[6] J. L. Naus, 'The French Royal Court and the Memory of the First Crusade', *Nottingham Medieval Studies*, 55 (2011), 49–78; M. G. Bull, 'The Capetian Monarchy and the Early Crusade Movement: Hugh of Vermandois and Louis VII', *Nottingham Medieval Studies*, 40 (1996), 25–46; C. Sweetenham, *Robert the Monk's History of the First Crusade* (Crusade Texts in Translation, 11; Aldershot, 2005), pp. 19–23.

[7] Cf. *Sacrorum conciliorum nova et amplissima collectio*, ed. J. D. Mansi, 55 vols (Paris, 1901–27), xx, 815; C. K. Gardner, 'The Capetian Presence in Berry as a Consequence of the First Crusade', in *Autour de la première croisade: actes du Colloque de la Society for the Study of the Crusades and the Latin East: Clermont-Ferrand, 22–25 juin 1995*, ed. M. Balard (Paris, 1996), pp. 75–6.

[8] For the long-term impacts on kingship of the early Capetians' crusading exploits see J. L. Naus, 'Negotiating Kingship in France at the Time of the Early Crusades', *French Historical Studies* (forthcoming). In terms of French kings in battle, it is worth considering that Charlemagne's legendary reputation was largely based on his performance as a war leader. Cf. M. Gabriele, *An Empire of Memory: The Legend of Charlemagne, the Franks, and Jerusalem before the First Crusade* (Oxford, 2011).

[9] *Sacrorum conciliorum nova et amplissima collectio*, xx, 937; *La Chronique de Saint-Maixent 751–1140*, ed. and trans. J. Verdon (Les classiques de l'histoire de France au moyen âge, 33; Paris, 1979), p. 154; Bull, 'Capetian Monarchy', 36–40.

the *Gesta Francorum* to erase this negative aspect of Hugh's career is worthy of close attention.[10] Where the *Gesta* recorded Hugh's departure in a short note, 'Hugh went but he never came back', Robert changed the story, claiming that 'once Hugh had carried out his mission to the emperor, he died unexpectedly'.[11] Hugh did not die on his mission to Constantinople, of course, and given Robert's heavy reliance on the testimony of returning crusaders, his monastery of Saint-Remi's location near Hugh's domain, and the general interest among churchmen in Reims in all matters Capetian, it is difficult to believe that Robert was simply unaware of the royal brother's fate. Rather, we can reasonably infer that Robert knew of Hugh's return to France in 1098, knew of his actual death in 1102 while trying to fulfil his original vow, and conflated these two episodes in his chronicle with the aim of expunging Hugh's flight from the historical record.

Robert not only erased the negative aspects of Hugh's crusading; he also added material manifestly designed to inflate the memory of Hugh's standing in the post-crusade political climate of northern France. In his description of Bohemond receiving news of the crusade, for instance, Robert singled out Hugh's royal status, noting that the Norman warlord 'was told by his sources about the princes: Hugh the Great, brother of King Philip of France was the standard-bearer and leader of the great army'.[12] Of course, one must allow for the fact that Robert was writing in northern France and would have been more likely to go into detail about local crusaders. But the fact that Hugh's royal status is inserted into Robert's text on several occasions, and that the corresponding passages in the *Gesta* make no such reference, is a good indication of the author's resolve to bolster Hugh's leadership role on the crusade in every way possible.[13] In a more telling instance, Robert reworked a story from the *Gesta Francorum* that described a prophecy made by the mother of Kerbogha, the Turkish governor of Mosul. She tells her son, who at that moment was planning an attack on the Christians at Antioch, that if he fought against the crusaders he would be defeated. In an attempt to understand his situation better, Kerbogha questions his mother on various points about the Christian faith. 'Are not Bohemond and Tancred the gods of the Franks?', he asks in the *Gesta Francorum*.[14] Robert makes a slight but crucial alteration: 'Are Hugh the standard-bearer and the Apulian Bohemond, and the knight Godfrey [of Bouillon] their gods?'[15] By the time Robert was writing his chronicle at the end of the first decade of the twelfth century, Bohemond and Godfrey had become arguably the two most famous crusading heroes. The substitution of Hugh's name for Tancred's is therefore best understood as an attempt to insert the king's brother into this elite group. In other words, what we get is a picture of what the crusade *ought* to have looked

---

10 Cf. AA v.3, pp. 340–2; *GF*, p. 72.
11 *GF*, p. 72; RM vii.20, p. 837.
12 RM ii.3, p. 740.
13 For discussion see Bull, 'Capetian Monarchy', 36–40.
14 *GF*, pp. 55–6.
15 RM vi.12, p. 813.

like from the king's perspective and (by extension) from that of a monk from Reims, a writer whose city was in the business of promoting sacral kingship.[16]

If theological refinement and literary polish had been Robert's sole aims, then surely these alterations would have been unnecessary. In fact, at times they could have quite an opposite effect. In one instance Robert's erasure of the names of several deserting French knights disrupts quite significantly the flow of the original *Gesta* text.[17] It is possible, of course, that, like Guibert of Nogent, Robert was simply fleshing out the *Gesta's* narrative with details learned from returning crusaders, though it is unlikely that veterans, particularly those from the region around Reims which is not far from the Vermandois, would have been so grossly misinformed about Hugh's fate at Constantinople. Indeed, charter evidence from Molesme makes plain that at least some departing on the 1101 expedition were aware of Hugh's shameful return to France in 1098.[18] Moreover, while we possess little evidence for Hugh's reception upon his return to Crépy-en-Valois in 1098, if we compare his case to the widespread knowledge of other high-profile deserters such as Stephen of Blois, it is difficult to accept that Robert seriously believed he could alter the historical record with deletion and addition.[19] People would have recognized his deception very quickly, and Robert went out of his way in the beginning of his text to establish his credibility as an author.[20] In searching for a fuller understanding of Robert's text, therefore, we must seek an explanation that marries the text's strong theological underpinning with its pro-Capetian tenor. One way to do this is by considering the *Historia Iherosolimitana* in light of Reims's relationship with the French kings, in particular the city's central role in promoting Capetian dynasticism.

The issue of royal legitimacy had been a central concern for the Capetian court from the time that Hugh Capet usurped the throne from the Carolingians at the end of the tenth century.[21] Although the smoothness with which the Capetians held onto power is remarkable, nevertheless sufficient anti-Capetian feeling existed for several spiritual centres to feel compelled to defend the new royal dynasty by producing texts and crafting rituals designed to demonstrate the solid foundations of Capetian rule.[22] In return, the religious houses enjoyed various benefits from the royal court, ranging from economic incentives to ecclesiastical immunities.[23] Over the course of the eleventh century, such rewards were

---

[16] Cf. N. L. Paul, 'A Warlord's Wisdom: Literacy and Propaganda at the Time of the First Crusade', *Speculum*, 85 (2010), 534–66.

[17] See Robert's erasure of a list of four crusaders from the Île-de-France who, according to the *Gesta Francorum*, fled from the siege of Antioch: *GF*, pp. 56–7.

[18] *Cartulaires de l'abbaye de Molesme*, ed. J. Laurent, 2 vols (Paris, 1907–11), ii, no. 7, p. 13, in which a departing crusader records his intention to follow Hugh to the east as part of the 1101 expedition.

[19] Cf. J. A. Brundage, 'An Errant Crusader: Stephen of Blois', *Traditio*, 16 (1960), 390–2.

[20] RM *apologeticus sermo*, pp. 721–2.

[21] K. F. Werner, 'Die Legitimität der Kapetinger und die Entstehung des *Reditus regni Francorum ad stirpem Karoli*', *Die Welt als Geschichte*, 12 (1952), 214; M. Bloch, *Feudal Society*, trans. L.A. Manyon, 2 vols (Chicago, 1961), ii, 383–93.

[22] See e.g. 'Historia Francorum Senonensis', *MGH SS* ix, 364–9.

[23] Cf. J.-F. Lemarginer, 'Le monachisme et l'encadrement religieux des campagnes du royaume de France situées au nord de la Loire, de la fin du Xe à la fin du XIe siècle', in *Le istituzioni*

lucrative enough to foster a keen competition between leading monasteries across northern France for the king's attention. In addition to the well-documented textual programme at Saint-Benoît-sur-Loire (the abbey known as Fleury) and the creation of a royal necropolis at Saint-Denis, various religious institutions at Reims worked to make their city the centre of royal sacrality on the basis of the coronation ritual and, as concerns the present discussion, the abbey of Saint-Remi's possession of a phial containing holy chrism used in that ceremony.[24] On this point it is worth noting that Reims was unique among religious centres in that the city's link to the French kings was shared among several institutions. Thus, interest in the Capetians was not limited to a single religious house, but rather the city *en masse* was a place where the health of Capetian dynasticism was taken very seriously.

The special relationship between Reims and the French kings was old, beginning in the final years of the fifth century, when St Remigius, bishop of Reims, baptized Clovis and thus converted the king and (by extension) all of France to Roman Christianity.[25] According to popular legend, on the assigned day Remigius and Clovis both arrived at the church to celebrate the latter's baptism. As they reached the presbytery, the cleric carrying the holy chrism was blocked by the massive crowd from reaching the bishop. Remigius intervened with impassioned prayer, and suddenly a white dove appeared carrying in its beak a phial filled with holy chrism.[26] The baptism thus proceeded, and in the long term the sacrality of the French monarchy was forever attached to the city of Reims and its patron. Of course, Reims's eventual status as a sacred city was based on more than the legend of Clovis's baptism.[27] It took the work of Hincmar, archbishop of Reims from 845 until 882, to fully realize the city's exceptional role in French king-making. Through a carefully orchestrated translation of St Remigius's relics to a new home in the church of Saint-Remi and the production of a widely read Life of the saint, Hincmar introduced his patron to a national audience. Most crucially for our purposes is that part of this effort involved the reinforcement of the Clovis legend by means of coronation ritual. Specifically,

---

ecclesiastiche della 'Societas Christiana' dei secoli XI–XII: Diocesi, pievi e parrocchie (Miscellanea del centro di studi medioevali, 8; Milan, 1977), pp. 363–75; *idem*, 'L'exemption monastique et les origines de la réforme grégorienne', in *A Cluny: Congrès scientifique. Fêtes et cérémonies liturgiques en l'honneur des saints abbés Odon et Odilon 9-11 juillet 1949* (Dijon, 1950), pp. 288–340.

[24] For Fleury see B. H. Rosenwein, T. Head, and S. Farmer, 'Monks and their Enemies: A Comparative Approach', *Speculum*, 66 (1991), 779–80; R.-H. Bautier, 'La place de l'abbaye de Fleury-sur-Loire dans l'historiographie française du IX au XII siècle', in *Etudes ligériennes d'histoire et d'archéologie médiévales*, ed. R. Louis (Auxerre, 1975), pp. 23–33. For Saint-Denis and the Capetians see G. Spiegel, *The Chronicle Tradition of Saint-Denis: A Survey* (Brookline, 1978).

[25] Cf. C. Carozzi, 'Du baptême au sacre de Clovis selon les traditions rémoises', in *Clovis: histoire & mémoire, le baptême de Clovis, son echo à travers l'histoire*, ed. M. Rouche, 2 vols. (Paris, 1997), ii, 29–44; P. Depreux, 'Saint Remi et la royauté carolingienne', *Revue historique*, 578 (1991), 235–60.

[26] Le Goff, 'Reims, City of Coronation', pp. 196–8; M.-C. Isaïa, *Remi de Reims: Mémoire d'un saint, histoire d'une église* (Histoire religieuse de la France, 35; Paris, 2010), pp. 87–113.

[27] M. Bur, 'Reims, ville des sacres', in *Le sacre des rois: Actes du colloque international d'histoire sur les sacres et couronnements royaux* (Reims, 1985), pp. 39–48; R.-H. Bautier, 'Sacres et couronnements sous les Carolingiens et les premiers Capétiens', in his *Recherches sur l'histoire de la France médiévale: des Mérovingiens aux premiers Capétiens* (London, 1991), pp. 7–56.

while crowning Charles the Bald king of Lotharingia in Metz in 869, Hincmar for the first time highlighted his patron's role in Clovis's baptism and his church's role in establishing a continuous line of legitimate French kings.[28] In so doing, Hincmar effectively associated the legitimacy of French kingship with the coronation ceremony performed by the archbishop of Reims. And thus, from this point forward, all future archbishops of the city claimed the exclusive right to crown successive French kings. Part of this was a claim to act as dispenser of the holy chrism, which was housed in Saint-Remi and miraculously replenished before the coronation of each new monarch. The city's status as the giver of royal sacrality was thus based on the twin acts of coronation and unction.

The relationship was strengthened further over the course of the eleventh century, as the archbishop of Reims enjoyed an unprecedented monopoly over performing the coronation ritual of the Capetian kings. In June 1017 at Compiègne Archbishop Arnulf crowned Robert's son Hugh as associate king. Following Hugh's untimely death, in 1027 Ebles of Roucy celebrated the coronation of the future Henry I. And then on 23 May 1059 Archbishop Gervais celebrated the coronation of Philip I. The last of these neatly demonstrated Reims's growing status as an ecclesiastical-royal city by weaving together several of the elements discussed above into a single display of status. Archbishop Gervais presided over a group of bishops and abbots gathered to witness the young king's coronation. Notable among them was Abbot Herimar of Saint-Remi, who had likely overseen the transfer of the phial of oil from his abbey to the church of Our Lady, where the ceremony was to be performed. Henry I signalled his assent to the election of his son, at which point the crowd agreed. Gervais then placed the staff of St Remigius in Philip's hand, anointed him with the holy oil, and proclaimed him king.[29]

The period of Philip's reign marked a crucial step forward in the relationship between Reims and the Capetians. In December 1089, Pope Urban II officially recognized the rights of the archbishops 'to consecrate, anoint and ordain' both the king and queen, at once lending papal endorsement to the legend of Clovis's baptism and the modern coronation ceremony.[30] For his part, Philip demonstrated a clear affection for Reims, and particularly Saint-Remi.[31] In a telling act of 1090, the king remarked upon St Remigius's status as an apostle of the French and his decision to support his patron's house. The act notes that 'though we must defend the holy church as a whole, we more especially decided to grant our protection to St Remigius ... because he was chosen by God as apostle of the Franks, and because he exerts his patronage on our crown and kingship by

---

[28] Isaïa, *Remi de Reims*, pp. 575–91; J. M. Wallace-Hadrill, 'History in the Mind of Archbishop Hincmar', in *The Writing of History in the Middle Ages: Essays Presented to R. W. Southern*, ed. R. H. C. Davis and J. M. Wallace-Hadrill (Oxford, 1981), pp. 43–79.

[29] For the coronation ceremony see R. A. Jackson, *Ordines Coronationis Franciae: Texts and Ordines for the Coronation of Frankish and French Kings and Queens in the Middle Ages* (Philadelphia, 1995), pp. 217–32, esp. 230–2.

[30] P. Demouy, *Genèse d'une cathédrale: Les archevêques de Reims et leur église aux XIᵉ et XIIᵉ siècles* (Langres, 2005), pp. 564–74.

[31] Spiegel, *Chronicle Tradition*, p. 28.

apostolic authority'.[32] Against such a background, it was perfectly reasonable for religious institutions in Reims to expect a continued close relationship to the French kings, one that fundamentally turned on the right of the archbishop to celebrate the coronation ritual

Considering this last point, it is easy to see how and why the coronation of Louis VI by the archbishop of Sens at Orléans in 1108 introduced disequilibrium into this relationship and threatened Reims's continued status as a sacred city. The events surrounding the coronation are well recorded in contemporary sources. King Philip had been 'day to day losing ground' before he finally died at Melun near the end of July 1108.[33] Louis was present at his father's deathbed, and accompanied the 'grand procession' that escorted his body on the roughly 120-kilometre journey to Orléans, from where the king was taken to Fleury for burial.[34] Precedent would have dictated that Louis next summon the archbishop of Reims, Ralph the Green, to celebrate his coronation; indeed, if he had followed in his father's footsteps, Louis would have travelled to Reims for the ceremony. But neither of these conditions was met. Rather, Louis was crowned at Orléans on 3 August by the archbishop of Sens in a ceremony hastily organized by the famous canonist Bishop Ivo of Chartres.[35]

According to Abbot Suger of Saint-Denis, the reason for this was that a 'conspiracy of wicked men would have excluded him [from ascending the throne]' had Louis tried to make the journey to Reims.[36] Although he does not say for sure, this is most likely a reference to Louis's half-brother Philip, who had worked against the young prince for several years and who, in 1110, would lead an open rebellion against the king. Political expediency may have justified the breach of precedent in Suger's mind, but not so for the archbishop of Reims, Ralph the Green. Shortly after the ceremony took place, his representatives arrived at Orléans and argued that the ceremony was invalid.[37] They further demanded that it be performed again at Reims, under Ralph's direction. This was quite a diplomatic and political challenge for the young king to face, and it was only settled by the careful assuaging of Ivo of Chartres, who, in a series of letters, acknowledged the historical role of the archbishop of Reims as king-maker while at the same time outlining the special circumstances that had demanded Louis's speedy coronation at Orléans.[38] In the end, Ivo persuaded the pope of his argument, and Ralph was forced to agree. But this does not mean that the archbishop and his supporters were pleased. Indeed, from this point onward

---

[32] *Recueil des actes de Philippe Ier, roi de France (1059–1108)*, ed. M. Prou (Paris, 1908), no. 120, pp. 305–6.

[33] Suger, *Vie de Louis VI le Gros*, ed. and trans. H. Waquet (Les classiques de l'histoire de France au moyen âge, 11; Paris, 1929), pp. 80–2.

[34] *Ibid.*, p. 84; A. Erlande-Brandenburg, *Le Roi est mort: Étude sur les funérailles, les sepultures et les tombeaux des rois de France jusqu'à la fin du XIIIe siècle* (Geneva, 1975), pp. 73–5.

[35] Suger, *Vie de Louis VI*, pp. 84–8; OV, vi, 154.

[36] Suger, *Vie de Louis VI*, pp. 84–8.

[37] *Ibid.*

[38] Ivo of Chartres, Letter concerning the coronation of Louis VI, in *Recueil des historiens des Gaules et de la France*, ed. M. Bouquet *et al.*, 24 vols (Paris, 1737–1904), xv, 144.

they worked hard to ensure that such an affront to Reim's status was not suffered again.[39]

Scholars have hitherto not considered a potential link between the coronation of Louis VI and the pro-Capetian tone of the *Historia Iherosolimitana*. The primary reason for this is that the text has been typically given a *terminus ante quem* of 1106 or 1107, at least a year before Louis's coronation. The case for this date is based on a widespread belief that the *Gesta Francorum* and its Benedictine progeny were produced in co-ordination with Bohemond of Antioch's 1105–6 trip to Italy and France to recruit for an upcoming expedition against the Byzantine empire.[40] As the argument goes, Bohemond distributed copies of the *Gesta Francorum* as he made his way around northern France. Each of the Benedictine chroniclers then attempted to drum up further support for the Norman's endeavour by reworking the *Gesta* into more theologically refined works of propaganda, presumably helping potential recruits better understand the providential events in which they could participate. In the particular case of Robert, Carol Sweetenham has suggested that Reims's historical connection to the French kings may have motivated Robert's pro-Capetian insertions and deletions because in 1106 Bohemond had married Constance, Louis VI's younger sister.[41] Scholars have found further support for a date around 1107 in an 1108 German text known as the *Magdeburger Aufruf*, which Knoch carefully linked to the *Historia Iherosolimitana* though various textual parallels, thereby suggesting that Robert's text must have been written before 1108 to arrive in Germany by that date.[42] Recently both of these positions have been challenged. Nicholas Paul has convincingly demonstrated that the *Gesta Francorum* and its by-products were not examples of propaganda produced in the wake of Bohemond's 1105–6 trip to France.[43] Moreover, Marcus Bull and Damien Kempf, in their new edition of the *Historia Iherosolimitana*, point out that the textual parallels on which Knoch based his argument are, in fact, much thinner than previously realized.[44] Thus, we are free to consider a later date for the *Historia Iherosolimitana*, one that better explains the internal evidence of the text.

Bull and Kempf suggest a date of completion around 1110 and posit the possibility that Robert had seen an early draft of Guibert of Nogent's *Gesta Dei per Francos*, which was begun in 1107–8. This 1110 date raises the distinct possibility that Robert was substantially influenced by the 1108 coronation celebration at Orléans. Scholars know very little about Robert other than what he tells us in

[39] It is worth noting that they were successful in this effort, and Louis VI ultimately returned to family precedent, having his sons crowned at Reims.

[40] Cf. A. C. Krey, 'A Neglected Passage in the *Gesta* and its Bearing on the Literature of the First Crusade', in *The Crusades and Other Historical Essays Presented to Dana C. Munro by His Former Students*, ed. L. J. Paetow (New York, 1928), pp. 57–78.

[41] Sweetenham, *Robert the Monk's History of the First Crusade*, p. 6.

[42] P. Knoch, 'Kreuzzug und Siedlung: Studien zum Aufruf der Magdeburger Kirche von 1108', *Jahrbuch für Geschichte Mittel- und Ostdeutschlands*, 23 (1974), 6–21.

[43] Paul, 'A Warlord's Wisdom', 534–66.

[44] See *The Historia Iherosolimitana of Robert the Monk*, ed. D. Kempf and M. G. Bull (Woodbridge, 2013), pp. xxxv–xxxviii. I am grateful to Professor Bull for sharing his thoughts on this subject.

the *apologeticus sermo* that prefaces his text. Towards the end of that section, he notes that he was a monk at the monastery of Saint-Remi and was writing his text at a priory that belonged to the abbey.[45] This is important for the present discussion because, as we have seen, the abbey of Saint-Remi played a crucial role in the royal coronation, housing the phial of chrism and thus providing one of the most important ritual elements. In practice this means that the abbot of Saint-Remi had to be present to deliver the oil at each coronation. Historically, this is one of the crucial matrices of power that defined Saint-Remi's status in the French ecclesiastical hierarchy. Thus, it is reasonable to suppose that an event which challenged the right of the archbishop to crown the kings of France would cause an equal state of tension among the monks of Saint-Remi. Moreover, unlike a house like Saint-Denis, which had its status reaffirmed on a regular basis as numerous pilgrims passed through the royal necropolis, the coronation ceremony on which Reims built its sacred reputation was an act performed only infrequently, and thus the prospect of being upstaged was that much more injurious.

If Robert was partly motivated to write a pro-Capetian version of the First Crusade by the events surrounding the 1108 Orléans coronation, the question of what he hoped to achieve remains. Or posed more effectively, we might ask who he intended to read this text. It is possible, as Sweetenham posits, that the *Historia Iherosolimitana* was a royal commission, but this is unlikely.[46] For one thing, despite the large number of surviving manuscripts of the *Historia*, few of them emanate from the Capetian heartland, and almost none was produced before 1150.[47] If Robert intended to impress the royal court, he would probably have been sadly disappointed. In addition, since Hugh of Vermandois ultimately did fulfil his crusading vow as part of the 1101 crusade, had Philip or Louis commissioned the work they would have surely had Robert include details of this later expedition rather than fabricate his death at Constantinople; in many ways it would have been a much easier (and more believable) way of exonerating the royal brother.

A more likely explanation is that the *Historia Iherosolimitana* was directed at various high-ranking churchmen in northern France. It was this group, after all, who in 1110 needed reminding of the historical connection between Frankish/ French identity, Capetian legitimacy, and the city of Reims. Critically, these are all points on which Robert touches. As we saw above, Reims's status as *ville sacre* was based on its historic connection to the French king. By definition, therefore, it was also closely tied to the status of the French king himself as ruler of *Francia* and legitimate successor to Clovis. Anything that called either of these points into question would have been a potential problem, but by the same token anything that extolled the royal connection to St Remigius would be welcome.

I do not doubt that Robert hoped his text would enjoy a positive response among members of the royal court, but I also believe that the evidence suggests

[45] RM *apologeticus sermo*, p. 722.
[46] Sweetenham, *Robert the Monk's History of the First Crusade*, p. 6.
[47] See *The* Historia Iherosolimitana *of Robert the Monk*, ed. Kempf and Bull, pp. xlii–xlvii.

that he had a wider audience in mind. This explanation also fits with the limited details we know of Robert's career. Scholars have long speculated that Robert was actually the onetime Abbot Robert of Saint-Remi, though there is little concrete evidence to support this claim.[48] Whether true or not, Robert the author was indeed writing in a priory away from the main abbey, suggesting that he had fallen afoul of his brethren in Reims. The opportunity to further his monastery's status would have been an appealing one to a monk trying to remake his own reputation.

Members of the French church had been competing for the king's favour for the better part of the eleventh century. Reims had been a central figure in this competition, and following the events of the 1108 coronation the city's royal connection (and thus status as a sacred place) was unquestionably strained. Placed in such a political and cultural context, Robert the Monk's *Historia Iherosolimitana* is best approached not only as evidence of the reception of the First Crusade in the west, but also as an indication of the value of situating the crusading movement in ongoing and vigorous scholarly debates about medieval discourses of political authority, cultural transformation and social development. Indeed, it demonstrates that the study of the crusades is an optimal route into a comprehensive understanding of structures and operation of power in the High Middle Ages and should be studied accordingly.

---

[48] Sweetenham, *Robert the Monk's History of the First Crusade*, p. 3.

TOWARDS A TEXTUAL ARCHAEOLOGY OF
THE FIRST CRUSADE

Damien Kempf

The unusually rich repertoire of historical narratives prompted by the First Crusade remains, in many ways, uncharted territory. Primarily used by historians as mere 'sources', as repositories of facts, since the foundations of crusading history as a genre in the nineteenth century, these texts have shaped the constitution of a particular type of historiography that unceasingly seeks to tell and retell a story that was told in different forms by its contemporaries.[1] One can still clearly hear nowadays strong echoes of Heinrich von Sybel's programmatic agenda (back in the early 1840s) to 'penetrate into the facts and reach the *kernel* from inside'.[2]

Many questions thus remain to be answered with regard to the historiographical florescence that characterized the aftermath of the conquest of Jerusalem in July 1099. Recent research has shed more light on the contexts in which specific texts were composed, the social and cultural conditions governing their production, but few studies have yet tackled the question of their impact. Who exactly read these texts? What happened to them? What were their repercussions on the society, the culture, and the people of the period? How were they interpreted, and appropriated, by later readers? In other words, what is the story, or what are the stories, behind the story?

In order to address these issues, one needs to move away from a static conception of texts as data, and consider them instead in their dynamic function as literary works, shaped by their intersection with specific actors at different times. As Hans-Robert Jauss remarked, 'a literary work is not an object which stands by itself and which offers the same face to each reader in each period. It is not a monument which reveals its timeless essence in a monologue. It is much more like an orchestration which strikes ever new chords among its readers and which frees the text from the substance of the

---

[1]   See M. G. Bull and D. Kempf, 'L'histoire toute crue: La Première Croisade au miroir de son histoire', *Médiévales*, 58 (2010), 151–60.

[2]   H. von Sybel, *Geschichte des ersten Kreuzzugs* (Düsseldorf, 1841), p. 3. My emphasis.

words and makes it meaningful for the time.'[3] However, the orchestration may just be conducted in an empty hall and strike no chord at all; there is indeed no guarantee that a text, whatever its content and inner value, finds a particular audience: 'in contrast to a political event, a literary event has no lasting results which succeeding generations cannot avoid. It can continue to have an effect only if future generations still respond to it or rediscover it – if there are readers who take up the work of the past again or authors who want to imitate, outdo, or refute it.'[4]

Of all the narratives of the First Crusade, no one could have suspected that generations of readers would have so favourably reacted to Robert the Monk's *Historia Iherosolimitana*, and made it the undoubted best-seller chronicle of the events that led to the conquest of Jerusalem in 1099. The remarkable success of the text, which totals over eighty Latin manuscripts (to which one must add numerous translations in the vernacular), can be compared to widely known medieval writings such as Gregory of Tours's *Histories*, Vincent de Beauvais's *Speculum Historiae* or the *Grandes Chroniques de France*, and indicates that the text had a much more powerful impact than any other First Crusade narrative.[5] The geographical distribution of the *Historia* proves as unexpected as its wide dissemination: despite its heavy recasting of the crusade as a French achievement, the text, against all apparent odds, enjoyed a great success in the German territories from the mid-twelfth century onward, especially in circles close to the emperor Frederick Barbarossa (1152–90). How Robert's francocentric chronicle of the First Crusade became the focus of interest in Germany is the topic of this paper. But, before addressing this issue in detail, we first need to introduce the text and its author.

Compared to other chroniclers of the First Crusade, little is known about Robert. The only information we have derives from the prefatory autobiographical remarks in the *apologeticus sermo* that opens the *Historia Iherosolimitana*:

> A certain abbot called B., distinguished by his knowledge of literature and his upright behaviour, showed me a history which set out this material. Partly because it did not include the beginning of the crusade which was launched at the Council of Clermont ... partly because the composition was uncertain and unsophisticated in its style and expression ... he instructed me, since I had been present at the Council of Clermont, to add the beginning which was missing and improve its style for future readers.[6]

---

[3] H.-R. Jauss, 'Literary History as a Challenge to Literary Theory', *New Literary History*, 2 (1970), 10.

[4] *Ibid.*, 11.

[5] A complete list of Latin manuscripts (eighty-four in total), extending from the twelfth to the sixteenth centuries, is to be found in the introduction to the new edition of the text by Marcus Bull and myself: *The Historia Iherosolimitana of Robert the Monk* (Woodbridge, 2013), pp. lxv–lxxiv. In comparison, most chronicles of the First Crusade survive in between five and ten manuscripts.

[6] RM *apologeticus sermo*, p. 721. Unless otherwise noted, I draw upon C. Sweetenham's fine translation of the text: *Robert the Monk's History of the First Crusade* (Crusade Texts in Translation, 11; Aldershot, 2005), p. 75.

Acknowledging at the end of the *apologeticus sermo* that readers might wish to know who wrote the text, he goes on to identify himself as Robert, a monk of 'a cloister of a certain cell of St Remigius'.[7] The exact identities of both Robert and the abbot B., on the orders of whom Robert composed the *Historia Iherosolimitana*, prove problematic. We know that the abbey of Saint-Remi was, between 1096 and 1097, ruled by a Robert, a former monk of the abbey of Marmoutier. Robert appears to have been elected contrary to the wishes of Bernard, his abbot at Marmoutier, and the dispute between the two men eventually led to Robert's excommunication at the council of Reims in 1097. It was only thanks to the support of influential ecclesiastical figures such as Abbot Baldric of Bourgueil that the decision was reversed by Pope Urban II, and Robert henceforth joined the priory of Saint-Oricle at Sénuc, which belonged to Saint-Remi. On the assumption that Robert the author was the Robert, abbot of Saint-Remi, it would be difficult to identify abbot B. with Bernard of Marmoutier given their antagonistic relationship. Baldric in fact appears to be a more probable option. But it could as well be that Robert the author was only a monk of Saint-Remi working on behalf of his abbot (the cartulary of the abbey lists a couple of Roberts amongst the monks belonging to the community in the early twelfth century).[8]

The date of the composition of the text is as uncertain as its author's identity. It is usually believed to have been composed in the years 1106–7, partly because of alleged textual relationships between the *Historia* and the so-called *Magdeburger Aufruf*, a letter written in 1107 in the name of the archbishop of Magdeburg and other Saxon prelates and princes to a number of German ecclesiastical and lay magnates. However, a close examination of the two texts does not sustain such a hypothesis. Moreover, the way in which Robert refers to King Philip I of France (d. 1108) in the past tense suggests a later date, c. 1109–10.[9]

At any rate, the text that Robert set out to revise because of its 'unsophisticated style' most likely refers to the *Gesta Francorum*, which Guibert of Nogent and Baldric of Bourgueil also undertook to amend around the same time. Like his two contemporaries, Robert did much more than simply correct the prose of his model. In addition to including Urban II's sermon at the Council of Clermont in November 1095, which is absent from the *Gesta*, he reshaped the entire narrative in terms of two governing principles. First, Robert sets the events of the First Crusade in a strong theological framework, interpreting the expedition, or rather 'pilgrimage' as he refers to it, as God's will: 'Since the creation of the world,' he writes in the prologue, 'what more miraculous undertaking has been there, other than the mystery of the redeeming Cross, than what was achieved in our own

---

[7] RM *sermo apologeticus*, p. 722; trans. Sweetenham, *Robert the Monk's History*, p. 75.

[8] Cartulary of the abbey, Archives départementales de la Marne, 56 H 87, fols. 2v–3. On the thorny issue of the authorship of the text, see *The* Historia Iherosolimitana *of Robert the Monk*, ed. Kempf and Bull, pp. xvii–xxxiv.

[9] See G. Constable, 'Early Crusading in Eastern Germany: The Magdeburg Charter of 1107/8', in his *Crusaders and Crusading in the Twelfth Century* (Farnham, 2008), pp. 197–214. Cf. *The* Historia Iherosolimitana *of Robert the Monk*, ed. Kempf and Bull, pp. xxxv–xxxviii. The text is edited by W. Wattenbach in 'Handschriftliches', *Neues Archiv der Gesellschaft für ältere deutsche Geschichtskunde*, 7 (1882), 624–6.

time by this journey of our own people to Jerusalem? For this was not the work of men: it was the work of God.'[10] The most significant events, and in particular the conquest of Jerusalem, which is presented as the ultimate goal of the crusaders, are explained in the light of Old Testament precedents, and understood as the typological realizations of biblical prophecies. Quoting the Book of Isaiah, Robert explains: 'We have found this and many other things in the books of the prophets which fit exactly the context of the liberation of the city in our era.'[11]

Interpreted as a major event within the history of salvation, the 'liberation' of Jerusalem from Muslim domination was also achieved because of the Franks' special status, as the prologue, which cleverly alters Psalm 33:12, asserts: 'What king or prince could subjugate so many towns and castles, if not the blessed nations of the Franks whose God is the Lord, and the people whom he has chosen for his own inheritance?'[12] As God's chosen people, the Franks thus appeared as the natural leaders of the expedition that led them to conquer the city of Christ: 'The earthly Jerusalem was forsaken by God in our era and held in odium because of the evil of its inhabitants. But when it so pleased God, he led the Frankish race from the ends of the earth with the intention that they should free her from the filthy Gentiles.'[13]

The Franks as the chosen people of God is a recurrent theme in the narrative. Moreover, their prestigious Carolingian ancestry is on several occasions asserted; first, and significantly, in the words of Urban II, whose sermon at Clermont launching the crusade is the first extended narrative set-piece in the *Historia*: 'May the deeds of your ancestors move you and spur your souls to manly courage – the worth and greatness of Charlemagne, his son Louis and your other kings who destroyed the pagan kingdoms and brought them within the bounds of Christendom.'[14] Following the pope's speech, the text presents Godfrey of Bouillon, one of the leaders of the First Crusade and the first Latin ruler of Jerusalem in 1099, as a highly distinguished soldier who followed 'the same route as Charlemagne the incomparable king of the Franks once followed on his pilgrimage to Constantinople'.[15]

The overtly Frankish flavour of the text is hardly surprising given the historical ties uniting the abbey of Saint-Remi to the French monarchy. By presenting the expedition to Jerusalem as the re-enactment of Charlemagne's 'pilgrimage' to Constantinople, and celebrating the greatness of the Frankish emperor as a model for the crusaders, Robert was echoing contemporary attempts to attach Capetian rulership to the prestige of the Carolingian dynasty, thereby legitimizing the claims of the royal dynasty to expand their rule over a much divided kingdom of western Francia. Even though the French king, Philip I, had not taken the cross after his excommunication by the pope (an event Robert significantly leaves unmentioned), some influential members of Philip's family

[10] RM *prologus*, p. 723; trans. Sweetenham, *Robert the Monk's History*, p. 77.
[11] RM ix.26, p. 882; trans. Sweetenham, *Robert the Monk's History*, pp. 213–14.
[12] RM *prologus*, p. 723; trans. Sweetenham, *Robert the Monk's History*, p. 77.
[13] RM ix.26, p. 882; trans. Sweetenham, *Robert the Monk's History*, p. 213.
[14] RM i.1, p. 728; trans. Sweetenham, *Robert the Monk's History*, p. 80.
[15] RM i.5, p. 732; trans. Sweetenham, *Robert the Monk's History*, p. 84.

participated in the expedition, such as his brother, Hugh the Great, whose relatively mediocre fate (he departed from the crusade in the summer of 1098) is turned by Robert into a heroic tale.[16] Introduced as 'the standard-bearer' of the French army, Hugh's deeds are always interpreted as examples of royal military strength and just conduct, thereby displaying the intrinsic virtues of the Capetian line. As Robert notes: 'Hugh was a credit to the royal blood from which he sprang because of the integrity of his conduct, his refined bearing and his courage.'[17] Even Bohemond of Taranto, the famous southern Italian Norman leader who had allied himself with the Capetian monarchy by marrying Philip's daughter in 1106, now exemplifies the grandeur of the French: 'He had inherited the highest principles from his French father; but they were tainted by elements from his Apulian mother.'[18]

The rewriting of Hugh's deeds, and the particular attention devoted to members of castellan families from the royal principality, firmly connect the composition of Robert's *Historia* with the royal court.[19] The abbey of Saint-Remi was dedicated to Remigius, the saint believed to have brought about the conversion of the Frankish king Clovis in the fifth century.[20] The abbey kept the holy ampulla, vessel of the oil supposedly sent from heaven with which Clovis was anointed, a miraculous event that distinguished French kings from the other monarchs of western Christendom, making the king of France God's vicegerent. Since the investiture of Hugh Capet in 987, the archbishops of Reims had been overseeing the coronation of the Capetian line.[21] This privilege was confirmed by Urban II in a letter of 1089 to Rainold, archbishop of Reims:

> First and foremost we confer upon you and your successors the power to conse-
> crate the kings of France; so that, just as St Remigius, having converted Clovis to
> the faith, is known to have instituted the first Christian king in this kingdom, so

---

[16]   See M. G. Bull, 'The Capetian Monarchy and the Early Crusade Movement: Hugh of Vermandois and Louis VII', *Nottingham Medieval Studies*, 40 (1996), 39–42, 43; L. Russo, 'Richerche sull'"Historia Iherosolimitana" di Roberto di Reims', *Studi Medievali*, 3rd ser. 43 (2002), 663–71; J. L. Naus, 'The French Royal Court and the Memory of the First Crusade', *Nottingham Medieval Studies*, 55 (2011), 71–4.

[17]   RM ii.1, p. 739; trans. Sweetenham, *Robert the Monk's History*, pp. 89–90.

[18]   RM viii.15, p. 855; trans. Sweetenham, *Robert the Monk's History*, p. 191. Contrary to what Sweetenham suggests, the comment is not a later addition but part of the main text.

[19]   Compare, for instance, Robert's treatment of William the Carpenter, viscount of Melun, who is said to come 'from royal stock' and have 'acquired the name of "Carpenter" because nobody wanted to take him on in battle', and whose desertion from the battlefield is played down (RM iv.12, pp. 781–2; trans. Sweetenham, *Robert the Monk's History*, pp. 127–8), with Guibert of Nogent's negative depiction of a man 'powerful in words, but less so in action...a man who set out to do things too great for him'. When he joined the crusade he 'took from his poor neighbours the little that they had to provide himself shamefully with provisions for the journey': GN iv.7, pp. 178–9; trans. R. Levine, *The Deeds of God Through the Franks* (Woodbridge, 1997), p. 79.

[20]   J. Goy, 'Les reliques de saint Rémi apôtre des Francs', in *Clovis: histoire et mémoire. Le baptême de Clovis, son écho à travers l'histoire: Actes du colloque international d'histoire de Reims*, ed. M. Rouche (Paris, 1997), pp. 649–57.

[21]   See J. Le Goff, 'Reims, City of Coronation', in *The Construction of the French Past: Realms of Memory*, ed. L. D. Kritzman, trans. A. Goldhammer, 3 vols (New York, 1996), iii, 193–251.

you and your successors, who serve in the place of St Remigius in the church of Reims by God's will, may perform the function of anointing and ordaining the king or the queen.[22]

Philip I showed a remarkable devotion to the saint. The fact that he called his son Louis suggests that he aimed to make the latter a new Clovis; it is noteworthy that Louis's first diploma (he was not even nine years old) was for Saint-Remi in 1090.[23] It is in fact possible that the Capetian perspective of Robert's *Historia* was in part a reaction against the decision by Louis, upon succeeding Philip on the throne, to be consecrated not at Reims, as was customary, but at Orléans, thereby threatening to weaken the historical ties between the Capetian dynasty and the saint.

In light of the *Historia*'s explicit agenda to promote the Capetian monarchy, it might, at first sight, seem all the more surprising to note the apparent absence of influence that Robert's text had on subsequent royal historiography. In the eleventh and early twelfth century, there was as yet no centralized effort to write the history of the dynasty. Rather than at court, such history was written in different monastic centres, the most important of which were Saint-Remi, Fleury and Saint-Denis. Already by the final decades of the eleventh century, the monks of Saint-Denis had crafted a legendary 'Journey of Charlemagne to Jerusalem' (*Descriptio qualiter Karolus Magnus*), an account of Charlemagne's supposed expedition to liberate Jerusalem and receive the imperial crown from Constantinople.[24] In addition, the common destiny shared by the monastery and the French crown was materially symbolized by the identification of the royal banner (the so-called oriflamme), which the French kings received from the monastery as its vassals for the Vexin, with Charlemagne's flag, described in the *Chanson de Roland* as an 'orie flambe'.[25] When Louis VI faced the threat of an invasion by Henry V of Germany in 1124, he went to Saint-Denis and declared Dionysius the special patron of the realm, an obvious attempt to dislodge St

---

[22] Urban II, 'Epistolae et privilegia', *PL* cli, 310: 'Primam praeterea praecipuamque tibi tuisque successoribus potestatem contradimus Francorum reges consecrandi: ut sicut B. Remigius ad fidem Clodoveo converso primum illi regno regem christianum instituisse cognoscitur; ita tu quoque tuique successores, qui ejusdem S. Remigii vice in Remensi ecclesia Domino disponente fungimini, ungendi regis et ordinandi sive reginae prima potestate fungamini.'

[23] See M.-C. Isaïa, *Remi de Reims: Mémoire d'un saint, histoire d'une Église* (Histoire religieuse de la France, 35; Paris, 2010), p. 725 n. 3.

[24] *Descriptio qualiter Karolus Magnus clavum et coronam Domini a Constantinopoli Aquisgrani detulerit qualiterque Karolus Calvus hec ad Sanctum Dyonisium retulerit*, ed. G. Rauschen, in *Die Legende Karls des Grossen im 11. und 12. Jahrhundert* (Leipzig, 1890), pp. 103–25. On the text, see R. Grosse, 'Reliques du Christ et foires de Saint-Denis au XIe siècle: à propos de la *Descriptio clavi et corone Domini*', *Revue d'histoire de l'Église de France*, 87 (2001), 357–8; idem, *Saint-Denis, zwischen Adel und König: Die Zeit vor Suger (1053–1122)* (Beihefte der Francia, 57; Stuttgart, 2002), pp. 42–54; M. Gabriele, 'The Provenance of the *Descriptio Qualiter Karolus Magnus*: Remembering the Carolingians in the Entourage of King Philip I (1060–1108) before the First Crusade', *Viator*, 39 (2008), 93–118.

[25] See G. M. Spiegel, *The Past as Text: The Theory and Practice of Medieval Historiography* (Baltimore, 1997), p. 124.

Remigius from that position.[26] Similarly, Louis VII, before his departure for the Second Crusade in 1147, went to Saint-Denis to receive the oriflamme as his war standard, as reported by Odo of Deuil, Louis's chaplain.[27] By the twelfth century, the monastery of Saint Denis had acquired a political significance within the symbolism of the French monarchy that came to rival and, in many ways, to displace the abbey of Saint-Remi, even to the extent of its arguing that the royal coronation should be held at Saint-Denis, an attempt that never succeeded despite the fact that the abbey had custody of the royal crown. The abbey's aggressive propaganda, which aimed at making Saint-Denis the official focus of Capetian identity and historical memory, might thus have overshadowed contemporary efforts by the monks of Saint-Remi to establish themselves in a similar position. This would help to explain why Robert's text found so little echo in pro-Capetian historiography (from the twelfth century onwards largely produced at the abbey of Saint-Denis) and account for the apparent absence of early French manuscripts of the *Historia* in places closely connected with the French monarchy. In this connection, it is worth noting that the lavish manuscript (Bibliothèque Nationale de France, lat. 14378) that was presented to King Louis VII by William, a veteran of the 1096–9 campaign, included the First Crusade narratives of Fulcher of Chartres and Raymond of Aguilers and the history of the principality of Antioch by Walter the Chancellor, but not Robert's *Historia*, which moreover does not appear to have been consulted by Odo of Deuil, Abbot Suger's confidant, as part of his preparations for the Second Crusade.[28]

In contrast to the relative insignificance of Robert's text within the corpus of Capetian historiography, one finds an unexpected and indeed triumphant progress of the *Historia* through German-speaking areas from the mid-twelfth century onwards. Most early German manuscripts are to be found in Bavaria, and in particular in newly-established communities connected with the Cistercian movement such as Zwettl, Sittich and Schäftlarn.[29] It appears probable that it was thanks to the Cistercians that Robert's text found its way so quickly from Reims into Germany. We have strong evidence of an early French Cistercian interest in the *Historia Iherosolimitana* in the twelfth century, as is shown by copies produced at the major communities of Cîteaux, Clairvaux and Orval. Such an

---

[26] Suger, *Vie de Louis VI le Gros*, ed. and trans. H. Waquet (Les classiques de l'histoire de France au moyen âge, 11; Paris, 1929), p. 220.

[27] Odo of Deuil, *De Profectione Ludovici VII in Orientem*, ed. and trans. V. C. Berry (New York, 1948), p. 16.

[28] See J. Rubenstein, 'Putting History to Use: Three Crusade Chronicles in Context', *Viator*, 35 (2004), 131–68; J. P. Phillips, 'Odo of Deuil's *De profectione Ludovici VII in Orientem* as a Source for the Second Crusade', in *The Experience of Crusading, Volume One: Western Approaches*, ed. M. G. Bull and N. J. Housley (Cambridge, 2003), pp. 83–4. It is also important to point out that, unlike other chronicles, Robert's does not seem to have been reworked by descendants of prominent French nobles who participated in the expedition.

[29] The abbey of Schäftlarn housed a community of Premonstratensians, an order of canons that was heavily influenced by Cistercian ideals and organizational practice. For an overview of Cistercian monasteries in Bavaria, see F. Prinz, 'Die innere Entwicklung: Staat, Gesellschaft, Kirche, Wirtschaft', in *Handbuch der bayerischen Geschichte: I: Das Alte Bayern*, ed. M. Spindler (Munich, 1981), pp. 487–8.

interest can be explained by the strong Cistercian involvement, and in particular the role of their leader, Bernard of Clairvaux, in the promotion of the Second Crusade (1145–9). In Germany, Bernard's relentless preaching persuaded King Conrad III, at first reluctant because of conflicts with the papacy and his nobility, to take the cross.[30]

The German participation in the crusade and the active role taken by the Cistercians in its preparation help to account for the presence of the *Historia Iherosolimitana* in Germany.[31] One figure in particular appears to have been instrumental in the dissemination of the text: Otto of Freising, Conrad III's half-brother, who was one of the most fervent advocates of the Second Crusade in Germany. Destined for a clerical career, Otto had studied in Paris before joining the Cistercian community of Morimond, in Champagne, in the early 1130s; he subsequently rose to become its abbot. Morimond was one of the four principal daughter houses of Cîteaux along with La Ferté, Clairvaux and Pontigny. The abbey grew rapidly and established numerous foundations in other countries. In Germany, it was responsible for the creation of new communities in Bavaria, where we find several manuscript copies of Robert's text.[32] It was precisely for Bavaria, where he had been appointed bishop of Freising, that Otto left Morimond in 1138. It would seem to be no coincidence that the earliest datable German manuscript of Robert's text was produced by a religious community (Reichersberg, then under the leadership of the renowned theologian Gerhoh) with close connections to Otto.[33]

Nor is it coincidental to find an important copy of Robert's text produced at Schäftlarn, an abbey which had been reformed by Otto. This manuscript, now preserved in the Vatican Library (Vat. Lat. 2001), was offered by Provost Henry to Frederick Barbarossa on the eve of the emperor's departure for the Third Crusade. On the colour frontispiece, the German monarch is depicted as a crusader, with his chest emblazoned with the cross. On his left, Henry is humbly presenting the manuscript to the emperor. The inscription surrounding the image urges Barbarossa to fight the Muslim leader Saladin, who had captured

---

[30] See G. Constable, 'The Second Crusade as Seen by Contemporaries', in his *Crusaders and Crusading in the Twelfth Century* (Farnham, 2008), pp. 229–300. A different view is expressed by J. P. Phillips, 'Papacy, Empire and the Second Crusade', in *The Second Crusade: Scope and Consequences*, ed. J. P. Phillips and M. Hoch (Manchester, 2001), pp. 15–31.

[31] For the German response to the Second Crusade, see J. P. Phillips, *The Second Crusade: Extending the Frontiers of Christendom* (New Haven, 2007), pp. 80–1, 83–97, 102, 128–35.

[32] See E. Krausen, 'Morimund, die Mutterabtei der bayerischen Zisterzen', *Analecta Sacri Ordinis Cisterciensis*, 14 (1958), 334–45; M. Parisse, 'La formation de la branche de Morimond', in *Unanimité et diversité cisterciennes*, ed. N. Bouter (Saint-Étienne, 2000), pp. 87–101. See also J. Burton and J. Kerr, *The Cistercians in the Middle Ages* (Woodbridge, 2011), pp. 36–7.

[33] The Benedictine abbey of Reichersberg was a dependency of the bishopric of Passau, whose bishop at the time of the Second Crusade, Conrad, was Otto of Freising's brother. For the provenance of the manuscript, see M. Tischler, 'Handschriftenfunde zu den Werken Liudprands von Cremona in bayerischen und österreichischen Bibliotheke', *Zeitschrift für bayerische Landesgeschichte*, 64 (2001), 59–82. Sylvia Schein remarks that Gerhoh, the provost of Reichersberg between 1132 and 1169, uses Robert's *Historia* when referring to the conquest of Jerusalem in his commentary on the Psalms: S. Schein, *Gateway to the Heavenly City: Crusader Jerusalem and the Catholic West (1099–1187)* (Aldershot, 2005), p. 31.

Jerusalem after a long siege on 2 October 1187.[34] This is a famous image, which is often reproduced in books relating to Barbarossa and the crusades. Less known, however, are the verses that close the manuscript, and which were added by the same hand following the end of Robert's text. Henry is directly addressing the emperor: if the quality of the manuscript, he says, does not correspond to courtly standards, it is because it was made in haste as Henry did not want to delay the exercise of royal power – that is, he did not want to delay Barbarossa's départure for the Holy Land.[35] He implores the emperor to accept the book and to follow the same successful path as the leader of the First Crusade Godfrey of Bouillon. One could hardly find a better expression of the symbolic power of books as both embodiment and proclamation of authority.

The terrible fate of the German contingent at the outset of the Second Crusade, comprehensively defeated by the Turks in October 1147, must have left a bitter memory in the mind of the young Frederick Barbarossa, who had accompanied his uncle Conrad III, and certainly accounts for his powerful commitment to promoting the Third Crusade (1189–92).[36] News of Saladin's conquest of much of the Latin East had prompted a papal call for a new crusade, to which Barbarossa responded immediately. This happened just after the emperor had finally come to terms with Pope Clement III, following several decades of tense relations between the empire and the papacy. 'By the end of March 1188, Frederick had defeated his enemies on every front. At home, all resistance had come to an end, in Italy there was no city or noble who could have challenged the emperor's might ... and the new pope was a loyal ally.'[37] Though at an advanced age (he was by now in his sixties), the emperor was then in a strong political position – stronger than any of his predecessors – to focus his attention on the disastrous situation in the Holy Land. He devoted much time and energy to gathering together a formidable army, overshadowing both Philip Augustus of France and Henry II of England by the scale of his preparations for the crusade. Barbarossa's army was far different from those seen previously on the major crusades: more structured, more experienced and better disciplined. It was also

---

[34] The complete inscription reads: 'Hic est depictus Rome Cesar Fridericus/Signifier Invictus celorum Regis amicus Cesar magnificus pius augustus Fridericus de terra domini pellat gentem Saladini Heinricus prepositus amen/Nulli pacificum Sarraceno Fridericum dirigat iste liber ubi sit locus a nece liber.' For the date of the manuscript, see *The Historia Iherosolimitana of Robert the Monk*, ed. Kempf and Bull, pp. xlv–xlvii.

[35] Fol. 68v: 'Ne studio segni fieret dilatio regni/Veloci dextra codex hic intus et extra/Est consummatus, non ut decuit decoratus/Aule regali nichilominus imperiali.'

[36] On Frederick Barbarossa, see J. Ehlers, 'Friedrich I. Barbarossa (1152–1190)', in *Die deutschen Herrscher des Mittelalters: Historische Portraits von Heinrich I. bis Maximilian I*, ed. B. Schneidmüller and S. Weinfurter (Munich, 2003), pp. 258–71; and now K. Görich, *Friedrich Barbarossa: Eine Biographie* (Munich, 2011). On Barbarossa and the crusade, see R. Hiestand, 'Kingship and Crusade in Twelfth-Century Germany', in *England and Germany in the High Middle Ages*, ed. A. Haverkamp and H. Vollrath (Oxford, 1996), pp. 235–65; *idem*, '"Precipua tocius christianismi columpna": Barbarossa und der Kreuzzug', in *Friedrich Barbarossa: Handlungsspielräume und Wirkungsweisen des Staufischen Kaisers*, ed. A. Haverkamp (Vorträge und Forschungen 40; Sigmaringen, 1992), pp. 51–108; E. Eickhoff, *Friedrich Barbarossa im Orient: Kreuzzug und Tod Friedrichs I.* (Tübingen, 1977).

[37] M. Pacaut, *Frederick Barbarossa*, trans. A. J. Pomerans (London, 1970), p. 194.

probably the largest crusading army ever to leave Europe, with tens of thousands of men. Despite the careful preparation and large numbers of troops, however, the emperor was never to complete or return from the expedition, dying on 10 June 1190 on his way to Antioch.

While scholars have emphasized Barbarossa's lifelong yearning to participate in a new crusade following the failure of the Second Crusade, they often neglect to mention that his reign was, right from the day of his coronation on 9 March 1152, already dedicated to the idea of crusading. As Otto of Freising, who was the emperor's uncle and the author of his biography, the *Gesta Friderici imperatoris*, reports, it was 'on that Sunday on which *Laetare Jerusalem* is sung that he was escorted by the bishops from the palace [of Aachen] to the church of the blessed Mary', and was there crowned by Arnulf, archbishop of Cologne, 'seated on the throne of the realm of the Franks that was placed in that same church by Charles the Great'.[38] After the liberation of Jerusalem in 1099, the liturgy of the Sunday of 'Laetare Jerusalem' (the fourth Sunday in Lent, the introit of the mass for which begins 'Rejoice Jerusalem') had been adapted to celebrate the feast of the conquest of the Holy City, on 15 July.[39] The Sunday of 'Laetare' therefore became closely associated with the crusade. From the very beginning, then, imperial authority, construed as the renewal of the Carolingian empire, was connected with the idea of crusading. Significantly, it was also on that day that Barbarossa and many nobles took the cross, in the presence of a papal legate, at the Diet of Mainz in 1188.

The contested canonization of Charlemagne was also part of Barbarossa's efforts to establish a new *sacrum imperium*.[40] After the transfer of the relics of the Three Kings (or Magi) from Milan to Cologne in 1164, Barbarossa arranged for Charlemagne to be canonized with great pomp by the antipope Paschal (III) in 1165, in Aachen, an event that was probably orchestrated by Rainald of Dassel, archbishop of Cologne and archchancellor of Italy, and one of the emperor's most influential advisers.[41] The publically staged canonization of Charlemagne – Barbarossa is said to have himself elevated the relics of the king – was followed by the composition of a new *Vita Karoli Magni*.[42]

[38] Otto of Freising, *The Deeds of Frederick Barbarossa*, trans. C. C. Mierow (New York, 1953), pp. 116–17.

[39] See Schein, *Gateway to the Heavenly City*, pp. 20–3.

[40] A. A. Latowsky, *Emperor of the World: Charlemagne and the Construction of Imperial Authority, 800–1229* (Ithaca, 2013), p. 281; R. Folz, *Le Souvenir et la légende de Charlemagne dans l'Empire germanique médiéval* (Paris, 1950), p. 207.

[41] On Rainald of Dassel, see now P. Godman, 'Transmontani: Frederick Barbarossa, Rainald of Dassel, and Cultural Identity in the German Empire', *Beiträge zur Geschichte der deutschen Sprache und Literatur*, 132 (2010), 200–29, with bibliography.

[42] See L. Vones, 'Heiligsprechung und Tradition: Die Kanonisation Karls des Großen 1165, die Aachener Karlsvita und der Pseudo-Turpin', in *Jakobus und Karl der Große: Von Einhards Karlsvita zum Pseudo-Turpin*, ed. K. Herbers (Tübingen, 2003), pp. 89–106; R. Folz, 'La chancellerie de Frédéric Ier et la canonisation de Charlemagne', *Le moyen âge*, 70 (1964), 13–31; J. Petersohn, 'Saint-Denis – Westminster – Aachen: Die Karls-Translatio von 1165 und ihre Vorbilder', *Deutsches Archiv für Erforschung des Mittelalters*, 31 (1975), 420–54; B. Bastert, 'Heros and Heiliger: Literarische Karlbilder im mittelalterlichen Frankreich und Deustchland', in *Karl der Große und das Erbe der Kulturen*, ed. F.-R. Erkens (Berlin, 2001), p. 208. The *Vita Karoli Magni* has been edited by G. Rauschen in *Die Legende*, pp. 17–93.

Interestingly, the interplay between these two important aspects of the emperor's strategy to legitimate and to enhance his imperial authority – his crusading aspirations and the sacralization of the Carolingian emperor – is reflected in some contemporary manuscripts that associate Robert's *Historia Iherosolimitana* with Einhard's *Life* of Charlemagne. This textual combination is first found in the Viennese manuscript produced at Reichersberg in the early 1150s, and appears again in another manuscript produced in the late twelfth century (St Gallen, Stiftsbibliothek, 547). Even though Barbarossa never managed to reach Jerusalem, his legacy as a devoted and vigorous leader of the Third Crusade left a lasting imprint on the medieval European imagination, a legacy mirrored in the remarkable success of Robert's *Historia Iherosolimitana* in the German empire, where it was widely disseminated up to the sixteenth century. The close connection between the emperor and the *Historia* was hermeneutically 'sealed' in a manuscript produced at the abbey of Sittich in the early 1180s (Wolfenbüttel, Herzog August Bibliothek, Helmst. 206). The manuscript originally contained Robert's chronicle and Otto's *Deeds of Frederick Barbarossa*, making it the earliest extant copy of the emperor's biography, to which a later twelfth-century scribe added the *Epistola de morte Friderici*, a short letter composed immediately after the death of the emperor that describes the crusaders' journey through Asia Minor.[43]

Despite its obvious Capetian overtones, readers such as Gerhoh of Reichersberg, Otto of Freising or Frederick Barbarossa undoubtedly found in Robert's *Historia* an echo of contemporary issues that ensured it a significant impact in Germany. 'Oppressed by so poignant a memory of the past, so violent an onslaught of the present woes, and so great a fear of future perils' (as Otto of Freising puts it), these men always regarded the new expeditions to the east in the light of what their illustrious predecessors had achieved, a perception informed by their reading of Robert's theologico-political view of the First Crusade, understood as a miraculous event led by the chosen people of the Franks.[44] As the 1099 conquest of Jerusalem remained a forceful symbol of the united Christian forces against the Muslim infidels, the *Historia Iherosolimitana*, along with the other narratives of the crusade, contributed to the development of crusading ideas in western Europe and to the construction of a mythical vision of Jerusalem, 'navel of the Earth' and 'indestructible glory of the heavenly kingdom'.[45]

---

[43] Edited by A. Chroust, *Quellen zur Geschichte des Kreuzzuges Kaiser Friedrichs I* (MGH Scriptores rerum Germanicarum, n.s. 5; Berlin, 1928), pp. 173–8. Trans. G. A. Loud, *The Crusade of Frederick Barbarossa: The History of the Expedition of the Emperor Frederick and Related Texts* (Crusade Texts in Translation, 19; Farnham, 2010), pp. 169–72. We have only two manuscripts of the *Epistola*, the second being Turin, Accademia delle Scienze, 193 (the text is to be found on fols. 1–3v).

[44] Otto of Freising, *The Two Cities: A Chronicle of Universal History to the Year 1146 A. D.*, trans. C. C. Mierow, ed. A. P. Evans and C. Knapp, rev. K. F. Morrison (New York, 2002), p. 445.

[45] RM i.2, p. 729; trans. Sweetenham, *Robert the Monk's History*, p. 81. On Jerusalem during the crusading period, see Schein, *Gateway to the Heavenly City*; A. H. Bredero, 'Jerusalem in the West', in his *Christendom and Christianity in the Middle Ages: The Relations Between Religion, Church, and Society* (Grand Rapids, MI, 1994), pp. 79–104; G. Stroumsa, 'Mystical Jerusalems', in *Jerusalem: Its Sanctity and Centrality in Judaism, Christianity and Islam*, ed. L. I. Levine (New York, 1998), pp. 349–70.

ROBERT THE MONK AND HIS SOURCE(S)

Marcus Bull

This paper considers the written source material that was used by the author known to us as Robert the Monk when he composed his account of the First Crusade, the *Historia Iherosolimitana*.[1] Its aim is to throw some light on where this texts sits within the patterns of influences and borrowings that connect many of the narratives about the First Crusade written in the Latin Christian tradition. A further aim, though constraints of space preclude a detailed examination, is to suggest that the close study of texts such as that by Robert, a work that both drew upon a guide source and itself served as a source in its turn, requires an in-depth consideration of questions of reader response and authorial creativity if we wish to understand the dynamics that energized the burst of writing about the First Crusade in the early decades of the twelfth century.[2]

It goes without saying that before a text can inform the writing of another work, it must be read. But read in what ways? Those who read a narrative of the First Crusade with the specific intention of themselves crafting another text on the same subject cannot be taken as a representative sample of all its readers, for they must have brought to the act of reading unusually heightened sensitivities as to matters of both content and form. The well-known derogatory remarks made by Baldric of Bourgueil, Robert the Monk and Guibert of Nogent about their guide text, what we know as the *Gesta Francorum*, represent an unusually overt but probably not atypical set of authorial postures with respect to material that is being effaced and replaced; the writers of what were

---

[1] See *The Historia Iherosolimitana of Robert the Monk*, ed. D. Kempf and M. G. Bull (Woodbridge, 2013), esp. pp. ix–xli, liv–lvi.

[2] For the narrative outpouring that followed the First Crusade, see R. Hiestand, 'Il cronista medievale e il suo pubblico: alcuni osservazioni in margine alla storiografia delle crociate', *Annali della Facoltà di Lettere e Filosofia dell'Università di Napoli*, n.s. 15 (1984–5), 207–27; S. B. Edgington 'The First Crusade: Reviewing the Evidence', in *The First Crusade: Origins and Impact*, ed. J. P. Phillips (Manchester, 1997), pp. 55–77; J. Flori, *Chroniqueurs et propagandistes: Introduction critique aux sources de la Première croisade* (Hautes études médiévales et modernes, 98; Geneva, 2010). See also J. P. Phillips, *The Second Crusade: Extending the Frontiers of Christendom* (New Haven, 2007), pp. 19–28.

announced as new, improved saints' Lives resorted to very similar authorial self-fashionings as against older texts that were considered stylistically or substantively deficient.[3] On the one hand, to read a text with the aim of oneself producing a superior substitute was doubtless to overread, compared to those of one's peers who simply represented the text's 'regular' reading public; that is, to combine sustained attention to the substance of the narrative, its plot and characters, with a relentless clause by clause policing of the interplay between the discourse on the page and the storyworld underneath it.[4] Many readers may have selectively brought this sort of acuity to their reading of particularly inviting or challenging passages in a text, but few could have maintained it over the course of a long and complex work. On the other hand, the sensitivities of that small minority of readers who read in order to rewrite must have borne some fairly close relationship to the actual or anticipated responses of their own hoped-for readership, given that the author of the new text would have aspired to communicate his own vision to his readers clearly and efficiently. The various accommodations and compromises that the authors of derivative accounts of the First Crusade made between their individual reading of their source text or texts and their ambitions to fashion a new telling, a new illocutionary act, drove the choices that they made about distinctive plot content and narratorial voice, while they also sought out secure foundations in shared cultural referentia that would have been available to their contemporary readership. In addition, the more crowded the 'market' for Latin narratives of the First Crusade became, especially in what swiftly emerged as the single most important centre of production and demand, the northern French-speaking world – and the market was certainly getting crowded by c. 1110, when Robert the Monk was completing his version, and quite cluttered by c. 1120 – the greater the need for authors of the latest tellings to attend to the cultural situatedness and reader reception of their texts.

It is important to remember that all the narrative histories of the First Crusade written in the decades after 1099, however reliant on other texts, constitute creative, expressive acts. We perhaps devote too much attention to these texts' interrelationships as understood in terms of the movement between them of capsule data, propositional content that can be readily translated from its original language and, critically, expressed in paraphrase.[5] Two objections to such an emphasis suggest themselves. First, this sort of approach too quickly sunders the propositional content of the narrative from its textuality, its embodiment of a language act. Second, it underestimates the extent to which the presentation of propositional content in a given text can become interwoven with the author's

---

[3] For the influence of authorial postures typical of hagiography on those who revised the *Gesta Francorum*, see *Gesta Francorum et aliorum Hierosolimitanorum*, ed. and trans. M. G. Bull (Oxford, forthcoming).

[4] For the concept of overreading, see H. Porter Abbott, *The Cambridge Introduction to Narrative*, 2nd edn (Cambridge, 2008), pp. 89–90.

[5] See M. G. Bull, 'The Relationship Between the *Gesta Francorum* and Peter Tudebode's *Historia de Hierosolymitano Itinere*: The Evidence of a Hitherto Unexamined Manuscript (St. Catharine's College, Cambridge, 3)', *Crusades*, 11 (2012), 1–17.

sensitivity to the scripts that govern many of the social interactions instantiated in the plot – in other words, expectations as to the ways in which a situation should properly play out rather than how it did or did not transpire in actuality.[6] Interpenetrating the play of scripts and sometimes indistinguishable from them on the page are the constraints and conventions, the horizons of expectation, attendant upon an author's choice of literary genre.[7] And beyond all this there is the question of the individual author's personal cognitive engagement with the storyworlds that the reading of a source text would have been able to cue and guide but never wholly determine and delimit. As one constructs a storyworld in the acts of reading and recall, and then narrates that storyworld back to oneself or to others, one must confront the fact that all narratives, even the most pains-takingly detailed, are one part solid matter and ninety-nine parts void. Most of what could potentially be said goes unstated and is left to the reader to infer. All retellings of even the most familiar stories, therefore, must reconstitute their subject matter creatively to some degree, and in ways that are far from adequately captured if we simply impose upon them evaluative binaries such as true–false, historical–fictional and original–derivative.

The focus of the remainder of this paper is on one configuration of First Crusade texts that nicely illustrates these general remarks. Specifically, the question to be addressed is the relationship between Robert the Monk's history of the crusade and the *Historia Vie Hierosolimitane* by Gilo of Paris and a contin-uator sometimes known as the Charleville Poet, specifically those portions of the text composed by Gilo.[8] The fact that there are some close affinities between Robert's history and the *Historia Vie Hierosolimitane* has been recognized since at least the nineteenth century.[9] A clear understanding of the relationship between the two works was, however, hindered by lingering confusion over the pattern of authorship within the latter text.[10] The respective contributions by Gilo and the Charleville Poet are not wholly consecutive: they are interwoven within the nine books that constitute the *Historia Vie Hierosolimitane* in its fullest surviving form.[11] The problem of attribution was not fully resolved until the appearance in 1997 of Christopher Grocock and Elizabeth Siberry's edition, which clarified

---

[6]   For examples of Robert the Monk's expansion upon the story logic of the *Gesta Francorum*, or the addition of vivid 'reality effect' details that seem too incidental to have originated in information supplied by former crusaders, see RM iii.10, p. 761 (the women bringing water during the battle of Dorylaeum draw it from a river running nearby); iv. 22, p. 788 (it is the younger elements, *juvenes*, of the crusade army who exhume the Turkish dead outside Antioch); vi.3, p. 806 (Cassianus flees Antioch dressed in dirty rags); vi.12, p. 812 (the dialogue between Kerbogha and his mother takes place in a private room); vii.14, p. 832 (the grass set alight during the battle of Antioch burns quickly because it had been dried by the summer heat). Many more such examples could be cited.

[7]   For the idea of a narrative's script, see J. Gavins, 'Scripts and Schemata', in *Routledge Encyclopedia of Narrative Theory*, ed. D. Herman, M. Jahn and M.-L. Ryan (London, 2005), pp. 520–1; R. C. Schank, *Tell Me a Story: Narrative and Intelligence* (Evanston, IL, 1995), pp. 7–12.

[8]   For the dual authorship of the fullest extant version of the *Historia Vie Hierosolimitane*, see *HVH*, pp. xiii–xxiv.

[9]   See the remarks of the *HVH*'s earlier editors in *RHC Occ* v, cxliv.

[10]   See *HVH*, pp. liii–lvii.

[11]   *HVH*, pp. xiii–xviii.

which portions of the poem were the work of which author, and by extension separated out the question of the two authors' respective sources.

It is the relationship between Robert's history and the original portions of the *Historia Vie Hierosolimitane*, that is to say Gilo's composition, that directly concerns us here. The similarities between them are evident on several textual levels: in shared details unique to them among all the extant First Crusade narratives; in similarly emplotted action sequences; and in shared moments of scenic dilation and emphasis.[12] In particular, attention has been drawn to the fact that Robert's text is prosimetric; one of Robert's verses is identical to a line in the *Historia Vie Hierosolimitane*, and several other of Robert's verse passages show substantive, thematic and lexical similarities to passages situated at equivalent plot points in Gilo's text.[13] This led Grocock and Siberry to argue that Robert and Gilo drew upon a now-lost common source text, in verse, a view more circumspectly followed by Carol Sweetenham in her translation of the *Historia Iherosolimitana* and recently endorsed by Jean Flori.[14] What this hypothesis suggests is that there existed a substantial verse telling of the First Crusade, or at least of selected highlights of it, which was in circulation before Robert wrote his history around 1110.[15] If this were the case, it would have important implications for our understanding of the morphology of the First Crusade as a narratable property in the years after 1099, that is, the sequence in which different literary forms commended themselves as suitable and effective vehicles for the telling of the story of the crusade. There are, however, strong reasons for doubting the existence of such a lost shared source.

First, there is an odd misstep in Grocock and Siberry's discussion that conjures up a phantom verse text which the very evidence adduced in support of it in fact fails to establish. Robert's history is prefaced by an *apologeticus sermo* that briefly explains the circumstances in which the text came to be written and the author's aims in writing it. It is useful to quote this in full:

Universos qui hanc istoriam legerint, sive legere audierint et auditam intellexerint, deprecor ut, cum in ea aliquid inurbane compositum invenerint, concedant veniam, quia hanc scribere conpulsus sum per obedientiam. Quidam etenim abbas, nomine B., litterarum scientia et morum probitate preditus, ostendit michi unam istoriam secundum hanc materiam, sed ei admodum displicebat, partim quia initium suum, quod in Clari Montis concilio constitutum fuit, non habebat, partim quia series tam pulcre materiei inculta iacebat, et litteralium compositio dictionum inculta vacillabat. Precepit igitur michi ut, qui Clari

---

[12] See *Robert the Monk's History of the First Crusade: Historia Iherosolimitana*, trans. C. Sweetenham (Crusade Texts in Translation, 11; Aldershot, 2005), pp. 29–35.

[13] The shared line ('Partim predati partimque fuere necati') occurs at *HVH* v.38, p. 100 and *RM* iv.1, p. 776.

[14] *HVH*, pp. lviii–lx; *Robert the Monk's History*, trans. Sweetenham, pp. 29–35; Flori, *Chroniqueurs*, pp. 129–30. Sweetenham's detailed discussion in places shades towards the argument that, rather than utilizing a common source, Robert in fact drew upon Gilo's work or a text very close to it.

[15] For the date of Robert's text, which is closely bound up with the question of the author's identity, see *The* Historia Iherosolimitana, ed. Kempf and Bull, pp. xvii–xli.

Montis concilio interfui, acephale materiei caput preponerem et lecturis eam accuratiori stilo componerem. Ego vero, quia notarium non habui alium nisi me, et dictavi et scripsi; sic quod continuatim paruit menti manus, et manui penna, et penne pagina. Et fidem satis prestare potest et levitas carminis et minime phalerata compositio dictionis. Unde si cui academicis studiis innutrito displicet hec nostra editio, ob forsitan quia pedestri sermone incedentes plus iusto in ea rusticaverimus, notificare ei volumus quia apud nos probabilius est abscondita rusticando elucidare quam aperta philosophando obnubilare. Sermo enim semper exactus, semper est ingratus, quia quod difficili intellectu percipitur, aure surdiori hauritur. Nos vero plebeio incessu sic volumus progredi nostrum sermonem, ut quivis cum audierit speret idem; et si forte idem esse temptaverit, longe separetur ab idem. Si quis affectat scire locum quo hec istoria composita fuerit, sciat esse claustrum cuiusdam celle sancti Remigii constitute in episcopatu Remensi. Si nomen auctoris exigitur, qui eam composuit, Robertus appellatur.[16]

Grocock and Siberry equate the phrase *levitas carminis* that occurs at around the mid point of this passage – literally 'the lightness of the poem' – with the *istoria* of the First Crusade that Robert says he was shown by an Abbot 'B' along with the request that he produce a replacement text that would remedy the omission of the Council of Clermont as the crusade's inaugural moment and efface the maladroit written style of the original. It is generally acknowledged that the text to which Robert must be referring is an eyewitness account of the crusade, the *Gesta Francorum*, in a form very close to those in which it now survives.[17] Grocock and Siberry, however, differentiate the guide text mentioned by Robert from the *Gesta Francorum*, which they relegate to the status of another of Robert's sources; and, on the basis of Robert's mention of *levitas carminis*, they further suppose that the deficient exemplar shown to Robert was a verse account of the crusade.[18]

The construction *levitas carminis*, however, appears at the point in the *sermo* at which Robert has already dealt with the abbot's introduction to him of the deficient telling of the crusade, and has now proceeded to reflections upon his own act of writing, specifically the circumstances in which he worked and his authorial ambitions. He has deictically moved on, or 'popped', from a scene played out in the past between the abbot and himself-as-character, to a plea for approval that is made in the narratorial now and is directed by the implied author constructed by the *sermo*, an honest, workaday toiler in the literary field named Robert, to the implied reader, who is duly cued to understand this self-fashioning as the ethical priming for the narrative that follows.[19] Robert mobilizes the

---

[16] RM, pp. 721–2. The orthography and punctuation of this quotation follow those in the equivalent passage in *The* Historia Iherosolimitana, ed. Kempf and Bull, p. 3.

[17] See the helpful discussion of the relationship between the *Gesta Francorum* and the *Historia Iherosolimitana* in *Robert the Monk's History*, trans. Sweetenham, pp. 12–27. See also *The* Historia Iherosolimitana, ed. Kempf and Bull, pp. xii–xiii.

[18] HVH, pp. lix–lx.

[19] For the concept of the implied author, see now the comprehensive survey in T. Kindt and H.-H. Müller, *The Implied Author: Concept and Controversy* (Narratologia, 9; Berlin, 2006).

well-worn humility topos to excuse his claimed stylistic shortcomings and to validate his text's authority as a function of its unfancy attention to clarity and simplicity. To this end, *levitas carminis* is invoked in the context of Robert's staged self-deprecation; to some extent the phrase gestures back towards and invites comparison with the clumsy (*inculta*) writing in the source text that Robert mentions, but it also enters a differentiating note of greater authorial artifice. Unlike the author of the source text, Robert presents himself as in control, crafting his self-deprecation: the phrase *levitas carminis* is thus linked to what Robert terms his text's unsophisticated composition (*inurbane compositum*) and unadorned delivery (*minime phalerata compositio dictionis*); and later in the passage the same idea is resumed and reinforced in a reference to his work's plain style (*pedestri sermone*), in the repetition of the verb *rustico* as a metaphor for the act of writing straightforwardly, and in Robert's insistence upon his work's common-or-garden plodding quality (*plebeio incessu*). It is perhaps arguable that the term *levitas carminis* is making specific reference to the standard of the verse passages in the *Historia Iherosolimitana*, in contrast to the unadorned diction that characterizes the prose. But given that verse accounts for a very small proportion of the total text, ninety lines within some 34,000 words, much the more plausible reading is that *carmen* is used either figuratively or metonymically to refer to the stylistic craft on display throughout the whole work. In other words, the reference to *carmen* in this passage is not to a poem about the First Crusade that Robert must have had before him as he wrote the *Historia Iherosolimitana*.

There remains the fact, however, that there are substantial similarities between the *Historia Iherosolimitana* and the *Historia Vie Hierosolimitane*. Moreover, as Carol Sweetenham has observed, the verse passages in Robert's text mostly occur within those sequences in which there are especially close parallels with Gilo's account.[20] Globally, most of the similarities that can be identified emerge from a comparison between Gilo's text and Robert's prose passages; necessarily so, for as we have seen prose is the dominant medium in the *Historia Iherosolimitana*. But for our immediate purposes it is worth focusing our attention on Robert's use of verse because this has seemed to lend particular support to the case for close affinities between the two texts and to corroborate the suggestion that there was a shared source. It is as if the verse delivery of the supposed shared source, in addition to inspiring in Gilo a like-for-like poetic adaptation, impressed itself on Robert to the extent that it intermittently burst through onto the surface of his prose discourse.[21]

The presence of verse passages within a work, however, cannot simply be a reflex of the use of verse in its source or sources, so we need to be clear about exactly how and why Robert switches to verse from time to time. Where, then, does the verse fit within the *Historia Iherosolimitana* as a whole? As already noted, there are some ninety lines of verse in total, almost all of which are hexameters. They are distributed across thirty sequences that range in length from one

---

[20] *Robert the Monk's History*, trans. Sweetenham, pp. 29–33.
[21] For prosimetric texts, see P. Dronke, *Verse with Prose from Petronius to Dante: The Art and Scope of the Mixed Form* (Cambridge, Mass., 1994).

line to thirteen lines; six or fewer lines is the norm. There is every indication that the verses were part of Robert's authorial design, although it is always important to bear in mind that, when we look at a prosimetric text on the printed page, modern editorial and typographical conventions exaggerate, or at least significantly misrepresent, the visual impact that the same text in manuscript form would have made upon a medieval reader. In manuscripts of Robert's text, which are not unusual in this respect, there may be some setting off of the verse sequences by means of *punctus* and capitals, but on the whole they are run more or less seamlessly into the arrangement and articulation of the surrounding text; the presence of verse would thus have announced itself to the reader mainly through the metre, probably aided by voiced or breathed reading, and through shifts in diction, tense and person, as well as intertextual reference.[22] Most of the verse passages in the *Historia Iherosolimitana* advance the plot, albeit on generally the smallest action-by-action scale, and their omission would consequently disrupt the reader's tracking of the story logic.[23] Importantly, the verses do not function as deictic shifters to cue apostrophes to the reader or other overt narratorial utterances.[24] It is true that there is a strong narrative voice within the *Historia Iherosolimitana*, in part an appropriation of the narrator's interventions in the *Gesta Francorum*, in part Robert's own introductions.[25] But the verse passages are not a privileged discursive vehicle for narratorial reflection, that is to say a platform upon which the narrator climbs in order to step out of the immediate narrative moment and pronounce upon the meaning of the action or the motives and qualities of the actors.[26] Robert's narrator shifts position with respect to the action many times and a range of focalization forms is deployed,

---

[22] For the manner in which the verse portions are rendered in the manuscripts of Robert's text, see *The* Historia Iherosolimitana, ed. Kempf and Bull, p. lx.

[23] E.g. RM iii.4, p. 757; iii.6, p. 759; iii.9, p. 760; iii.13, pp. 762–3; iv.1, p. 775; vi.10, p. 810; viii.11, p. 831; viii.4, p. 846; viii.7, p. 849; ix.15, p. 873.

[24] For a partial exception see RM iii.14, p. 763, an offering of thanks for the crusaders' victory at Dorylaeum which is voiced by the narrator, not the crusaders.

[25] See e.g. RM ii.19, pp. 749–50 in which the excuses made for the leaders' swearing of oaths to the emperor in *GF*, p. 12 are amplified; RM iii.8, p. 759, where the narrator's confession of ignorance concerning the meaning of Turkish battle cries ('et clamosis vocibus nescio quid barbarum perstridere') resumes the narratorial posture expressed, less economically, in *GF*, p. 18 ('coeperunt stridere et garrire ac clamare, excelsa uoce dicentes diabolicum sonum nescio quomodo in sua lingua'). RM iv.1, p. 775 echoes the sentiment articulated in *GF*, p. 21 that the Turks were worthy foes but for their faith, but the context is shifted from the battle of Dorylaeum to the beginning of the siege of Antioch. RM v.10, p. 798 retains the image of a thinly smiling Bohemond in *GF*, p. 45 when he is seemingly thwarted in his plans for controlling Antioch, but introduces a note of sarcasm on his part. For instances of the narratorial voice for which the *Gesta Francorum* offers no direct point of comparison, see RM iv.12, p. 781; iv.13, p. 782; vi.1, p. 805; vii.7, p. 827; vii.23, p. 839; viii.2, p. 844. In a similar vein are a number of truisms offered about the nature of warfare: RM iv.7, p. 779; viii.4, p. 845; ix.3, p. 864.

[26] It is noteworthy that at RM iii.15, p. 764 a single line of verse concludes a passage describing the collection of spoils from the battlefield of Dorylaeum on the day after the battle, effectively bookending the narration of the battle as an event, before Robert shifts register to reflect (in prose) upon the larger matter of the role of the crusaders as instruments of the divine will.

as one would expect in a text of considerable length and complexity, but the verse is not conspicuously there to faciliate this process.[27]

It is possible that in a few instances, in particular in cases where a verse line is syntactically connected to the prose adjacent to it, the verse as a discrete piece of the text's architecture began not with Robert himself but with a copyist anterior to the extant manuscript transmission, sensitized by Robert's willingness to include hexameters and attuned to hearing metrical patterns in the prose.[28] On the other hand, in almost all of the cases of single-line verse and *a fortiori* in instances of two or more lines, the verse passages express grammatically complete ideas.[29] They sometimes announce themselves by such means as the use of the historic present tense and the rendering of agents in the singular as synecdoches or personifications of a collectivity.[30] The distribution of the verse passages is revealing. The first two books of the *Historia Iherosolimitana*, of nine, contain no verses. Book III has no fewer than thirty-six lines spread across fifteen sequences, half the total number of such sequences in the whole work. Thereafter, Books IV–IX limit themselves to fewer instances, between two and four per book, and to fewer total lines: fourteen, eleven, two, eight, seven and twelve, respectively.

The abruptness of the shift between Books I–II and Book III is therefore particularly noteworthy. It is to be explained with reference to changes in subject matter and attendant tone. Books I and II recount the beginnings of the First Crusade, including of course the Council of Clermont, and deliver the crusaders as far as Constantinople. Book III begins with the crusaders crossing the Bosphorus, and moves swiftly to the siege of Nicaea and the clashes of arms that took place during it, the first hostilities between the main crusade armies and Muslim opponents. Although Robert has already given an account of the Peasants' Crusade, its evident failures precluded elevated treatment.[31] But now the collective might of the main crusade, which will constitute the principal agent

---

[27] It is important to distinguish between the verse embedded within the body of the text and those verse rubrics that form one (intermittent) part of the two levels of rubrication familiar from the arrangement of the *Historia Iherosolimitana* in the *RHC*: see e.g. i.1, p. 727; i.5, p. 731; i. 9, p. 734; ii.1, p. 739; ii.3, p. 740; ii.10, p. 744; iii.2, p. 756; iii.5, p. 758; iii.29, p. 771; iv.20, p. 786; v.8, p. 796; vi.7, p. 808; vi.12, p. 811; vii.1, p. 821; vii.8, p. 827; viii.4, p. 845; viii.16, p. 855; viii.17, p. 856; ix.6, p. 866; ix.8, p. 867; ix.9, p. 868; ix.13, p. 871; ix.16, p. 873; ix.26, p. 881. The *RHC* editors confected the familiar disposition of the text by blending and harmonizing the readings of various manuscripts, thereby forcing the text-as-presented into a form that receives no warrant from the earliest manuscript evidence. (This includes what is in fact the over-division of Robert's nine books into the numerous, brief chapters that have become the text's apparent 'signature' articulation.) The verse rubrics would seem to have begun life as marginalia (the consistencies in many of their internal rhyme schemes suggesting these were largely the work of one scribe or scriptorium) which subsequently migrated into the text. For the status of the rubrics and the manipulation of the text by the *RHC* editors, see *The* Historia Iherosolimitana, ed. Kempf and Bull, pp. xlix–l, liii–lvi.

[28] See RM iii.8, p. 760; iv.1, p. 776; viii.7, p. 848; viii.4, p. 865.

[29] See e.g. RM iii.6, p. 759; iii.9, p. 760; iii.13, pp. 762-3; iv.1, p. 775; vi.10, p. 810; vii.11, p. 831; viii.4, p. 846; viii.7, p. 849; ix.15, p. 873.

[30] RM iii.13, p. 762: 'Sed miles Christi prosternit eos nece tristi'; vii.24, p. 840: 'Miles ut ascendit murum, fit celsior hoste / Hostis et ille fuit viribus inferior'.

[31] RM i.5–13, pp. 731–6.

in the narrative arc of all that follows, is assembled, finds itself in hostile territory, and functions in an overt and sustained military mode, thereby nudging the discursive registers of the text closer to the epic.[32] Although what is said in the verse sequences is generally bland, they make a contribution to this epic tone, more by the fact of their presence than by virtue of the amount of propositional content that they deliver. This helps to explain the distribution pattern that we have noted: Robert can shift into verse once the plot of the crusade offers up large-scale combat, but then in later books seemingly learns to appreciate that less was perhaps more when it came to seeding the prose with verse reinforcements of the text's epic-mindedness. We do not know enough about the circumstances in which Robert wrote his history to be categorical on this point, nor indeed whether he wrote its books in the order in which they appear, though this must be likely; but a trajectory in his authorial design seems to emerge across the sequence Books I–II, Book III, and then Books IV–IX.

The epic mood accentuated by Robert's verse passages is evident, for example, in their references to battles, sieges and the breaking of camp, in the imagery of dawn breaking and armies preparing themselves in the first light of day, and in some of the animal similes for which Robert shows a particular fondness.[33] Similarly, part of the *planctus* of the widow of Walo of Chaumont, killed during the siege of Antioch, is in verse, as are rhetorical questions tauntingly directed by the narrator to Turks in headlong flight.[34] To a large extent, therefore, the verse sequences contribute towards one of the main narrative projects of the *Historia Iherosolimitana* as against its source the *Gesta Francorum*, which is to enhance the length, detail, richness of imagery, and story logic of the sequences describing armed conflict, while also accentuating their epic resonances.[35] (The *Gesta Francorum* is sketchy in its handling of fighting, briefly sandwiching actual moments of armed encounter between longer descriptions of the build-up and the aftermath, that is the flight or death of the losing side and the victors' taking of booty.)[36]

It is important to note that making a comparison between Robert's text and Gilo's portions of the *Historie Vie Hierosolimitane* is not a case of matching like against like. The action narrated in Gilo's text begins at Nicaea and ends between the fall of Jerusalem and the battle of Ascalon. Compared to the *Historia Iherosolimitana*, the *Gesta Francorum*, and indeed every telling of the First Crusade that is wholly or substantially in prose, Gilo's text is far less directed

---

[32] For the insistent signalling of the epic mood once the action picks up in Book III, see e.g. RM iii.3, pp. 756–7 (unkempt mothers fleeing with their children); iii.4, p. 757 (glistening weapons); iii.5, p. 758 (the laments of the besieged); iii.7, p. 759 (animals graze on lush grass); iii.8, p. 760 (dispatch of a swift messenger).

[33] See e.g. RM iii.3, p. 756; iii.4, p. 757; iii.6, p. 759; iii.9, p. 760; iii.11, p. 761; iii.13, pp. 762–3; iv.1, p. 775; v.12, p. 800 (in which the character Pirrus himself refers to the breaking of dawn); ix.4, p. 865; ix.15, p. 873.

[34] RM iii.12, p. 762; v.7, p. 795.

[35] For a useful overview of the *Historia Iherosolimitana*'s principal substantive and thematic departures from the *Gesta Francorum*, see *Robert the Monk's History*, trans. Sweetenham, pp. 15–26.

[36] I aim to pursue this question further in an article-length study of the *Gesta Francorum*'s indebtedness to the plot architectures and lexis of biblical battle narratives.

towards providing an account of the crusade as a single and continuous process articulated by interlinking episodes of different sorts. The gapping is of a different order, disavowing any appearance of homology between the completeness of the crusade as an event and a beginning–middle–end completeness in the manner of its telling.[37] It was precisely this gappiness, of course, that opened up the large spaces for the so-called Charleville Poet to insert substantial additional blocks of narrative into the text. Gilo's story content is shaped by more pronounced swings between pause and ellipsis, to apply Gérard Genette's terms for the two extremes among the ways in which text 'time', its amplitude relative to the duration of what is narrated, compares to the time taken by events in the storyworld.[38] In more specific terms, Gilo's narrative of the crusade is mostly an anthology of battle and siege set pieces, a sort of edited highlights that sacrifices much of the colligations, situational variety and plot architecture of other accounts in order to open out scenes over which like-minded connoisseurs of classical epic verse familiar with Lucan, Virgil, Ovid and the *Ilias Latina* could linger. It is revealing, for instance, that Gilo's text fast-forwards from the battle of Dorylaeum to the crusaders' arrival outside Antioch, then foreshortens the intervals between the set-piece passages of arms that take place during the siege.[39] Gilo's interruptions of the plot rhythms that prose tellings of the crusade normalized mean that his work is predominantly devoted to those same sorts of moments of scenic battle array, opportunities for individual displays of prowess, and clichéd epic images, such as the dawn's first rays, a widow's mourning, and animal similes, in which verse surfaces in the *Historia Iherosolimatana*.[40] It is Gilo's limited range of diegeses and plot situations, not a lost common source, that explains the fact that most of Robert's verse passages occur where the plot arcs of the two texts are at their closest.

Although more work remains to be done on the lexical and substantive correspondences between Gilo's work and the prose sections of the *Historia Iherosolimitana*, as well as important differences in their respective emphases such as the relative prominence afforded Bohemond and Godfrey of Bouillon, much the most plausible hypothesis is that Gilo used Robert's text as a source. This was a highly selective and intermittent borrowing that varied in its depth and range, and was seldom sustained over long sequences given both the demands of the verse form and the preference for battle-centred plot situations that has been noted. It is not exactly clear when Gilo wrote his part of the *Historia*

---

[37] For gapping, see the helpful discussion in D. Herman, *Story Logic: Problems and Possibilities of Narrative* (Lincoln, NE, 2002), pp. 66–9. See also M. Steinberg, *Expositional Modes and Temporal Ordering in Fiction* (Bloomington, 1978), esp. pp. 50–5, 129–58, 236–46; L. Doležel, *Heterocosmica: Fiction and Possible Worlds* (Baltimore, 1998), pp. 169–84.

[38] See G. Genette, *Narrative Discourse: An Essay in Method*, trans. J. E. Lewin (Ithaca, NY, 1980), pp. 33–5, 86–112; cf. S. Chatman, *Story and Discourse: Narrative Structure in Fiction and Film* (Ithaca, NY, 1978), pp. 67–78.

[39] See *HVH*, pp. 92, 98 for Gilo's pronounced compression of the interval (in reality July–October 1097) between the battle of Dorylaeum and the beginning of the crusaders' siege of Antioch. The Charleville Poet exploits the foreshortening to add intervening narrative (pp. 92–6) that includes the well-known episode of Godfrey of Bouillon's encounter with a bear.

[40] See e.g. the treatment of the battle of Dorylaeum in *HVH* iv.157–330, pp. 80–90.

Vie Hierosolimitane, but a dating to the second decade of the twelfth century is suggested by the fact that Book IX, which is one of Gilo's, concludes with the remark that he was writing while resident in Paris.[41] Gilo entered Cluny at some point before his career took him to Rome, where he became cardinal bishop of Tusculum.[42] If we work from the assumption that Gilo joined the papal entourage during or soon after Pope Calixtus II's visit to Cluny in January 1120, Gilo must have entered Cluny no later than 1119. We know very little about the transmission and reception of Robert's history in the period immediately after it was written: the earliest extant manuscripts date from the mid twelfth century.[43] But the fact that Gilo was living in Paris for at least some of the time before he entered Cluny put him in a good position to come by a copy of the *Historia Iherosolimitana*. A noteworthy feature of Robert's authorial project was to slant the story of the crusade in directions favourable to the Capetian monarchy; he also demonstrates a clear interest in crusaders from the Île-de-France, not just his own region of Champagne.[44] It is therefore likely that copies of Robert's history were circulating in or around Paris when Gilo was there, and that one such copy either piqued his interest in attempting a telling of the crusade in verse or supplied helpful additional material for a project already in gestation.

Appeals to lost works as links in textual chains are sometimes a necessary methodological move, but can risk muting important questions about the authorial craft on show within those narratives that do survive. This is the case with the First Crusade narrative corpus. It is easy to imagine missing-link texts doing much of the creative work that got the crusade from lived collective experience to a discourse or discourses that delivered the lexical sets, the cast of agents, the plot architectures, the acceptable genre borrowings and all that made the crusade narrativizable. But we should not underestimate the contributions of the narratives that are extant. There is plenty of evidence that reveals that the *Historia Iherosolimitana* is a skilfully crafted and cleverly conceived work, the poetics of which do not require that Robert drew upon a second guide text alongside the *Gesta Francorum*. In the first place, one can point to the imagination on display in the many passages that are self-evidently based on corresponding sequences in the *Gesta Francorum*, but which amplify the diegesis, clarify gaps in the story logic, enlarge upon character motivation, layer by means of subordination and more nuanced conjunction the *Gesta Francorum*'s paratactic beating out of the action rhythm, and establish more overt cause-and-effect connections.[45] These are not instances of Robert reacting to new sources

---

[41] *HVH* ix.374–5, p. 252: 'Hec ego composui, Gilo nomine, Parisiensis / Incola …'. Cf. the editors' remarks on dating in *HVH*, p. xxiv: their conjecture that the text was written 'probably in the first decade' of the twelfth century cannot be squared with the likely dating of Robert's text.

[42] See R. Hüls, *Kardinäle, Klerus und Kirchen Roms, 1049–1130* (Tübingen, 1977), pp. 142–3.

[43] *The Historia Iherosolimitana*, ed. Kempf and Bull, pp. xlii–xlvii.

[44] See *The* Historia Iherosolimitana, ed. Kempf and Bull, pp. xvi, xxxix–xl; J. L. Naus, 'The French Royal Court and the Memory of the First Crusade', *Nottingham Medieval Studies*, 55 (2011), 49–78.

[45] See e.g. RM iii.1, p. 755 (more detail on the construction of the road to Nicaea than that supplied by *GF*, p. 14); iii.22, p. 768 (the metaphor of the crusaders thirsting for Turkish blood suggested

of information but the products of cognitive response and imagination: Robert as reader is processing the *Gesta Francorum*'s storyworld, and as writer resolving the incompletenesses and inconsistencies that he finds there. Second, there is the question of the substantial amount of detail, including discrete scenes and characters, unique to the *Historia Iherosolimitana*.[46] Much of this probably reached Robert from other sources, including orally transmitted memories. But we should be careful not to construct an image of Robert's authorial posture as wholly passive and reactive, a recycling of content upon which others had already done the difficult and interesting creative work. Robert was perfectly capable of building a lot from a little and even of what we would consider making things up.

Third, as we have seen, the verse sequences in the *Historia Iherosolimitana* are not in the nature of isolated and contrastive moments of counterpoise set off against the prose. They rather take in one particular formal direction engagements with acoustic effects, rhyme, rhythm and clausal balance that inform the whole text. In part, the text achieves such effects by reacting to, or riffing off, similar features in the *Gesta Francorum*. For example, the most ambitious instance of patterned alliteration in the *Gesta Francorum* occurs in a description of the Orontes flowing red with Turkish blood after one sanguinary battle with the crusaders:

> Unda uero rapidi fluminis undique uidebatur fluere rubea Turcorum sanguine.[47]

This calls forth in the *Historia Iherosolimitana* a more complex amalgam of alliteration, assonance and clausal rhyme as it expands the diegesis, adding to it the focalizing shared gaze of horrified observers that is merely hinted at in the *Gesta Francorum*'s invitation to the reader, in its use of *uidebatur*, to process the scene by means of picturing its appearance:

> Cruor effusus sanguineum flumini dabat colorem, cunctisque cernentibus magnum incutiebat horrorem.[48]

In most instances, however, the text's effects are not cued by its source but are of its own devising. From Book III, for example, there is a sequence that mimics some aspects of verse in its use of the present tense and rhyme, beginning with the breaking of dawn and then evoking the panic and distress of the inhabitants

by *GF*, p. 25 is replaced by the desire to drench the earth with their blood); iii. 28, pp. 770–1 (the crusaders' travails in crossing the Taurus mountains are amplified relative to *GF*, p. 27, with increased focalization through the crusaders' perceptions); iv.15, p. 784 (the leonine simile and image of banners inspired by *GF*, pp. 36–7 is generalized to the mass of crusaders rather than attached specifically to Robert fitz Girard); vii.14, p. 833 (the simile of the abattoir suggested by the account of the battle of Ascalon in *GF*, p. 96 is transferred to the battle of Antioch and intensified by the image of spurting blood). Cf. RM iii.18, p. 766, in which the description of the crusaders picking ears of corn mutes the evocation of Luke 6:1 found in *GF*, p. 23. See also n. 6 above.

[46] See the useful list in *Robert the Monk's History*, trans. Sweetenham, pp. 17–18.

[47] *GF*, p. 41.

[48] RM iv.21, p. 787.

of Nicaea in epic terms before describing the Byzantine emperor's cunning manipulation of their plight:

> Quod ubi imperatori nuntiatur, admodum inde gratulatur; sed et inde mente concipit fraudem, ut deinceps parturiat iniquitatem: iubet ut suis ciuitas reddatur, Turcis integra fiducia tribuatur, et ad se Constantinopolim conducantur.[49]

As this example suggests, one of the *Historia Iherosolimitana*'s favoured compositional devices is the rhymed clause, typically appearing in pairs and frequently sustained over long stretches of text. In numerous such instances the prosody nudges still further towards some of the effects of verse in combining rhyme with matching clausal syllable totals. For example, from Book VIII a sequence of thirteen-syllable clauses:

> altumque silentium intus habebatur, nec ullius uocis sonus audiebatur[50]

In Book IX an example of paired sixteen syllables, reinforced by internal rhyme:

> Hora uesperi bello incompetens diremit litem, et nox superueniens utrisque contulit quietem[51]

These passages illustrate an attention to vocalization and acoustic effect that subtends all the text and situates the verse sequences securely within the discursive design of the whole. Robert the Monk did not need a source text in verse to inspire him to offer up occasional hexameters, just as he did not need this putative source to compensate for gaps in imagination and creativity between what the *Gesta Francorum* offered by way of raw material and the sort of historiographical vision anticipated by the *apologeticus sermo*. There was no common source; Gilo of Paris used the *Historia Iherosolimitana*. For his part, Robert doubtless drew on many sources of information and inspiration, but on only one substantial written account of the crusade, the *Gesta Francorum*, as well as on a stylistic posture towards form and content, and towards the priority of form over content, that we historians are sometimes too wary of acknowledging in the narrative sources that we consult.

---

[49] RM iii.5, p. 758.
[50] RM viii.10, p. 852.
[51] RM ix.3, p. 864.

REWRITING THE HISTORY BOOKS: THE FIRST CRUSADE AND THE PAST

William J. Purkis

In c. 1110 a French cleric known as Robert the Monk set out the reasons why he had begun to compose his *Historia Iherosolimitana*, a Latin prose narrative of the First Crusade that would go on to become the most widely-copied and extensively-circulated history of the expedition in the medieval west.[1] Taking his cue from those historians who had contributed to the composition of the Old and New Testaments, Robert wrote in the *Historia*'s prologue of 'how pleasing it is to God that a record should be made for his faithful people when he carries out any miraculous work on earth that has been arranged to take place for all time'. He then went on, famously, to identify the First Crusade as being comparable in significance with God's creation of the world and Christ's redemption of mankind on the cross, before offering what seems to be a very personal response to the events of the 1090s:

> The more carefully one reflects on it, the more fully is the mind astounded by it. For this was not the work of men; it was the work of God. And so it ought to be commended in writing, as much for the present as for the future, so that Christians will have their hope in God strengthened; and so that they will be encouraged to praise him more eagerly in their minds.[2]

In writing these words, Robert demonstrated clearly his understanding of the impact that the crusade had had on Latin Christians in the years after the conquest of Jerusalem in 1099. Taking this sentiment as its point of departure,

---

[1] M. G. Bull, 'Robert the Monk', in *Christian–Muslim Relations: A Bibliographical History: Volume 3 (1050-1200)*, ed. D. Thomas, A. Mallett *et al.* (Leiden, 2011), pp. 312–17.

[2] RM *prologus*, p. 723. For similar authorial perceptions on the future utility of crusade narratives, see, for example, FC *prologus*, pp. 115–16; RA, p. 35; and BB *prologus*, p. 10. These hopes were materialized in the manuscript presented to King Louis VII of France by William Grassegals: see J. Rubenstein, 'Putting History to Use: Three Crusade Chronicles in Context', *Viator*, 35 (2004), 131–68.

this paper seeks to gauge the cultural significance of the First Crusade for western European elites in the twelfth and thirteenth centuries by examining, first, a range of immediate responses to the expedition's novelty and achievements; and, second, by exploring the ways in which the expedition was subsequently used as a reference point by various writers when describing other instances of conflict, both real and imagined, both present and past. In so doing, the paper seeks to demonstrate how history came to be written (and rewritten) to reflect and refract the memory of the First Crusade.

Robert the Monk was by no means alone among his contemporaries in believing that the events of 1096–9 held a monumental significance. Indeed, a sense of wonder at the crusade's achievements is palpable across all of the earliest accounts that were composed by those who had participated in the expedition, with the northern French cleric Fulcher of Chartres celebrating the conquest of Jerusalem in his *Historia Hierosolymitana* with the following words, for example:

> O time so long desired! O time more memorable than other times! O deed before all other deeds! ... And this [deed] was truly memorable, and rightly remembered, because everything that our Lord God Jesus Christ did and taught in this place, as a man living among men, was restored and renewed in the memory of the faithful. And this same deed, which I believe the Lord wished to be carried out by his people, his beloved children and family, will resound and endure in the memory of all peoples until the end of time.[3]

Similarly, the Provençal priest Raymond of Aguilers illustrated plainly the mood after the conquest of Jerusalem when he wrote of:

> A new day, a new joy, a new and perpetual happiness; the completion of our labour and devotion required new words and new songs from everyone. I declare that this day will be celebrated by all generations to come because all our suffering and hardship was transformed into joy and exultation.[4]

But, if anything, this feeling of excitement was even more pronounced for those who, like Robert the Monk, were writing 'theologically refined' histories of the expedition back in western Europe as the magnitude of the crusaders' achievements began to sink in.[5] Guibert of Nogent stated in the preface to his *Dei gesta per Francos* (c. 1109) that he was writing 'about this glory of our time',[6] before

---

3   FC i.29, pp. 305–6.

4   RA, p. 151. See also *Epistulae et chartae ad historiam primi belli sacri spectantes: Die Kreuzzugsbriefe aus den Jahren 1088–1100*, ed. H. Hagenmeyer (Innsbruck, 1901), p. 157, where Anselm of Ribemont describes the ferocity of the battles fought at Antioch as 'unheard of' (*inauditus*). For the significance of the 'immediate present' in the participant narratives for the crusade, see M. G. Bull, 'The Eyewitness Accounts of the First Crusade as Political Scripts', *Reading Medieval Studies*, 36 (2010), 29–30.

5   See esp. J. S. C. Riley-Smith, *The First Crusade and the Idea of Crusading* (London, 1986), pp. 135–52.

6   GN *praefatio*, p. 80.

going on to explain in the first of his seven books that he intended to write about 'the recent and incomparable victory of the expedition to Jerusalem, whose glory for those who are not totally foolish is such that our times may rejoice in a fame that no previous times have ever merited.'[7] For Guibert the crusade was, as is so well known, an opportunity instituted by God 'in our time' as 'a new way of earning salvation,'[8] and his sense of the crusade's novelty, and of the historical significance of his era, is evident throughout the text. He wrote repeatedly, for example, about the importance of 'new times,'[9] in which God had intervened in the affairs of 'modern men' (*moderni*),[10] and argued for the distinctiveness of the first crusaders' deeds, both in terms of comparing them with all past achievements and any potential future undertakings:

> No land on earth will ever see soldiers of such nobility fighting together. If you wish, I shall relate the story of every kingdom, speak of battles done everywhere; none of these will be able to equal either the nobility of the force of these men ... Let us rejoice then in the battles they won, undertaken purely out of a spiritual desire, granted by a divine power, which had never before appeared, but was made manifest in modern times [*tempora moderna*] ... Thus, I say, we cannot offer examples from the past to match this, nor do we think that anything like this will occur in the future.[11]

More generally, of course, the explosion of historical writing inspired by the First Crusade is indicative of contemporary ideas about the campaign's significance,[12] and similar sentiments to those quoted here were expressed in correspondence[13]

---

[7] GN i.1, p. 86. Translation from R. Levine, *The Deeds of God through the Franks* (Woodbridge, 1997), p. 28.

[8] GN i.1, p. 87.

[9] See, for example, GN ii.10, p. 126; vii.9, p. 282; vii.21, p. 305. See also RM ix.26, p. 882, where Robert describes the crusade's success as the fulfilment of scriptural prophecy 'in our times' (*in nostris aetatibus*).

[10] GN vii.21, p. 305.

[11] GN iii.8, p. 148; vii.1, p. 267; vii.23, p. 312. Translations from Levine, *The Deeds of God*, pp. 63, 124, 147. See also GN v.24, pp. 226–7, where contrasts are drawn between the siege of Antioch and the siege of Troy, and vii.22, p. 308, where Guibert affirms the distinctiveness of the crusaders' achievements.

[12] See S. B. Edgington, 'The First Crusade: Reviewing the Evidence', in *The First Crusade: Origins and Impact*, ed. J. P. Phillips (Manchester, 1997), pp. 55–77; J. P. Phillips, *The Second Crusade: Extending the Frontiers of Christendom* (New Haven and London, 2007), pp. 17–36; C. J. Tyerman, *The Debate on the Crusades* (Manchester, 2011), pp. 7–36; M. G. Bull, 'The Western Narratives of the First Crusade', in *Christian-Muslim Relations: A Bibliographical History: Volume 3 (1050–1200)*, ed. D. Thomas, A. Mallett *et al.* (Leiden, 2011), pp. 15–25.

[13] In their letter to the west composed in September 1099 (*Die Kreuzzugsbriefe*, p. 168), the crusade's leaders stated that 'God has accomplished through us what he promised in ancient times'. Similarly, in a letter sent to the clergy of France in December 1099 (*Die Kreuzzugsbriefe*, p. 175), Pope Paschal II wrote that 'in our times almighty God has deigned to snatch the eastern Church from the hands of the Turks'. And at around the same time Archbishop Manasses of Reims wrote to Bishop Lambert of Arras (*Die Kreuzzugsbriefe*, p. 175), informing him that 'Jerusalem stands on high with joy and gladness, which it has so gloriously received from God in our times'.

and subsequently filtered into broader narrative histories, such as those composed in the 1120s and 1130s by the Anglo-Norman writers William of Malmesbury, Henry of Huntingdon and Orderic Vitalis.[14]

One indicator of the way in which contemporaries conceived of the primacy of the First Crusade is the evidence to suggest that, even from a very early stage, the expedition was regarded as the start of a sequence of military campaigns and thus allocated a numerical 'first-ness'.[15] With reference to the crusade of 1101, for example, Guibert of Nogent clearly distinguished this expedition from that which had reached Jerusalem in 1099, which he referred to as 'the previous army' (*prior exercitus*).[16] As has been shown elsewhere, the fact that this subsequent campaign was such a disaster only served to reinforce the 'miraculous' qualities of its predecessor;[17] according to Guibert, its leaders believed 'that they could do new things and do them better than those who had preceded them', but, as he went on to illustrate, 'such a slaughter of Christians of both sexes took place, so much money, clothing, gold and silver was taken, that this one victory was enough to recompense the Turks for the losses inflicted upon them by the first expedition' (*prima expeditio*).[18] Similarly, Fulcher of Chartres referred to 1096 as 'the year in which the Franks who seek Jerusalem first passed through Rome' and to the crusade of 1101 as 'the second pilgrimage of the Franks' (*de secunda Francorum miserabili peregrinatione*).[19] The significance of the First Crusade for Fulcher can also be seen from the fact that certain events in his *Historia* are dated by reference to their distance in time from the 1090s; thus the twenty-sixth chapter of his third book concludes with the phrase 'Thus far our deeds have run for twenty-four years / Since the beginning of the renowned journey of pilgrims

---

[14] See Phillips, *The Second Crusade*, pp. 23–4. For the idea that the mid-twelfth-century Cistercian chronicler Otto of Freising regarded the First Crusade as 'a radical political change in history', see H.-W. Goetz, 'The Concept of Time in the Historiography of the Eleventh and Twelfth Centuries', in *Medieval Concepts of the Past: Ritual, Memory, Historiography*, ed. G. Althoff, J. Fried and P. J. Geary (Cambridge, 2002), p. 148 and n. 39.

[15] See M. G. Bull, 'The Roots of Lay Enthusiasm for the First Crusade', *History*, 78 (1993), 353–4. More generally, see G. Constable, 'The Numbering of the Crusades', in his *Crusaders and Crusading in the Twelfth Century* (Farnham, 2008), pp. 353–6 (and cf. the comments on p. 354). See also the remarks of H. E. Mayer, *The Crusades*, trans. J. Gillingham, 2nd edn (Oxford, 1988), p. 314 n. 117; J. S. C. Riley-Smith, *The Crusades: A History*, 2nd edn (London, 2005), p. xxv; N. Jaspert, *The Crusades*, trans. P. G. Jestice (London, 2006), p. 47; G. Constable, 'The Historiography of the Crusades', in his *Crusaders and Crusading in the Twelfth Century*, p. 24; and J. Rubenstein, *Armies of Heaven: The First Crusade and the Quest for Apocalypse* (New York, 2011), pp. xi, 343 n. 1. But cf. C. J. Tyerman, *The Invention of the Crusades* (Basingstoke, 1998), esp. pp. 8–29, where it is argued that 'The First Crusade only appeared as the beginning of a coherent movement retrospectively when that movement was constructed after 1187' (p. 12); and P. E. Chevedden, 'The Islamic View and the Christian View of the Crusades: A New Synthesis', *History*, 93 (2008), 181–200, which offers an alternative approach to the 'first-ness' of the First Crusade.

[16] GN vii.24, p. 314.

[17] Riley-Smith, *The First Crusade*, pp. 120–34.

[18] GN vii.24, p. 315. Translation from Levine, *The Deeds of God*, p. 148.

[19] FC i.5, pp. 148–9; ii.16, p. 428. Contrasting examples of the numbering of contingents on the First Crusade are cited in J. S. C. Riley-Smith, *The First Crusaders, 1095–1131* (Cambridge, 1997), p. 109.

from every region.'[20] A decade or so later Orderic Vitalis showed a similar sense of historical perspective to Fulcher and Guibert when he described Bohemond of Taranto's crusade of 1106 as 'the third departure of westerners for Jerusalem' (*tercia profectio occidentalium in Ierusalem*).[21]

A further measure of the cultural impact of the First Crusade is the evidence to suggest that ideas and rhetoric associated with the expedition's preaching and narrativization began to seep into the works of other twelfth-century writers from a relatively early date. The memory of the First Crusade was certainly being appropriated by Archbishop Diego of Compostela in 1125, for example, when he called upon the Iberian warrior classes to take the fight to the Almoravids 'just like the knights of Christ, the faithful sons of the holy Church, [who] opened the way to Jerusalem with much labour and spilling of blood';[22] it is possible that this declaration also inspired King Alfonso I of Aragon to identify similarities between the First Crusade's liberation of the Holy Sepulchre and his own military campaigns in the Ebro valley in the 1120s.[23] And it was not only war against Muslims that acquired a crusading character. In 1107/8, for example, in the text commonly known as the 'Magdeburg charter', the warriors of eastern Germany were incited to go to war with their pagan neighbours with the deeds of the first crusaders being upheld as a worthy example for them to follow;[24] and around twenty years later Orderic Vitalis portrayed Helias of La Flèche's defence of his patrimony in the county of Maine as a kind of domestic crusade.[25]

But these appropriations of the crusade's memory could be retrospective too, and certain writers soon began to project images and ideas associated with crusading onto cognate activities, such as inter-faith conflict and Jerusalem pilgrimage, that had taken place before 1095.[26] In a charter from 1118, for example, the canons of Toussaint described how Fulk Nerra, an eleventh-century count of Anjou, had gone on pilgrimage to the Holy Sepulchre out of a desire '[to follow] the precept of the Lord where he said: *If any man will come after me, let him deny himself and take up his cross and follow me*', a passage which would seem to bear the direct influence of ideas associated with the crusade preaching of the 1090s.[27] Similarly, in an anonymous twelfth-century biography of Bishop Altmann of Passau, it was recorded that those who had set out for the east on the great German pilgrimage of 1064–5 had 'abandoned

[20] FC iii.26, p. 693: 'Gesta quater senos currunt hucusque per annos / Post iter inceptum peregrinis undique notum.'

[21] OV, iii, 182.

[22] *Historia Compostellana*, ii.78, ed. E. Falque Rey (Corpus Christianorum, Continuatio Mediaeualis, 70; Turnhout, 1988), p. 379.

[23] See W. J. Purkis, *Crusading Spirituality in the Holy Land and Iberia, c.1095–c.1187* (Woodbridge, 2008), pp. 129–38.

[24] See G. Constable, 'Early Crusading in Eastern Germany: The Magdeburg Charter of 1107/8', in his *Crusaders and Crusading in the Twelfth Century*, pp. 197–214.

[25] OV, v, 228–32.

[26] For a broader consideration of anachronism in eleventh- and twelfth-century historiography, see Goetz, 'The Concept of Time', esp. pp. 153–63.

[27] F. Comte, *L'Abbaye Toussaint d'Angers des origines à 1330: étude historique et cartulaire* (Angers, 1985), no. 102, p. 147.

their homes, families and material possessions, and through the hard road followed Christ, carrying the cross'.[28] Jonathan Riley-Smith has described this as 'a descriptive phrase prefiguring the crusaders',[29] but given that the text from which it originates was probably composed in the 1120s it seems more likely that, as with the Anjou charter, the statement is indicative of the spiritual mood at the time of composition rather than that of the earlier period to which it makes reference.[30]

A more dramatic example of this process of the invention of 'proto-crusaders' is to be found within Geoffrey of Monmouth's *Historia regum Britannie*, which was composed in the 1130s.[31] Geraldine Heng has recently suggested a number of ways in which Geoffrey's work and portrayal of King Arthur might be understood to be informed by the history and historiography of the First Crusade,[32] describing, for example, his depiction of 'an Arthur who serviceably defeats monstrosities from a crusading history that is integrally intertwined with the Anglo-Norman past and present',[33] and identifying the presence of Arab, African and Oriental enemies in the armies with which he engaged.[34] Elsewhere, parallels are drawn between Geoffrey's account of the processes of Arthurian state formation and the early settlement of the Latin East, which is characterized as 'a colonial experiment for which the cultural rescue and popularity of Arthur's deeds offer ideological support'.[35] Here, 'the exhausted empire of the Romans' is understood to represent the beleaguered Byzantine Empire of Geoffrey's own times: 'the Arthurian empire, like the empire of the crusader states, is a newly arrived, virile alternative to the superannuated empire of the (Eastern) Romans, who are mockingly derided through metaphors of gender also used by the *Gesta Francorum*'.[36] In this context, certain passages of Geoffrey's text become more explicable, such as the description of how, immediately before the battle

---

[28] 'Vita Altmanni episcopi Pataviensis', *MGH SS* xii, 230.

[29] Riley-Smith, *The First Crusaders*, p. 29 n. 21.

[30] For the date, see E. Joranson, 'The Great German Pilgrimage of 1064–1065', in *The Crusades and Other Historical Essays Presented to Dana C. Munro by his Former Students*, ed. L. J. Paetow (New York, 1928), p. 8. For another possible example of eleventh-century Jerusalem pilgrims being characterized as proto-crusaders by twelfth-century writers, see C. Morris, *The Sepulchre of Christ and the Medieval West: From the Beginning to 1600* (Oxford, 2005), pp. 144–6.

[31] Geoffrey of Monmouth, *The History of the Kings of Britain*, ed. M. D. Reeve, trans. N. Wright (Woodbridge, 2007), with discussion of the date at p. vii.

[32] G. Heng, *Empire of Magic: Medieval Romance and the Politics of Cultural Fantasy* (New York, 2003). Heng's point of departure (pp. 2–3) is that elements of Arthurian legend emerged in response to the traumatic experience of cannibalism on the First Crusade. For an alternative approach that contextualizes cannibalism as an act of holy war, see J. Rubenstein, 'Cannibals and Crusaders', *French Historical Studies*, 31 (2008), 525–52.

[33] Heng, *Empire of Magic*, p. 41.

[34] *Ibid.*, pp. 43, 47, 50–1, which builds on J. S. P. Tatlock, 'Certain Contemporary Matters in Geoffrey of Monmouth', *Speculum*, 6 (1931), 206–20.

[35] Heng, *Empire of Magic*, p. 46. The idea that the Latin East was 'a colonial experiment' is not unproblematic; see R. Ellenblum, *Crusader Castles and Modern Histories* (Cambridge, 2007).

[36] Heng, *Empire of Magic*, pp. 46, 48–9. On this theme more generally, see A. Lynch, 'Imperial Arthur: Home and Away', in *The Cambridge Companion to the Arthurian Legend*, ed. E. Archibald and A. Putter (Cambridge, 2009), pp. 171–87.

of Bath in 516, the warriors of Arthur's army were 'marked with the sign of the Christian faith' and inspired by the words of what was in effect a crusade sermon. Arthur's 'proto-crusaders' were instructed that to fight for the defence of their countrymen and their *patria* was an act of Christo-mimesis, in language that was clearly influenced by ideas that had proliferated in the narratives of the First Crusade:

> Fight for your country, ready to die for it if you must. Such a death means victory and the salvation of your souls. Whoever lays down his life for his fellow-Christians dedicates himself as a living sacrifice to God and patently follows Christ, who deigned to die for his brothers. If any of you falls in this battle, let his death, provided he does not shrink from it, be the repentance and cleansing of all his sins.[37]

Some of Heng's arguments are persuasive and her work certainly opens interesting avenues for further investigation; she does not consider, for example, which narratives of the crusade Geoffrey might have consulted or been exposed to as he composed his *Historia*.[38] But the suggestion that Arthur's deeds were actively being textualized to lend 'ideological support' for Latin settlement in the eastern Mediterranean is not entirely convincing;[39] it seems more likely that Geoffrey's *Historia* represents a passive appropriation of a popular and influential set of new ideas rather than anything more deliberate and propagandistic.[40] In this regard, Geoffrey's work, like the other examples cited above, seems to affirm the importance and distinctiveness of the events of the 1090s rather than to undermine them.[41]

That the First Crusade was a significant departure from what had come before can also be observed through consideration of another (more problematic) text, the so-called encyclical of Pope Sergius IV (1009–12), which purports to be an early-eleventh-century papal call for a military expedition to the east that was provoked by al-Hakim's destruction of the Holy Sepulchre in 1009.[42] As has been discussed elsewhere, the document contains many ideas associated with the preaching for the First Crusade – armed pilgrimage, Christo-mimesis, vengeance, the desire to restore Christian custody of the Holy Sepulchre and so forth – and it has often been regarded as a forgery, possibly produced at the

---

[37] Geoffrey of Monmouth, *History*, pp. 198–9. For commentary on this passage, see Tyerman, *The Invention of the Crusades*, p. 16; Heng, *Empire of Magic*, pp. 42–3; and Phillips, *The Second Crusade*, p. 27. For crusading as *imitatio Christi*, see Purkis, *Crusading Spirituality*, esp. pp. 30–47.

[38] See, for example, Heng, *Empire of Magic*, p. 331 n. 64, where it is stated that Geoffrey 'may or may not have read' Baldric of Bourgueil's *Historia Ierosolimitana*.

[39] Heng, *Empire of Magic*, p. 49. For the 'ideological value' of Arthurian legend for later medieval kings of England, see *ibid.*, pp. 58–9; and Lynch, 'Imperial Arthur', pp. 171–7.

[40] For reservations about the use of texts as 'propaganda', see now N. L. Paul, 'A Warlord's Wisdom: Literacy and Propaganda at the Time of the First Crusade', *Speculum*, 85 (2010), 534–66.

[41] Cf. Tyerman, *The Invention of the Crusades*, p. 16.

[42] See J. France, 'The Destruction of Jerusalem and the First Crusade', *Journal of Ecclesiastical History*, 47 (1996), 1–17.

Cluniac abbey of Moissac in the mid-1090s to provide a historical precedent for Pope Urban's campaign.[43] Although the status of this source as a late-eleventh-century text is no longer as secure as it once was,[44] its contents are certainly suggestive of the anxieties that might have surrounded the novelty of the crusade appeal in the 1090s.[45] To identify the crusade as a continuation of an earlier papal initiative, rather than as a distinct breach from the past, was one way of addressing any concerns that might have emerged among the ecclesiastical intelligentsia about the expedition's 'first-ness'; in this respect, assuming the encyclical was a product of the 1090s rather than an earlier text, it should perhaps be read alongside the sorts of apologetical treatises produced by or for many of the new religious orders of the twelfth century, who sought to dispel any accusations of novelty that might come their way, either by seeking to root their ways of life in earlier medieval monastic history or by claiming that their devotional practices were based on models drawn from the Old and New Testaments.[46] As it turned out, of course, the very success of the crusade, which was regarded as a manifestation of divine will, neutralized the potential for any such criticism and rendered such texts unnecessary,[47] which may explain why Pseudo-Sergius's encyclical did not receive a wider circulation and only survives in a single manuscript copy.[48] Nevertheless, the letter is certainly indicative of a contemporary willingness to play fast and loose with crusading historiography, should it be deemed necessary to do so.

Perhaps the greatest example of such creative approaches to the past is to be found within the *Historia Turpini*, the Latin text most commonly referred to as the *Pseudo-Turpin Chronicle*, the earliest surviving version of which was probably produced in Santiago de Compostela in c. 1140, wherein the emperor

---

[43] See A. Gieysztor, 'The Genesis of the Crusades: The Encyclical of Sergius IV (1009–12)', *Medievalia et Humanistica*, 5 (1948), 3–23, and 6 (1950), 3–34; H. E. J. Cowdrey, 'Pope Urban II's Preaching of the First Crusade', *History*, 55 (1970), 185; H. M. Schaller, 'Zur Kreuzzugsenzyklika Papst Sergius' IV', in *Papsttum, Kirche und Recht im Mittelalter: Festschrift für Horst Fuhrmann zum 65. Geburtstag*, ed. H. Mordek (Tübingen, 1991), pp. 135–53; M. G. Bull, *Knightly Piety and the Lay Response to the First Crusade: The Limousin and Gascony, c.970–c.1130* (Oxford, 1993), pp. 64–6; Morris, *The Sepulchre of Christ*, pp. 136–7; Purkis, *Crusading Spirituality*, pp. 45–7; M. Gabriele, *An Empire of Memory: The Legend of Charlemagne, the Franks, and Jerusalem before the First Crusade* (Oxford, 2011), pp. 141–3; S. A. Throop, *Crusading as an Act of Vengeance, 1095–1216* (Farnham, 2011), pp. 44, 196–7.

[44] See esp. the contrasting comments of Throop, *Crusading as an Act of Vengeance*, p. 197, and Gabriele, *An Empire of Memory*, pp. 141–2 and n. 45. It should be noted that if the encyclical *was* an authentic text, the contribution of Sergius IV to the development of the crusading idea was certainly not recognized in the 1090s.

[45] For the context, see B. Smalley, 'Ecclesiastical Attitudes to Novelty, c.1100–c.1250', in *Church, Society and Politics*, ed. D. Baker (Studies in Church History, 12; Oxford, 1975), pp. 113–31.

[46] See, for example, *Libellus de diversis ordinibus et professionibus qui sunt in aecclesia*, ed. and trans. G. Constable and B. S. Smith, rev. edn (Oxford, 2003). For a more general discussion, see G. Constable, *The Reformation of the Twelfth Century* (Cambridge, 1996), pp. 125–67. For the absence of similar legitimizing connections between the past and the present in the *GF*, *FC* and *RA*, see Bull, 'Eyewitness Accounts', 29–30.

[47] See Riley-Smith, *The First Crusaders*, p. 77.

[48] Morris, *The Sepulchre of Christ*, p. 137.

Charlemagne was reinvented as a kind of crusading superhero.[49] Connections between the Carolingian past and the crusading present were by no means unprecedented at the time of the text's composition; in c. 1099–1100 for example, the author of the *Gesta Francorum* had described how several contingents of first crusaders had 'travelled by the road to Constantinople which Charlemagne, the wonderful king of the Franks, built a long time ago',[50] an undertaking that Robert the Monk later dovetailed with the emperor's mythical pilgrimage to the Holy Land.[51] Elsewhere, Robert had Pope Urban II cite the military deeds of Charlemagne in his report of the Clermont sermon as heroic inspiration for the crusaders,[52] and in Ralph of Caen's account of the battle of Dorylaeum it was recorded of Robert of Flanders and Hugh the Great that 'if you beheld the fury of the counts, this one with a spear and that one with a sword, you would declare that Roland and Oliver had been reborn'.[53] In a recent survey of twelfth-century legends of Charlemagne, Jace Stuckey has argued that in these and other sources for the First Crusade the emperor was 'envisaged as the "prototypical" crusader, propagated as the model and progenitor for a "new" generation'.[54] But this almost certainly stretches the evidence too far,[55] and it is probably more fruitful to interpret these allusions in the same way that references in various First Crusade sources to the Israelites and the Maccabees have recently been characterized, that is as 'status-affirming similes' rather than attempts to draw explicit connections between the past and the present.[56] For these references to 'Carolingiana' in the narratives for the First Crusade are very different in tone from the overt recasting of Charlemagne as a proto-crusader in the Latin *Historia Turpini*, the contents of which were unquestionably coloured with the imagery and ideals of early crusading narratives. Here, Charlemagne was charged with liberating the Iberian peninsula (identified as the patrimony of St James) from Muslim oppression and reopening the pilgrim road to Compostela; he and his men were participating in an act of vengeance both for the sufferings Christ had endured during his Passion and for the hardships that had been inflicted upon the peninsula's Christian communities by its Muslim overlords; they were also portrayed as voluntary exiles who chose to endure suffering and expected to

---

[49] For the text, see *Liber sancti Jacobi: Codex Calixtinus*, ed. K. Herbers and M. Santos Noia (Santiago de Compostela, 1998), pp. 199–229; and *Historia Karoli Magni et Rotholandi ou Chronique du Pseudo-Turpin*, ed. C. Meredith-Jones (Paris, 1936).

[50] *GF*, p. 2.

[51] RM i.5, p. 732.

[52] RM i.1, p. 728.

[53] RC, c. 29, p. 627.

[54] J. Stuckey, 'Charlemagne as Crusader? Memory, Propaganda, and the Many Uses of Charlemagne's Legendary Expedition to Spain', in *The Legend of Charlemagne in the Middle Ages: Power, Faith, and Crusade*, ed. M. Gabriele and J. Stuckey (Basingstoke, 2008), p. 139. For the importance of Frankish identity and the Carolingian past in the late eleventh century, see now Gabriele, *An Empire of Memory*.

[55] The passage in Ekkehard of Aura's *Chronicon*, which reports the rumour that Charlemagne had come back to life to lead the expedition, is perhaps the exception that proves the rule: see Stuckey, 'Charlemagne as Crusader?', p. 137.

[56] Bull, 'Eyewitness Accounts', 30.

receive spiritual rewards for doing so, as was promised by Archbishop Turpin himself in a church council held in Reims; those who fell in battle would be honoured with the crown of martyrdom; and some of those who were destined to die for their faith were marked out by the miraculous appearance of the sign of the cross upon their flesh.[57]

The immediate contemporary resonance of Pseudo-Turpin's portrayal of Charlemagne as an exemplar of crusading piety emerges most clearly, however, from a text that was appended to the *Historia* in its primary manuscript (the *Codex Calixtinus*): a forged crusade encyclical, *Crebo dilectissimi*, which was spuriously ascribed to Pope Calixtus II (1119–24).[58] The encyclical opened by setting out the various justifications for war in twelfth-century Iberia in terms that are familiar from the *narrationes* of other crusading documentation – the desecration of churches, the persecution and enslavement of Christians and so on – before calling on the arms-bearers of the west to respond by taking the fight to peninsular Islam. Pseudo-Calixtus then offered an innovative framework by which such actions could be understood, recounting the deeds of Charlemagne and identifying Archbishop Turpin's offer of spiritual rewards to those who fought for the emperor in the eighth century as the inaugural event in what was depicted, erroneously, as a centuries-long history of crusading warfare:

> I ask you to understand how great is the need for you to go to Spain to subdue the Saracens, and how great the reward will be for those who go there willingly. For it is said that Charlemagne, the most famous king of the Franks, and more famous than any other king, led an expedition to Spain, and that after countless labours he defeated the infidel peoples; and that blessed Turpin, the archbishop of Reims and Charlemagne's comrade, having assembled a council of all the bishops of Gaul and Lotharingia in the city of Reims, with divine authority freed from the bonds of all their sins all those who were going (or would later go) to Spain to expel the infidel peoples, to defend Christianity, to liberate enslaved Christians, and to accept martyrdom for the love of God, as has been written [in the *Historia Turpini*]. All the popes who have come afterwards have confirmed this, all the way to our own time with the testifying of blessed Pope Urban, that illustrious man, who at the Council of Clermont in France, in the presence of around one hundred bishops, asserted the same when he proclaimed the journey to Jerusalem, as the codex of the *Ystoria Iherosolimitana* tells us.[59]

The schema identified here was therefore intended to suggest, like the production and content of the encyclical of Pseudo-Sergius IV, that the First Crusade was simply a continuation of a long-standing tradition of ideological violence between Christians and Muslims that had received papal endorsement for years.

---

[57] For a full discussion, see Purkis, *Crusading Spirituality*, pp. 150–65.

[58] For the text of the letter, see *Liber sancti Jacobi*, pp. 228–9. See also Calixtus II, *Bullaire*, ed. U. Robert, 2 vols (Paris, 1891), ii, no. 449, pp. 261–2.

[59] *Liber sancti Jacobi*, p. 229. M. G. Bull, 'The Capetian Monarchy and the Early Crusade Movement: Hugh of Vermandois and Louis VII', *Nottingham Medieval Studies*, 40 (1996), 43, suggests the final phrase was a reference to the work of Robert the Monk.

The author's intention seems to have been to undermine the significance of the First Crusade as a novel and defining moment in contemporary history and, as has been argued elsewhere, to legitimize crusading in Iberia by exaggerating its historical pedigree.[60] Nevertheless, the fact that the events of 1095 are identified directly in the source as an important event in crusading historiography, and that the Council of Clermont is in effect depicted as a re-enactment of the Council of Reims – or, rather, that the Council of Reims *is* the Council of Clermont, albeit located three hundred years earlier – certainly reinforces the argument that contemporaries were aware that Pope Urban's address marked a major turning point in the development of the Church's attitudes towards inter-faith violence.

Although the vision of the crusading past proffered in the *Historia Turpini* and Pseudo-Calixtus II's *Crebo dilectissimi* was inflected by particular Iberian circumstances, and possibly therefore of limited applicability to wider contemporary perspectives,[61] the texts' implicit recognition of the First Crusade as a key historical reference point was given more explicit expression in papal letters and other documentation from the twelfth and thirteenth centuries, which indicate that a sense of the expedition's primacy was retained by many western Europeans. In his general letter calling for the Second Crusade in 1145, for example, Pope Eugenius III began his appeal by rehearsing the narrative of events that had taken place some fifty years previously, and the form of words that he used was mostly adopted verbatim in papal crusade appeals for at least the next generation.[62] And even where there were differences in wording, such as in Pope Alexander III's *Inter omnia* (1169), papal writers continued to look back nostalgically to the First Crusade. In that text, for example, the pope described how:

> Long ago, when [Jerusalem] came under the power of the Saracens because of the sins of the Christian people, men of virtue rose up, and having wiped out and driven off the heathen, they restored the Holy Land to the faith of Christ once again. And after raising the banner of faith there, they returned the Sepulchre of the Lord to [the custody of] the Christian people.[63]

This interpretation of crusading historiography, which loaded the events of the 1090s with significance, was not just limited to the papal curia, however. As James Powell has argued, the contents of letters such as *Quantum praedecessores* and *Inter omnia* had 'a direct impact on the shaping of an historical vision

---

[60] Purkis, *Crusading Spirituality*, pp. 162–5.

[61] It should be noted, however, that the *Historia Turpini* was an immensely popular text, which survives in around 150 Latin manuscripts and was translated into many vernacular languages: see G. Spiegel, *Romancing the Past: The Rise of Vernacular Prose Historiography in Thirteenth-Century France* (Berkeley, 1993), pp. 55–98; and M. Cheynet, 'The Chronicle of Pseudo-Turpin', in *Christian–Muslim Relations: A Bibliographical History: Volume 3 (1050–1200)*, ed. D. Thomas, A. Mallett *et al.* (Leiden, 2011), pp. 455–77.

[62] Eugenius III, *Quantum praedecessores*, in R. Grosse, 'Überlegungen zum Kreuzzugsaufruf Eugens III. von 1145/46. Mit einer Neuedition von JL 8876', *Francia*, 18 (1991), 85–92. For commentary, see Phillips, *The Second Crusade*, pp. 36–60; Purkis, *Crusading Spirituality*, pp. 111–19.

[63] Alexander III, 'Epistolae et privilegia', *PL* cc, 600.

of the crusade movement among the elites',[64] and a number of twelfth- and thirteenth-century sources demonstrate the continued importance of the First Crusade as a touchstone for subsequent crusading activities.[65] With reference to the crusade of 1146–9, for example, Jonathan Phillips has recently identified three examples of the way in which this expedition was allocated a 'second-ness' by contemporaries, as has been done by many modern historians. In separate (and apparently independent) texts, the expedition was described variously as a 'second departure to Jerusalem', a 'second Jerusalem journey' and a 'second movement of Christians'.[66] In each case it seems reasonable to assume that the writers concerned were looking to the campaign of the 1090s as the 'second' crusade's numerical predecessor. Similarly, in the first decade of the thirteenth century the Cistercian chronicler Gunther of Pairis described how his abbot, Martin, had referred explicitly to the example of the first crusaders (especially Godfrey of Bouillon) as a source of inspiration in his preaching for the Fourth Crusade.[67] And in a sermon composed in the 1260s, Cardinal Odo of Châteauroux harked back to the 1090s when he wrote optimistically of the most recent cohort of crusaders that 'the Lord will compare them and will put them on a par with those ancient nobles who left the kingdom of Francia and conquered Antioch and the land of Jerusalem'.[68]

Yet it is also evident that by the early thirteenth century certain writers were able to conceive of other, quite distinct, historiographical frameworks by which crusading might be understood. A dramatically different conceptualization is offered, for example, by the Cistercian monk Caesarius of Heisterbach in his *Dialogus miraculorum*, which was composed between 1218 and 1223.[69] Caesarius described the deeds of a number of crusaders who had fought in

---

[64] J. M. Powell, 'Myth, Legend, Propaganda, History: The First Crusade, 1140–ca. 1300', in *Autour de la première croisade: Actes du colloque de la Society for the Study of the Crusades and the Latin East (Clermont-Ferrand, 22–25 juin 1995)*, ed. M. Balard (Paris, 1997), pp. 134–6. See also Constable, 'Historiography', p. 9.

[65] For the memory of the First Crusade in the recovery treatises produced after 1291, see A. Leopold, *How to Recover the Holy Land: The Crusade Proposals of the Late Thirteenth and Early Fourteenth Centuries* (Aldershot, 2000), pp. 61–2, 144–7. For papal memory of the First Crusade in the fifteenth century, see now N. Housley, 'Pope Pius II and Crusading', *Crusades*, 11 (2012), 219, 221–2, 226, 228.

[66] Phillips, *The Second Crusade*, p. 104. See also Constable, 'The Numbering of the Crusades', p. 355. In 1146 Bernard of Clairvaux referred to Peter the Hermit's exploits on 'the previous expedition' (*in priori expeditione*): see *Sancti Bernardi opera*, ed. J. Leclercq, H.-M. Rochais and C. H. Talbot, 8 vols (Rome, 1957–77), viii, no. 363, p. 317.

[67] Gunther of Pairis, *Hystoria Constantinopolitana*, ed. P. Orth (Spolia Berolinensia, 5; Hildesheim, 1994), p. 113.

[68] C. T. Maier, *Crusade Propaganda and Ideology: Model Sermons for the Preaching of the Cross* (Cambridge, 2000), pp. 154–5.

[69] Caesarius of Heisterbach, *Dialogus miraculorum*, ed. and trans. H. Schneider and N. Nösges, 5 vols (Fontes Christiani 86; Turnhout, 2009), cited hereafter as DM with the original book and chapter numbers; the modern volume and page numbers appear in brackets. For a full discussion of the DM as a source for medieval crusading historiography, see W. J. Purkis, 'Crusading and Crusade Memory in Caesarius of Heisterbach's *Dialogus miraculorum*', *Journal of Medieval History*, 39 (2013), 100–27.

'the first expedition to Jerusalem' (*in prima expeditione Jerosolymitana*),[70] 'the first expedition' (*in prima expeditione*),[71] or, simply, 'that great expedition' (*in ista magna expeditione*),[72] but, when he did so, he was referring to the events of the 1190s rather than to those of a century earlier; his 'first' crusade was what modern historians would normally refer to as the 'Third' Crusade. This designation is noteworthy, not least because it indicates that Caesarius privileged the significance of the Third Crusade over those expeditions that had preceded it. This is probably a reflection of the fact that the third crusaders were (once again) fighting for the recovery of Jerusalem from Islam; in other words, for Caesarius, the disastrous events of 1187 had marked a seismic disturbance in the historical narrative, which lent the expedition that was provoked by them an immense significance and thus a new 'first-ness'.[73] But it is striking that although Caesarius did include material relating to the crusading movement that clearly dates from the period before 1187 (such as a series of references to the crusade preaching of Bernard of Clairvaux), his 'crusade memory' did not seem to reach back as far as the 1090s. The First Crusade (as we know it) does not make a single appearance in the *Dialogus*, which is notable – particularly given that Caesarius did demonstrate historical awareness of the last decade of the eleventh century in the very first story of his collection,[74] and given that the First Crusade would seem to have offered a ready supply of morality tales and stories of the miraculous that would have been every bit as appropriate for his audience as the other crusading materials deployed in the *Dialogus*.[75] Of course it may simply be the case that because the Cistercians had had no involvement in the First Crusade it was not deemed a sufficiently fitting subject for inclusion in the *Dialogus*, or that, as far as Caesarius and his audience were concerned, more recent crusading campaigns were fresher in the memory and thus had a greater resonance.[76] Either way, Caesarius's reframing of crusading historiography is suggestive of a changing awareness of the First Crusade's significance at the turn of the thirteenth century, when the conquest of Jerusalem in 1187 was perhaps felt to be more momentous than that of 1099.[77]

---

[70] DM i.34 (Schneider i.300), x.46 (Schneider iv.1986), and x.63 (Schneider iv.2014).

[71] DM x.12 (Schneider iv.1920) and xi.23 (Schneider v.2104).

[72] DM ix.13 (Schneider iv.1774), although cf. Schneider iv.1774 n. 1656, where it is suggested that this phrase refers to the Fifth Crusade.

[73] See J. Richard, '1187: point de départ pour une nouvelle forme de la croisade', in *The Horns of Hattin: Proceedings of the Second Conference of the Society for the Study of the Crusades and the Latin East*, ed. B. Z. Kedar (Jerusalem, 1992), pp. 250–60; and Tyerman, *The Invention of the Crusades*, esp. pp. 14, 26–9.

[74] DM i.1 (Schneider i.206–8), which offers an account of the foundation of the Cistercian Order and refers to the pontificate of Urban II.

[75] See, for example, J. B. MacGregor, 'The First Crusade in Late Medieval *Exempla*', *The Historian*, 68 (2006), 29–48.

[76] DM xi.3 (Schneider v.2052). For the significance of 'communicative' and 'living' memory, see A. Kirk, 'Social and Cultural Memory', in *Memory, Tradition, and Text: Uses of the Past in Early Christianity*, ed. A. Kirk and T. Thatcher (Atlanta, 2005), pp. 5–6.

[77] See Y. Katzir, 'The Conquests of Jerusalem, 1099 and 1187: Historical Memory and Religious Typology', in *The Meeting of Two Worlds: Cultural Exchange between East and West during the*

While Caesarius's conceptualization of the crusades seems to have imposed narrower chronological boundaries on the movement's history, other thirteenth-century evidence suggests that some writers were willing to think in broader terms, above and beyond 1095, and to engage with some of the more pseudo-historical ideas discussed above. In a defence of the activity of crusading presented to the Second Council of Lyons in 1274, for example, Humbert of Romans sketched a rather different historical framework that certainly acknowledged the significance of the First Crusade but also placed it within a larger context.[78] Responding to the criticism that over the years too many Christians (and not enough Muslims) had died on crusades, Humbert encouraged his audience to adjust the chronological criteria by which such judgements about the ongoing viability of crusading could be made:

> I would reply that those who speak like this can only be considering contemporary or recent events ... But if those critics had read the ancient histories perhaps they would speak differently. For one reads that Charles Martel, going to the aid of the duke of Aquitaine, killed 370,000 Saracens who came against him with very little loss of his own men. One also reads that when Jerusalem was captured in the time of Godfrey of Bouillon the Christians rampaged so uncontrollably against the Saracens that at Solomon's Porch the blood of the slain came up to the horses' knees. Who could, moreover, count how many Saracens the army of Charlemagne killed in Spain? Charles himself attacked Spain twice to liberate it from the grip of the Saracens after Blessed James, whose votary he was, had appeared to him in a vision asking him to do this and summoning him to this task. So I beseech all men like them [i.e. the critics] to read and meditate on the chronicles and various histories, and they will find as they consider the facts about the wars fought in our times between Christians and Saracens, that the outcomes of these events were not disasters that ought to be blamed on the sins of modern Christians, but successes in which many more Saracens were killed by the Christians than vice versa.[79]

Although more research on thirteenth-century perspectives is needed, these works by Caesarius of Heisterbach and Humbert of Romans certainly suggest that, in spite of the 'first-ness' contemporaries attached to the First Crusade in the early years of the twelfth century, after 1187 there was no longer a universally acknowledged truth about that expedition's primacy that united the faithful of the medieval Catholic west.[80] In some respects this is not surprising because, as Caesarius of Heisterbach's work demonstrates, for all the retrospection and historical self-referentiality that was evident in many crusading-related texts

Period of the Crusades, ed. V. P. Goss (Kalamazoo, MI, 1986), pp. 103–13; Tyerman, *The Invention of the Crusades*.

[78] For the context, see J. E. Siberry, *Criticism of Crusading, 1095–1274* (Oxford, 1985), esp. pp. 14–15.

[79] Humbert of Romans, 'Opus tripartitum', in *Fasciculus rerum expetendarum et fugiendarum*, ed. E. Brown, 2 vols (London, 1690), ii, 192–3. Translation from L. and J. S. C. Riley-Smith, *The Crusades: Idea and Reality, 1095–1274* (London, 1981), p. 107.

[80] For the inclusion of Charlemagne in the pantheon of 'great crusading leaders' in the fifteenth century, see Housley, 'Pope Pius II and Crusading', 228.

from the early twelfth century onwards, crusading activities also often retained a sense of 'present-ness', with preachers and commentators frequently seeking to lend their immediate circumstances an air of especial historical importance. These sentiments may well have been amplified after 1187, with successive crusades seeking time and again to restore Latin custody over the holy places, and thus creating an increasingly heavy weight of expectation on the 'immediate present',[81] but they are to be found in the earlier period too. Indeed, the tensions between the crusading past and the crusading present are perhaps illustrated best in Bernard of Clairvaux's letters for the Second Crusade from 1146.[82] On the one hand, they indicate Bernard's awareness of the deeds of the first crusaders and of their utility as a source of inspiration, reminding his audience of the threat to the Holy Land and of the need to defend those places that had been won by 'the swords of the fathers';[83] on the other, the letters show a belief in the novelty and distinctiveness of his own times that is reminiscent of both Guibert of Nogent and Caesarius of Heisterbach. 'This time is like no other time that has come before', Bernard wrote to the duke and people of Bohemia, '[because] a new richness of divine mercy comes down from heaven. Blessed are those who find themselves to be alive in this year that is so pleasing to the Lord, this year of remission, this year of jubilee! I say to you: the Lord has not done this for any previous generation.'[84] Bernard therefore evidently retained a memory of the crusading past whilst also demonstrating an awareness of, or perhaps a hope and belief in, the significance of his own times.[85] He could not know, of course, that the 'miraculous' deeds of the 1090s that Robert the Monk had marvelled at a generation earlier were never to be repeated, either in his own lifetime or in those of any of the crusade propagandists who followed in his wake.

---

[81] See above, n. 4.
[82] For commentary, see Phillips, *The Second Crusade*, pp. 61–79; Purkis, *Crusading Spirituality*, pp. 86–98, 117–19; G. Constable, 'The Second Crusade as Seen by Contemporaries', in his *Crusaders and Crusading in the Twelfth Century*, pp. 259–81.
[83] *Sancti Bernardi opera*, viii, no. 363, p. 313.
[84] *Sancti Bernardi opera*, viii, no. 458, p. 435. Cf. GN vii.1, p. 267; DM x.47 (Schneider iv.1988–90).
[85] For another manifestation of this theme, see Constable, 'The Second Crusade', p. 251.

THE IDEAL OF KNIGHTHOOD IN ENGLISH AND FRENCH WRITING, 1100–1230: CRUSADE, PIETY, CHIVALRY AND PATRIOTISM

Laura Ashe

This paper seeks to re-examine a knotty problem: the extent and nature of the relation between the crusade movement and the knightly ideal of chivalry.[1] My focus is on the lay, aristocratic culture of the Anglo-Norman world, as revealed by twelfth- and early thirteenth-century vernacular texts, and the study arose from a serious and simple question: round about when and, much more importantly, how did knights stop thinking that, inasmuch as they were knights, they were going to hell?

Certainly a change can be observed. There is no shortage of evidence for aristocratic fears of damnation in the eleventh and twelfth centuries; any number of pious gifts and bequests are recorded with the urgent prayer that they might deflect the wrath of God for the sins of the benefactor and his ancestors.[2] Even more pointedly, hundreds of accounts survive of dreadful dreams and visions, including Orderic Vitalis's memorable story of the priest who encounters the tormented spirit of his dead brother, a knight:

'... pro peccatis quibus nimis oneratus eram immania supplicia pertuli. Arma quae ferimus ignea sunt, et nos foetore teterrimo inficiunt, ingentique ponderositate nimis opprimunt, et ardore inextinguibili comburunt.'... stupensque sic interrogauit, 'Vnde tanta coagulatio cruoris imminet calcaneis tuis?' At ille respondit, 'Non est sanguis sed ignis, et maioris michi videtur esse ponderis quam si ferrem super me Montem Sancti Michahelis. Et quia preciosis et acutis utebar calcaribus ut festinarem ad effundendum sanguinem, iure sarcinam in talis baiulo

[1] I am grateful to the Leverhulme Trust for the award of a Philip Leverhulme Prize which supported this research.
[2] C. Harper-Bill, 'The Piety of the Anglo-Norman Knightly Class', in *Proceedings of the Battle Conference on Anglo-Norman Studies II: 1979*, ed. R. A. Brown (Woodbridge, 1980), pp. 63–77, 173–6.

155

enormem, qua intolerabiliter grauatus nulli hominum depromere ualeo penae quantitatem.'[3]

Before he was compelled to modify his stance by military necessity and ambition, Gregory VII had observed simply that the profession of warrior, like that of the merchant, 'sine peccato exerceri non possit' ('may not be carried out without sin').[4] A century later, Peter of Blois represented Henry II bluntly complaining that 'tota enim militum vita in peccato est' ('the whole life of a knight is passed in sin').[5]

And yet by the fourteenth century, all this has changed. In Geoffroi de Charny's *Livre de chevalerie*, he promises that all forms and practices of chivalry are morally worthy: 'all such matters are honourable'. Of the men who devote themselves solely to jousting and the tournament circuit he says:

> Et pour ce que Dieu leur a donné tele grace de eulx si bien gouverner en celui fait d'armes, le prennent il si a gré que ilz en delaissent et entreoublient les autres mestiers d'armes, mais toutevoies est il mestier bon et bien avenant a faire et bel a regarder. Et pour ce di je qu'il est bien de le faire pour celi qui le fait, quant Dieu lui en donne tele grace du bienfaire; car tuit fait d'armes font bien a loer a tous ceulx qui bien y font ce qu'il y appartient de faire. Car je ne tieng qu'il soit nul petit fait d'armes fors que tous bons et grans, combien que li un des fais d'armes vaille miex que li autre.[6]

This is extremely pious, but only in one sense. It is confident that all martial prowess is a gift of God; and furthermore, that all uses of prowess, including tournaments, are a proper exercise of that gift. The tournament knight succeeds 'by the grace of God'. He is, surely, capable of going to heaven; there is nothing in the least sinful about his chosen profession.

---

[3] OV, iv, 246–8: "'I have endured severe punishment for the great sins with which I am heavily burdened. The arms which we bear are red-hot, and offend us with an appalling stench, weighing us down with intolerable weight, and burning with everlasting fire." … And horrified, [the priest] asked, "How do you come to have that great clot of blood around your heels?" His brother replied, "It is not blood, but fire, and it weighs more heavily on me than if I were carrying the Mont Saint-Michel. Because I used bright, sharp spurs in my eager haste to shed blood I am justly condemned to carry this enormous load on my heels, which is such an intolerable burden that I cannot convey to anyone the extent of my sufferings."'

[4] Gregory VII, *Das Register*, ed. E. Caspar, 1 vol in 2 (MGH Epistolae Selectae, 2; Berlin, 1920–3), VI.5b, p. 404; see H. E. J. Cowdrey, 'Gregory VII and the Bearing of Arms', in *Montjoie: Studies in Crusade History in Honour of Hans Eberhard Mayer*, ed. B. Z. Kedar, J. S. C. Riley-Smith and R. Hiestand (Aldershot, 1997), pp. 21–35.

[5] Peter of Blois, 'Dialogus inter regem Henricum II et abbatem Bonævallensem', *PL* ccvii, 987.

[6] *The Book of Chivalry of Geoffroi de Charny*, ed. and trans. R. W. Kaeuper and E. Kennedy (Philadelphia, 1996), p. 86: 'And because God has bestowed on them such grace as to conduct themselves well in this particular pursuit of arms, they enjoy it so much that they neglect and abandon the other pursuits of arms; that is not to deny that it is a good pursuit, attractive for the participants and fair to see. I therefore say that it is good to do for him who does it, when, by the grace of God he does it well; for all deeds of arms merit praise for all those who perform well in them. For I maintain that there are no small feats of arms, but only good and great ones, although some feats of arms are of greater worth than others.'

It thus seems necessary to consider how this change came about, and I began this project with a reasonably uncontroversial working hypothesis: that indeed it was the crusade movement that provided the spark, which lit the blue touchpaper on the notion that knighthood could be free of sin. Thus, one might imagine, was enabled the whole florescence of chivalrous ideology, and the elevation and celebration of the martial aristocracy. However, it is the argument of this paper that in fact the ideologies of the crusade movement offered surprisingly little to the culture of chivalry. As the idealization of knighthood gathered force in secular writing of the late twelfth and early thirteenth century, it engaged and negotiated with a variety of ideas. The crusade movement was a vital, but paradoxically challenging, and even potentially threatening ingredient in this mix. Nor did chivalry take the same path in both England and France. With a few exceptions, England's vernacular literature was curiously unengaged with the crusade for the best part of a century, and yet I will argue that the English romances developed a particularly distinctive and robust vision of the ideal knight. In comparison, French *chansons de geste* and romances trace a different pattern of development, both involved with and purposefully distanced from the crusade ideal.

The key literary text for the beginning of these developments is the *Song of Roland*, written c. 1100, and preserved in a late twelfth-century Anglo-Norman manuscript. Despite the earlier existence of some version of Roland's legend, the First Crusade seems to me to provide a cast-iron *terminus post quem* for the composition of the poem as we have it. *Roland* has thoroughly absorbed the popular view of Urban II's crusade promises, and glories in its exposition of God's active support for the Franks, and the welcoming of its hero into heaven as a martyr of holy war.

> Cleimet sa culpe, si priet Deu mercit:
> 'Veire Patene, ki unkes ne mentis,
> Seint Lazaron de mort resurrexis,
> E Daniel des leons guaresis,
> Guaris de mei l'anme de tuz perilz
> Pur les pecchez que en ma vie fis!'
> Sun destre guant a Deu en puroffrit;
> Seint Gabriel de sa main l'ad pris...
> Deus tramist sun angle Cherubin,
> E seint Michel del Peril;
> Ensembl'od els sent Gabriel i vint.
> L'anme del cunte portent en pareïs.[7]

Such certainties were not possible before the First Crusade. Looking one century earlier, we see Roland's predecessor Byrhtnoth in the Old English poem *The*

---

[7] *The Song of Roland*, ed. and trans. G. J. Brault, 2 vols (Philadelphia, 1978), ii, 146, ll. 2383–96: 'He confesses his sins and prays for God's pardon: "True Father, who never lied, who raised Saint Lazarus from the dead and protected Daniel from the lions, protect my soul from all perils for the sins that I have committed in my lifetime!" He offers his right glove to God; Saint Gabriel took it from his hand ... God sends his angel Cherubin and Saint Michael of the Sea of Peril; together with them comes Saint Gabriel. They carry the count's soul to paradise.'

Battle of Maldon, who dies in battle with the heathen Vikings, with a similarly fervent prayer that God might protect his soul from the devils who will come to claim it.

> 'Geþancie þe, ðeoda Waldend,
> ealra þæra wynna þe ic on worulde gebad.
> Nu ic ah, milde Metod, mæste þearfe
> þæt þu minum gaste godes geunne
> þæt min sawul to ðe siðian mote
> on þin geweald, þeoden engla,
> mid friþe feran. Ic eom frymdi to þe
> þæt hi helsceaðan hynan ne moton.'
> Ða hine heowon hæðene scealcas.[8]

No assurance is given, and the fate of Byrhtnoth's soul is left uncertain. If Byrhtnoth is asking a question, then it is Roland who is given the answer, brought by angels; it is an answer which the theology and popular reception of crusade had created.

Here the ideology of crusade has evidently brought about a fundamental transition, such that the warrior can be saved within the exercise of his profession; he can offer up his martial prowess to God, and be rewarded for it. The question which follows from this concerns what happens next. Does the transference of value work this rapidly and easily, such that Roland's superlative quality of *vassalage*, the service of his lord and of his God, for which he receives heavenly reward, becomes transmuted into the similarly morally elevated *chevalerie* of his later compatriots? In fact, I suggest not. In the long game of justifying the warrior's lifestyle, the glorious sacrifice of Roland is, ideologically speaking, a dead end. Because despite the apparently explosive effects of crusade theology, particularly in the aftermath of the First Crusade's spectacular success, its dispensations were really very tightly constrained.

As is well known, the twelfth-century authors who celebrated the glories of the new, Christian knighthood minced no words in damning the sins of worldly knights. Bernard of Clairvaux's praise of the Templars was constructed in terms of their difference from knights of the world:

> Novum militiae genus ortum nuper auditur in terris ... et saeculis inexpertum: qua gemino pariter conflictu infatigabiliter decertatur, tum adversus carnem et sanguinem, tum contra spiritualia nequitiae in coelestibus ... O vere sancta et tuta militia ... Quoties namque congrederis tu, qui militiam militas saecularem, timendum omnino, ne aut occidas hostem quidem in corpore, te vero in anima: aut forte tu occidaris ab illo, et in corpore simul, et in anima.[9]

---

[8] *The Battle of Maldon*, ed. D. Scragg (Manchester, 1981), p. 62, ll. 173–81: '"I thank you, Lord of nations, for all the joys which I have received on earth. Now I have, kind Creator, the greatest need that you might grant favour to my spirit, so that my soul may travel to you, ruler of angels, to go in peace into your power. I entreat you to ensure that the hellish enemy may not seize it." Then the heathen warriors cut him down ...'

[9] Bernard of Clairvaux, 'Liber ad milites Templi de laude novae militiae', *Sancti Bernardi opera*,

The worldly knight was sending his soul to hell, bedecked as it was with 'God knows what plumes and silks'. And nor was it enough, in fact, merely to be fighting in the right cause, as the disasters of the Second Crusade proved; it was possible to be a crusader and yet to be sinful, and hence presumably damned. Even the strongest statements of crusading theology are a long way from being a panacea for knighthood. Guibert of Nogent asserted that of those who died on crusade, 'si quas necesse fuerit peccatorum luere penas, sola sanguinis effusio omnem fuit potissima purgare reatum'.[10] But to be certain of being received into paradise, then, they must be utterly committed to the cause of the crusade; and they do have to die for it. These promises cannot aid them on their return home, to the harsh and material daily life of the martial aristocracy. Guibert's statement simply cannot be taken as an all-encompassing recuperation of knighthood; it is a promise which helps to persuade and encourage men to risk their lives, in that place, at that time, for that cause.

Thus we can return to the *Song of Roland*, and see why it could be so powerful, and yet so uninfluential on later chivalric literature. Because despite the work's intermittent triumphalism, the necessary implications of Christ-like self-sacrifice threaten to overwhelm the text. Roland *has* to die, and after his death the suffering Charlemagne is left behind, aged and in mourning, directed by God to never-ending battles in which his men will die and go to heaven. Notoriously, the poem ends with Charlemagne's weary and lonely cry 'Si penuse est ma vie!' ('How painful my life is!'). The *Song of Roland* gains a great deal of its literary power as a grand, heroic, and yet ultimately tragic vision; it does not offer a celebration or justification of the military aristocratic lifestyle *per se*. And indeed in only slightly later versions of the *Roland*, in late twelfth-century continental French and Italian manuscripts, the poem's emphases are subtly different: the later text irons out much of the ambiguity of the work, and makes Roland and his fellow knights significantly more orthodox and submissive to the Church in their piety.[11] They are thus thoroughly aligned with late twelfth-century *clerical* views of idealized Christian knighthood on crusade.

There then remains a problematic gap: for all crusading ideology's force, it does not offer to justify the knight in his aristocratic lifestyle, or in all his deeds of arms; only the knight fighting in a just war against pagans, who must himself be morally upright, chaste and virtuous, and have given up the world to take the cross; above all, the knight who gives up his life in the Christian

---

ed. J. Leclercq, H. M. Rochais and C. H. Talbot, 8 vols (Rome, 1957–77), iii, 214–15: 'A new kind of knighthood seems recently to have appeared on the earth … one unknown in ages past. It indefatigably wages a twofold combat, against flesh and blood and against a spiritual host of evil in the heavens … How truly holy and secure this knighthood … Whenever *you* march out, o worldly warrior, you have to worry that killing your foe's body may mean killing your soul, or that by him you may be killed, body and soul both.'

[10] GN iv.14, p. 191: 'If there was any need to suffer penalties for their sins, the spilling of their blood alone was a more powerful way of expiating all offences.'

[11] See *The Song of Roland: The French Corpus*, ed. J. J. Duggan *et al.*, 3 vols (Turnhout, 2005), Châteauroux-Venice 7 version [vol. 2], e.g. pp. 198, 258–9, ll. 1930–9, 3332–54; Aude has a much expanded role (by the evident influence of romance) and is similarly pious: p. 779, ll. 7365–83.

cause. And this gap has still not been bridged by the text heralded as the first real extant codification of chivalry, the deeply religious *Ordene de chevalerie* of around 1220, which is set against the backdrop of the Third Crusade. In it Hue de Tabarie, a French knight held prisoner by Saladin, is asked by the latter to explain the elaborate rituals of entry to knighthood. The anonymous clerical author celebrates knighthood as a mode of life within which a man may achieve salvation: but he does so by demanding of the knight a life of monkish virtue and restraint. Every stage of his explanation is unambiguously religious:

> Sire, cil bains ou vous baingniez,
> Il est a ce senefiez:
> Tout issi com li enfeçons
> Nes de pechiez ist hors de fons
> Quant de baptesme est aportez,
> Sire, tout ensement devez
> Issir sanz nule vilonie
> De ce baing, car chevalerie
> Se doit baingnier en honesté,
> En cortoisie et en bonté,
> Et fere amer a toutes genz. ...
> Sire, ceste robe vous done
> A entendre, ce est la somme,
> Que vous devez vo sanc espandre
> Por dieu et por sa loi desfendre ...
> Sire, par ceste çainturete
> Est entendu que vo char nete,
> Voz rains, vo cors entirement,
> Devez tenir molt saintement,
> Ausi comme en virginité
> Vo cors tenir en netëé.
> Luxure ne devez hanter,
> Quar chevaliers doit molt amer
> Son cors et netement tenir,
> Qu'il ne se puist en ce honir,
> Quar Diex het molt si fete ordure.[12]

---

[12] *The Anonymous Ordene de chevalerie*, ed. K. Busby (Utrecht Publications in General and Comparative Literature, 17; Amsterdam, 1983), pp. 108, 109, 110, ll. 113–23, 153–6, 175–87: 'Sire, this bath in which you are bathing signifies this: just as the child leaves the font free from sin when he is brought from baptism, Sire, so you should leave this bath without any wickedness, for knighthood should bathe in honesty, in courtesy, and in goodness, and be beloved of all people ... Sire, this [red] robe gives you to understand, quite simply, that you should spill your blood in order to defend God and his holy law ... Sire, this belt signifies that you should preserve in holiness your pure flesh, your loins, and your whole body, and keep your body pure, as in a state of virginity. You should not practise lechery, for a knight should cherish his body and keep it pure so that he does not incur shame therefrom, for God much hates suchlike filth.'

This is much closer in spirit to Bernard of Clairvaux than Geoffroi de Charny; it excludes much of aristocratic life, bringing knighthood into line with a Christian ideal, rather than the reverse. There is, then, a persistent chasm between the literature of crusading and the earliest texts of chivalric instruction, and the later ideology of chivalry. How was the gap bridged?

The romances of France and England play an important role in both tracing and feeding the development of chivalry; but I suggest that there is an equally important difference between the two literatures, over the twelfth and early thirteenth century. Crusade ideology is absorbed by the two literatures in contrasting ways, and their negotiations with the idea of Christian knighthood trace markedly different paths. Notable above all is the degree to which crusade ideas are both absorbed and resisted, appropriated and rejected. In fact, I suggest that twelfth- and thirteenth-century French literature presents the ideals of Christian knighthood and of courtly chivalry not as a functioning combination, but as divided and even opposed values.

It is now well acknowledged that the continental epic *chanson de geste* continued to develop during the twelfth and thirteenth centuries, alongside the romance.[13] Nevertheless, the high-pitched ideal of the *Chanson de Roland* is never matched again. Charlemagne is followed in the subsequent cycles of *chansons* by his failing son Louis, and the violent chaos and injustices of a world without effective kingship;[14] the bitterness, and eventually irony and mocking humour, of the later *chansons* share something with writings about the failed crusades, and failed crusaders. Moving from the *chansons de geste* to the continental French romance, there is still a pervasive pessimism about kings; if not weak and corrupt, as with Louis, they are weak and undermined, as in the French romances' incarnation of King Arthur, who is an enfeebled, inactive king, surpassed and cuckolded by Lancelot.[15]

Thus Lancelot is the key: in the continental romances, far distant from the crusading ideal, emerges the courtly, chivalric knight, a figure who seems to grow to fill the vacuum left by the enfeebled king. The romances were written for and patronized by the highest nobility in France, and culturally they conjure up the triumph of the aristocracy over royalty, in the ascendancy of the knight who surpasses his king. The continental romance knight goes on his own individual quests, to no wider purpose than augmenting his own reputation for chivalry and prowess. In so doing, however, the knight has no access to the usual tropes which would justify his actions. That is, the warrior Roland was defined by and rewarded for his service, his *vassalage*, of his lord king and his Lord God. Lancelot in contrast does not serve an ideal; therefore, and I suggest as a matter of logical development, instead he embodies one. Chivalry is itself Lancelot's purpose, and his significance.[16]

---

[13] S. Kay, *The Chansons de Geste in the Age of Romance: Political Fictions* (Oxford, 1995).

[14] See the comments of R. W. Kaeuper, *War, Justice, and Public Order: England and France in the Later Middle Ages* (Oxford, 1988), pp. 316–22.

[15] See for example the summary of R. Morris, *The Character of King Arthur in Medieval Literature* (Cambridge, 1982), pp. 123–4.

[16] I discuss the literary and historical implications of this phenomenon in my 'William Marshal,

Laura Ashe

This newly closed, self-sustaining system therefore combines and conflates knighthood, courtesy and nobility, in what I would regard as the archetype of early French chivalry. It can be seen fully codified in an early thirteenth-century text written – exceptionally for the period – not by a cleric but a knight, Raoul de Hodenc. This is the *Roman des eles*, 'romance of the wings', which refers to the 'wings' by which a knight may rise to glory: these two qualities are *largesse* and *courtoisie*. In an elaborate extended metaphor, each wing has seven 'feathers'. The seven feathers of largesse are all variations on the instruction to be as generous as possible, and indeed more so:

> La seconde est de tel afere
> Que hom qui veut larguesce fere
> Ne doit mie entendre a avoir,
> Ne que sa terre puet valoir.
> Ja chevaliers, se Diex me saut,
> Puis qu'il enquiert que soigles vaut,
> Ne montera en grant hautece;
> Ne cil n'est pas plains de proece,
> Ne d'onor ne de hardement,
> Qui plus ne done et plus despent,
> Et en folie et en savoir,
> Que sa terre ne puet valoir.[17]

The seven feathers of courtesy are a variety of guides to conduct. The first is, piously enough, to 'honour Holy Church', but the penalty for failure to do so is severe only in chivalric terms: 'Ne doit estre nommez cortois / Qui Eglise n'aime et honeure, / Que ja ne l'ert ne jor ne eure.'[18] The fate of the knight's soul is not at issue here; his relation with the Church is, like all of his social relations, governed and judged solely by courtesy and largesse. The other 'feathers' of courtesy are to avoid pride and boastfulness; to love joy – in particular, never to be nasty to minstrels or break up a party – and never to be envious, or to utter derisive or slanderous words. And the last, which takes up nearly a third of the whole poem, is love. This is perhaps what French chivalry is most famous for including, the idea that the state of being in love is itself improving: Raoul tells us that whatever qualities a man possesses, love will magnify and better them.

Lancelot and Arthur: Chivalry and Kingship', in *Anglo-Norman Studies XXX: Proceedings of the Battle Conference 2007*, ed. C. P. Lewis (Woodbridge, 2008), pp. 22–33.

17   Raoul de Hodenc, *Le Roman des Eles*, ed. K. Busby (Utrecht Publications in General and Comparative Literature, 17; Amsterdam, 1983), p. 35, ll. 161–72: 'The second (feather) is such that a man who wants to be generous should never look to possessions or to the value of his land. A knight, God protect me, will not rise to great heights if he inquires of the value of corn; nor is he full of prowess, honour, or bravery who does not, in folly or in wisdom, give and spend more than his land may be worth.'

18   *Ibid.*, p. 39, ll. 284–6: 'He who neither loves nor honours the Church should not be called courteous, for he will never be so.'

Here then is a highly independent, secular vision of chivalry; it has a great deal in common with the continental French romances, and not very much at all with contemporary and earlier religious writings which sought to confine honourable chivalry to chastity, piety and Christian self-sacrifice. Perhaps the most important cultural information this text gives us is the economic elitism of chivalry: only the very wealthiest noblemen could afford to practise liberality, and indeed idleness, on the scale Raoul prescribes. Thus French chivalric ideology elevated and celebrated behaviours available only to a very exclusive club of the higher nobility. It asserted both their independence from monarchy, and their qualitative difference from the other strata of society; and it encouraged the continued extravagance and liberality of their lifestyles, which offered great rewards to those who could please and impress their lords and patrons.

All this has notably little to do with the crusade. It may be the crusader knight who gave chivalry its status as a code, an order; but as it developed it kept only the framework and rituals, and little or none of the content. The romance knight Lancelot embodies his own chivalric perfection; he has no higher cause to fight for, and he is never sacrificed. Inevitably, then, this ideology was simply not robust enough to resist the demands of Christian teaching. If the purpose of chivalry is self-improvement and self-advancement, then by a process of inevitable logic, that had to be identified with the improvement of the soul. The figure of the voluntarily impoverished, self-sacrificing crusader knight hovers accusingly behind the celebrations of the court and tournament. And he finally emerges, in the romances, as the thoroughly Christian Grail Quest knight, who is chaste, virginal, self-denying, and whose virtue is once again crowned with death. His appearance is ideologically disastrous: the Grail Quest destroys the Arthurian court, exposes its apparent virtue as empty and static; Arthur's court is superseded by the court of heaven, and the greatest knights in the world are superseded by those who reject the world. Left behind are all the knights who fail to complete the Grail Quest, prevented by their sins, wrestling with their guilt, and embodied in the superlatively chivalric but sinful and tragically damned Lancelot.[19] The romances openly acknowledge this: in the thirteenth-century *Prose Lancelot*, the queen, in conversation with Lancelot, observes ruefully that 'Nostre Sire ne garde mie a la cortoisie del monde, kar cil qui est buens al monde est mals a Dieu.'[20] Thus the ideological vision of French chivalry, in the early thirteenth century, is still impotently, if intermittently, labouring under a consciousness of its own sin. It was not so in England.

This can be demonstrated with the brief example of one of the insular French romances: the *Romance of Horn* of Thomas, written around 1170.[21] This is the life

---

[19] For a fuller discussion of this, see L. Ashe, 'The Hero and his Realm in Medieval English Romance', in *Boundaries in Medieval Romance*, ed. N. Cartlidge (Cambridge, 2008), pp. 139–41.

[20] *Lancelot: roman en prose du XIIIe siècle*, ed. A. Micha, 9 vols (Paris, 1978-83), i, 152: 'Our Lord doesn't care in the least about worldly courtesy, so that one who is good in the eyes of the world is evil to God.'

[21] *The Romance of Horn*, ed. M. K. Pope (Anglo-Norman Texts, 9-10; Oxford, 1955); trans J. Weiss, *The Birth of Romance in England: Four Twelfth-Century Romances in the French of England* (Tempe, AZ, 2009), pp. 45–137.

story of Horn, whose country 'Suddene' – some part of England in the distant past – is invaded by pagans, Saracens, when he is a child. His father the king is killed, and he and twelve young companions are cast adrift at sea. They land in Brittany, and are there brought up at court, where Horn impresses everyone with his astonishing virtue, beauty and prowess, fighting off the invading pagans when they appear. The princess Rigmel falls in love with him; but accused of treachery by a jealous courtier, Horn sails again and this time reaches Ireland, where he once again impresses all (and has another princess fall in love with him), and again defeats the pagan armies. Finally, he returns to his own land and completes a final victory over the pagans, reclaiming his kingdom, before marrying Rigmel and ruling in peace.

In its Saracen enemies *Horn* is clearly influenced by the crusade movement, but its chief concerns do not lie there. Similarly, the hero is carefully constructed to possess all the qualities and virtues which are associated with French courtliness and chivalry: Thomas takes great pains to assure us that Horn is very beautiful, well-dressed and extremely attractive to women; and he digresses at length on his courtly and sporting accomplishments. Nevertheless, this too is no more than a decorative addition to Thomas's real focus. In order to explain the work's motivation, there are two important aspects to be considered.

The first concerns the continental ideals of courtly chivalry. It is vital to observe that, in as much as each appears in the text, courtly and chivalrous behaviours are directly *opposed* to crusading ideology, in an echo of that division visible in the continental literature. Whenever Horn is celebrated for his court-liness, and most strikingly when the two princesses are trying to seduce him, he rejects all praise and their loving advances. This life is a worthless distraction, he insists, in the most pious terms; it is only war he desires, to fight the pagans and reclaim his country:

> il n'ad soing d'amer, einz est en grant tristur
> Pur la triwe …
> Cinc aunz ot ja passé qu'il n'i aveit fet tur
> De ses armes porter: mut en iert de peior.
> Envers Deu en sun quoer en ad fet grant clamur:
> 'Ohi, Deus! …
> Dune mei vëeir tens, dunt joe su preecheur,
> K'encore puisse munter mun destrier milsoudur
> E espied depescier devant chastel u tur,
> Pur amisté de vus, desur gent paenur
> Qui taunt ont mort des miens: k'en seie vengeör.'[22]

---

[22] *Horn*, p. 99, ll. 2891–904: 'He cared nothing for love but instead was very dejected about the truce … For five years already there had been no expedition where he could carry arms, and he suffered much for it. In his heart he appealed to God: "Ah God! … let me see the day when I can foretell I can again mount my precious steed and break lances before castle and tower, for love of you, against the heathen killers of my people: let me avenge them."' Trans. Weiss, *Birth of Romance*, p. 97.

And when in battle a defeated pagan asks for mercy – asks, that is, for the kind of chivalrous restraint which Anglo-Norman knights in 1170 routinely granted one another – Horn does not oblige.

> Horn s'est mut corocié par le cop Marmorin ...
> Ja en dorra un cop, s'il poet, al barbarin ...
> Ne se pot cil tenir qu'il ne chaïst sovin
> Ausi lonc cum il fu el mi leu del chemin.
> E Horn nel esparnia, ki nel tint pur cosin,
> Ainz li trencha le chief veänt ces de sun lin.[23]

Thus Thomas represents the spirit of crusading as antithetical to the values of chivalry. Chivalry and courtliness are things one does at home, amongst kinsmen; the kind of war fought against pagans is total and unremitting: unchivalrous.

The second, and more important, observation I wish to make is to note the lack, in this romance, of an ever-present element in crusading ideology: that of self-sacrifice, self-denial and withdrawal from the world. This comes about because while Horn is a knight, he is rightfully a king. I suggest that it is this which justifies him, makes him favoured by God, and makes him entirely different from both Roland and Lancelot. In the context of his destiny, courtly chivalry is just an accomplishment – a set of qualities and knowledge of correct behaviours – which Horn possesses because they are good to have, while he goes about his greater purposes. Correspondingly, his destiny excludes the Christ-like death in battle. His significance, in contrast with the figures both of chivalric Lancelot and crusading Roland, is something else: it is that of the rightful king, the ruler, God's representative on earth, who defends the land, defeats enemies, brings about peace, gives law and justice. This hero is self-justified; he does not need to die to prove his moral worth; indeed, he cannot die because he is needed to rule. Where the crusader fights for Christ, with the promise that he becomes like Christ in his virtuous death, Horn fights with God's support, and is His representative on earth: the anointed king. So the highest good here is neither that of self-sacrifice to a Christian cause, nor that of self-advancement in the name of one's own reputation, but of self-advancement in the name of the land, justice, and peace.

Thus the knightly English king is justified where the French chivalric knight is not, and he lives where the crusader dies. I have argued elsewhere that the idealization of kingship is a fundamental component of Anglo-Norman culture, and it can be seen everywhere in the literature.[24] However, an obvious question arises. How does an ideal of kingship help develop an ideal of knighthood? Kings are different from

---

[23] *Horn*, p. 51, ll. 1519–36: 'Horn was enraged by Marmorin's blow ... now he would give the heathen a blow, if he could ... He could not stop himself falling prone, measuring his full length in the middle of the path. And Horn did not spare him, did not treat him like a kinsman, but cut off his head in front of his clan.' Trans. Weiss, *Birth of Romance*, p. 72.

[24] L. Ashe, 'The Anomalous King of Conquered England', in *Every Inch a King: Comparative Studies on Kings and Kingship in the Ancient and Medieval Worlds*, ed. C. Melville and L. Mitchell (Leiden, 2012), pp. 173–93.

knights; indeed, the conflicting interests of kings and nobility mark literary culture and historical events throughout the period. Nevertheless, the answer is simple and indeed ancient: if the king is justified, God's representative on earth, then the warrior who serves the king can be equally justified. John of Salisbury states this openly in his writing on warriors in *Policraticus*. For him warfare is a profession, following the classical image of the Roman legionary army; it is dependent upon training, intelligence, strategy and discipline. But then he moves to discuss the oath of knighthood, its selectivity and meaning, its status as an order:

> Verumtamen citra religionem sacramenti ex antiqua lege, nemo militiae cingulo donabatur ... Jurant equidem milites per Deum, et Christum ejus, et Spiritum sanctum, et per majestatem principis, quae secundum Deum humano generi diligenda est et colenda. (Nam cum quis legitimum accepit principatum, tanquam praesenti et corporali Deo, fidelis ei est praestanda devotio, impendendus pervigil famulatus) ... Cum vero hoc praestiterint jusjurandum, cingulo militari donantur, et privilegiis.[25]

In the context of the literature of crusading, this is much more important than it at first appears. John does not distinguish between the Christian soldier and the worldly soldier, as Bernard of Clairvaux does, but between those who have taken an oath, been properly trained, and serve the state; and those who have not – we assume, mercenaries. And, finally, he performs that vital connection we have been waiting for: the transference of Christian approval to the knight who fights in his own proper status and position.

> Sed ut faciant in eis judicium conscriptum, in quo quisque non tam suum, quam Dei, angelorum, et hominum sequatur ex aequitate et publica utilitate arbitrium ... sicut judicum est dictare judicium, ita et istorum faciendo exercere officium est. Utique gloria haec est omnibus sanctis ejus. Nam et haec agentes milites sancti sunt, et in eo fideliores principi, quo servant studiosius fidem Dei; et virtutis suae utilius gloriam promovent, quo fidelius Dei sui in omnibus gloriam quaerunt.[26]

Thus the warrior is justified by virtue of his place in John's vision of the *res publica*, of the properly governed nation, of the laws and rule of the just prince,

---

[25] John of Salisbury, 'Policraticus', *PL* cxcix, 599: 'No one will be given the belt of the soldier except under the terms of a sacred oath, according to the ancient law...The soldiers swear by God and His Christ and by the Holy Spirit and by the majesty of the prince, which according to God is to be respected and revered by the human race. (For when one accepts the lawful ruler, faithful devotion is to be offered to him just as the constant vigil of devoted service is offered to the person and body of God) ... Once they perform this oath-taking, they are given the belt and privileges of a soldier.' Trans. C. J. Nederman, *John of Salisbury: Policraticus* (Cambridge, 1990), pp. 114–15.

[26] 'Policraticus', 600–1: 'They serve in order that they may execute judgements assigned to them, according to which each attends not to his own will but to the will of God, the angels and men by reason of equity and the public utility ... just as judges prescribe judgements, so soldiers perform their duty by executing judgement. Above all, "this is the glory of all His saints" [Ps. 149: 9]. For those who act this way are saints and those who are most devoted in their faith in God serve the prince most loyally.' Trans. Nederman, *Policraticus*, pp. 116–17.

and the service both due to him and required in order to keep the peace and integrity of the realm.

Thomas Bisson has said that John's work cannot be regarded as a real theory of government.[27] But there is something significant here, and it had penetrated beyond the schools. When Jordan Fantosme wrote his poetic chronicle of the 1173–4 civil war, he confidently and tendentiously represented it as a foreign invasion fought off by courageous English defenders; and he contrasted the supposedly venal behaviour of these invaders – stealing, ravaging, looting – with that of his English baronial heroes, in whose mouths he placed speeches condemning such standard and accepted practices.[28] This is an ideal of the service of king and nation which leaves the question of the warrior's soul safely in the background, because the vital step has been taken. 'Ore pernez voz armes, mar serrez esmaié!':[29] there is nothing inherently wrong or sinful in the warrior's profession. Thus, in the literatures of England, ideologies flourished which justified the warrior, and promised him a reward in heaven, without drawing directly upon either the new crusading ideology or upon the continental French codifications of courtly chivalric behaviour. English writers observed both, and sometimes deployed them. But above all, they possessed a working structure which gave purpose and meaning to the fighting man, and to his place in the justly governed kingdom, which needed neither the high-pitched self-sacrifice of the crusading ideal nor the artificially constructed economic elitism of French chivalry.

The narrativization of early crusade ideas, in an immensely rich and varie-gated body of vernacular texts, necessarily brings with it multiple geographical, chronological and generic nuances. Later medieval knighthood came to a fruitful accommodation with crusade ideology, but in very many different, and sometimes conflicting and oppositional ways. I would like to end with several speculative conclusions. First, it seems that early crusading ideology, as written about by theologians and clerics, had surprisingly little to offer the warrior aristocracy in their quest to establish a working ideal for their own class and status. Second, I suggest that courtesy, and more specifically extravagant largesse, is not an incidental but a fundamental ingredient of French chivalry. It rendered the status of chivalric knight accessible only to the wealthiest aristocracy, and encouraged them in behaviours which enabled the younger sons of those families to support and establish themselves: that is, there was a strong economic motivation for this ideal.[30] The practice of courtly chivalry generated the materials for its own continued survival and success: the behavioural codes of chivalry allowed the formulation and distinctiveness of an elite class at the summit of society, and the

---

[27] T. N. Bisson, *The Crisis of the Twelfth Century: Power, Lordship and the Origins of European Government* (Princeton, 2009), p. 489.

[28] See L. Ashe, *Fiction and History in England, 1066–1200* (Cambridge, 2007), pp. 84–94, 98–102.

[29] *Jordan Fantosme's Chronicle*, ed. and trans. R. C. Johnston (Oxford, 1981), p. 130, l. 1761: 'Take up your arms and fear nothing!'

[30] Cf. the comments of J. Gillingham, 'Conquering the Barbarians: War and Chivalry in Britain and Ireland', in his *The English in the Twelfth Century: Imperialism, National Identity and Political Values* (Woodbridge, 2000), pp. 41–58.

power and status of that aristocracy in turn endowed chivalry with its aura of superiority, and a spreading influence throughout culture.

Thirdly, there is the matter of the French chivalric knight, who rises in the literature to fill the vacuum left by historiographical and fictional weak and ineffective kingship, in writings addressed to an aristocracy which resented the encroachments of royal power. This knight does not serve his king or any higher cause, and as such comes to embody and to symbolize the ideal of his own chivalric lifestyle. Inevitably then, I suggest that that ideal could not resist the implications of Christian instruction, and so this knight is juxtaposed – and unfavourably compared – with the fully Christian knight who completes the Grail Quest. Here can be seen a new form of integration between chivalric and crusading ideals.

In contrast, finally, there are the strangely dissonant voices of the writings of twelfth- and thirteenth-century England, in which warfare against pagans is considered properly unchivalric, and crusading and courtliness are treated as mutually exclusive. Texts such as the *Romance of Horn* can be seen to draw with magpie readiness on crusade motifs, and on the embellishments of courtliness and French chivalry; but their central purpose and power lie in their certainty that the defence, peace and governance of the realm is justification enough for the warrior who serves his lord. This is the ideal of English knighthood; it is somewhat different from *chevalerie*. And by the thirteenth century, indeed, this oddly bureaucratic ideal could appropriate the ideology of crusade to itself, as the various parties in the English baronial wars fought under the papal banner. In 1095 the warrior had been asked to serve on the crusade; within a century, the ideology of crusade was available in the service of the warrior.

INDEX

Printed in the United States
By Bookmasters